BARRON'S

601

Words You Need to Know for the

SAT

PSAT, GRE, State Regents, and other standardized tests

by

MURRAY BROMBERG

Principal
Samuel H. Wang High School, Queens, New York

JULIUS LIEBB

Assistant Principal, English
Andrew Jackson High School, Queens, New York

BARRON'S EDUCATIONAL SERIES, Inc.
Woodbury, New York • London • Toronto • Sydney

© Copyright 1981 by Barron's Educational Series, Inc.
Adapted from *Words With a Flair*

All inquiries should be addressed to:
Barron's Educational Series, Inc.
113 Crossways Park Drive
Woodbury, New York 11797

Library of Congress Catalog Card No. 81-4472

Paper Edition
International Standard Book No. 0-8120-2409-5

Library of Congress Cataloging in Publication Data
Bromberg, Murray.
 601 words you need to know for the SAT, PSAT,
GRE, state regents, and other standardized tests.

 Previously published as: Words with a flair. © 1979.
 Includes index.
 1. Vocabulary. I. Liebb, Julius. II. Title.
PE1449.B69   1981   428.1   81-4472
ISBN 0-8120-2409-5 (pbk.)   AACR2

PRINTED IN THE UNITED STATES OF AMERICA

6789   410   18 17 16 15 14 13 12

CONTENTS

Unit IV

INTRODUCTION

People who are planning to take Scholastic Aptitude Tests (SATs, PSATs), Comprehensive English Tests (Regents), Graduate Record Exams (GREs), and other standardized tests commonly study long lists of vocabulary words in preparation for the verbal portion of such tests. Although that is commendable, it is not economical. There are just too many words to study — and not enough time before a test to master all of them.

With that challenge in mind, we have carefully chosen 601 words which testmakers are fond of using. By concentrating on difficult-but-not-esoteric words at the level most commonly tested on the major exams, we have been able to produce a compact, manageable assortment of functional vocabulary words. Naturally, no one—not even the testmakers themselves—can predict precisely which words will turn up on a specific exam, but the words we've selected deal with topics and concepts considered vital for today's students. Mastering them, therefore, will be a valuable step toward readiness for your upcoming exam.

This book, therefore, was designed for the high school or college student who wants to be ready for an upcoming standardized test. It is also useful for the adult who is seeking self-improvement through independent study.

The testmaker who thought he could stump you with *etiology, jejune, leitmotif,* and *baleful* will be in for a surprise when you get through with *601 Words You Need to Know for the SAT.*

PRONUNCIATION KEY*

a	asp, fat, parrot	ə	represents
ā	ape, date, play		
ä	ah, car, father		*a* in ago
			e in agent
e	elf, ten, berry		*i* in sanity
ē	even, meet, money		*o* in comply
			u in focus
i	is, hit, mirror		
ī	ice, bite, high	ər	perhaps
ō	open, tone, go	ch	chin, catcher, arch
ô	all, horn, law	sh	she, cushion, dash
o͞o	ooze, tool, crew	zh	azure, leisure
oo	look, pull, moor	ŋ	ring, anger, drink
yo͞o	use, cute, few		
yoo	united, cure, globule		
oi	oil, oint, toy	H	German ich
ou	out, crowd, plow		
u	up, cut, color		

*Pronunciation Key used by permission. From *Webster's New World Dictionary*, Second College Edition. Copyright © 1978 by William Collins + World Publishing Co., Inc.

WORD LIST

Here are the 601 important words which you will encounter in this book. You might wish to go through the list now, placing a light checkmark next to those words which you think you know. Many students who are expected to do well on the verbal portion of the Scholastic Aptitude Test may find that they are sure of the meanings of 150 or more of these useful vocabulary words. Other readers, however, will discover that they have mastered fewer than 50 of them.

After you have worked your way through the forty lessons, come back to the list and see how many more checkmarks you can make.

Now, get started!

(The page number refers to the first page on which the new word appears.)

A

aberrant 30
abnegation 178
abscess 50
abscond 178
a cappella 129
accolade 80
acidulous 6
acrid 116
acrophobia 85
adagio 15
addle 116
ad hoc 129
adjudicate 63
ado 116
Adonis 25
affidavit 178
aficionado 35
agnostic 187
à la carte 164
alchemy 71
alienist 20
alms 116
altercation 178
amanuensis 20
ambivalent 134
amicus curiae 103
amplitude 75
amorphous 138
amulet 116
anachronism 39
anarchy 173
andante 15
anon 39
antaean 120
antebellum 39
antediluvian 39
anthropomorphism 30
antic 168
antipodal 159
aperture 116
aphasia 50
aphorism 182
apocalyptic 187
apocryphal 187

apostate 187
apotheosis 187
appellate 63
arcane 71
archaeology 90
archetype 30
argonaut 120
argot 150
arpeggio 15
arson 103
arteriosclerosis 50
askew 116
aspersion 150
assuage 164
atavism 39
atonement 58
augury 39
authoritarian 30
avant-garde 107

B

bacchanal 25
badinage 150
baleful 6
bane 43
barrio 35
barrister 103
bathos 145
battery 178
bauble 116
beadle 20
beguile 168
bellicose 6
benediction 187
bequest 178
bête noire 107
betimes 39
bevy 117
bibliophile 85
bicameral 58
biennial 39
bilious 6
bilk 117
biopsy 50
blasphemy 187
blithe 117

bombast 150
bonanza 35
bonhomie 168
bon mot 107
bon vivant 129
bourgeois 173
bovine 54
braggadocio 150
bravado 35
bravura 15
bucolic 134
bumptious 6
bureaucracy 173

C

cabal 10
cadaver 50
calliope 120
camaraderie 10
canon 154
captious 6
carcinogen 50
cardiology 90
careen 117
cartography 159
Cassandra 25
caste 10
catharsis 30
cause célèbre 178
caveat emptor 178
censure 150
chary 117
churlish 6
circumspect 67
claustrophobia 85
codicil 179
coiffure 112
collusion 63
comatose 50
comestible 164
complaisant 7
concierge 159
conclave 80
condiment 164
contiguous 179
contraband 179

contralto 15
contrite 7
contumacious 179
conundrum 71
convivial 7
cornucopia 25
cortege 10
cosmetologist 20
countermand 151
coup de grace 107
craven 7
crescendo 15
crotchety 134
cuisine 164
cul-de-sac 107
culinary 164
cyclopean 120

D

dalliance 168
debonair 7
Decalogue 58
decimate 58
de facto 129
deign 43
deist 188
demagogue 173
demarche 112
demography 30
demonology 71
demure 67
denouement 112
deposition 63
dermatologist 20
desperado 35
detente 10
deus ex machina 107
dichotomy 58
dilatory 134
dirge 80
disconsolate 134
disenfranchise 179
dispassionate 67
diurnal 40
divertissement 168
dogma 182

Words From Proper Names

Should you be pleased to be called a *maverick*?

Who might issue a *philippic* against a *philanderer*?

Why would *Procrustean* be an interesting name for a mattress company?

Is it acceptable to boast about a *Pyrrhic* victory?

Which literary figure do you recognize in the word *quixotic*?

---

jingoist
lothario
maverick
nemesis
philanderer
philippic
procrustean
protean
Pyrrhic
quixotic
saturnine
solecism
spoonerism
sybarite
tawdry

1. **jingoist** (jiŋ'-gō-ist)—one who boasts about his patriotism and favors a warlike foreign policy. In 1877, British Prime Minister Disraeli sent the fleet to Gallipoli to slow up the Russians. A singer wrote a ditty called "By Jingo" in honor of that action.
   a. The senator lost because his constituents rejected his *jingoistic* policies.
   b. *"Jingoism,"* to paraphrase Samuel Johnson, "is the last refuge of a scoundrel."

2. **lothario** (lō-ther'-ē-ō)—rake; seducer; lover. Lothario was an amorous character in an 18th-century play, *The Fair Penitent.*
   a. The aging playboy thought of himself as a sophisticated *lothario.*
   b. I tried out for the role of the young *lothario,* but they cast me as the butler.

3. **maverick** (mav'-ər-ik)—one who acts independently. Samuel Maverick was a Texas rancher who refused to brand his cattle as others were doing.
   a. When you defend unpopular causes, you get the reputation of being a *maverick.*
   b. The president said that he didn't want yes-men or *mavericks* in his cabinet.

4. **nemesis** (nem'-ə-sis)—agent of retribution; just punishment. In Greek mythology, the goddess Nemesis punished pretentiousness with her sword and avenging wings.
   a. No matter how great a team we fielded, little Calhoun Tech always proved to be our *nemesis.*
   b. Math is my *nemesis,* constantly reminding me that I'm not as bright as I imagine.

5. **philanderer** (fi-lan'-dər-er)—one who makes love insincerely; one who engages in passing love affairs. The word comes from the Greek *philandros* ("man-loving") but gained its current usage because many English playwrights gave the name to their romantic leads.
   a. When Mrs. Greene wanted to find out if her husband was a *philanderer,* she hired a detective.
   b. At the age of 40, Eric switched from part-time *philanderer* to full-time, domesticated husband.

6. **philippic** (fi-lip'-ik)—bitter verbal attack. Philip II of Macedon wanted to make Greece into a monarchy. He was opposed by the great orator, Demosthenes, who denounced Philip in devastating speeches which came to be known as *philippics.*
   a. My *philippic* against higher taxes was reported on the local radio station.

    b. The leader of the rent strike mounted the platform to deliver an effective *philippic* against the management.

7. **procrustean** (prō-krus′-tē-ən)—designed to secure conformity; drastic. An ancient Greek robber named Procrustes tied his victims to a bed and then, to make them fit the bed, stretched the short ones and hacked off the limbs of the taller ones.
    a. Our mayor takes various suggestions and gives them a *procrustean* treatment to fit his philosophy.
    b. Your *procrustean* attitude does not allow for disagreement.

8. **protean** (prōt′-ē-ən)—changeable; taking on different forms. In Greek mythology, Proteus was a sea god who could change his appearance at will.
    a. I resent your *protean* propensity for changing your mind whenever you feel like it.
    b. The stage designer received an award for his *protean* construction which lent itself to the play's various moods.

9. **Pyrrhic** victory (pir′-ik)—a victory which is exceptionally costly. Pyrrhus defeated the Romans in 279 B.C. but his losses were terribly heavy.
    a. The workers seemed to triumph at the end of the strike but it was a *Pyrrhic* victory.
    b. Although we won the championship, it was a *Pyrrhic* victory because of the crippling injuries we suffered.

10. **quixotic** (kwik-sät′-ik)—romantically idealistic; impractical. The Spanish novelist, Cervantes, brought this word into our language when he wrote *Don Quixote*. His hero went forth foolishly to tilt against windmills and help the downtrodden.
    a. Margo's *quixotic* behavior was upsetting to her family because she had always been so level-headed.
    b. The City Planning Commission's ideas were labeled *quixotic* by the skeptical editors.

11. **saturnine** (sat′-ər-nīn)—sluggish; gloomy; grave. The planet Saturn is so far from the sun that it was thought of as cold and dismal.
    a. Uncle Dave's constant *saturnine* expression drove my lively Aunt Pearl up the wall.
    b. While awaiting the jury's verdict, my client had a *saturnine* appearance.

12. **solecism** (säl′-ə-siz′m)—substandard use of words; violation of good manners. This word derives from the Greek inhabitants of the colony of Soloi who used a slangy dialect.
    a. There are some word forms that my teacher considers *solecisms* but I feel are acceptable.
    b. "Ain't she sweet" is a *solecism*—ain't it?

13. **spoonerism** (spōōn′-ər-iz′m)—an unintentional exchange of sounds. Reverend Spooner of New College, Oxford, occasionally twisted his words around when he got excited so that "conquering kings" came out as "kinkering congs."
    a. My cousin collects *spoonerisms* that he hears on the radio, and he hopes to publish them.
    b. The candidate's unfortunate *spoonerism* shocked his elderly audience and cost him their votes.

14. **sybarite** (sib′-ə-rīt)—one who is fond of luxury and soft living. Sybaris was a fabulously wealthy Italian city, symbolic of the good life.

a. Rudy was criticized for living as a *sybarite* while others of his family were starving.

b. The *sybarites* in Roman depictions are often eating grapes.

15. **tawdry** (tô'-drē)—cheap; gaudy; showy. This word can be traced to St. Audrey. Scarves called "St. Audrey's laces" were sold in England where the local people changed the pronunciation to *tawdry*. The quality of the scarves, which at first was good, deteriorated when they were mass produced for the peasant trade.

a. Marlene's *tawdry* taste in clothing was an embarrassment to her boyfriend.

b. The jewelry at Tiffany's can hardly be described as *tawdry*.

EXERCISES

I. Which Word Comes to Mind?

In each of the following, read the statement, then circle the word that comes to mind.

1. You want to rip into your neighbor for his bigoted remarks

(philanderer,   philippic,   protean)

2. A newspaper editorial calls for us to send the fleet to intimidate a Caribbean country

(jingoism,   spoonerism,   solecism)

3. All the girls own pantsuits except Betsy who prefers dresses

(maverick,   saturnine,   nemesis)

4. I heard of a scheme to provide $2000 for each American family

(lothario,   Pyrrhic,   quixotic)

5. Everyone at the meeting was forced to change his mind in order to agree with the chairman's philosophy

(tawdry,   sybarite,   procrustean)

II. True or False?

In the space provided, indicate whether each statement is true or false.

_____ 1. No one welcomes a *Pyrrhic* victory.

_____ 2. A *jingoist* is a hawk rather than a dove.

_____ 3. "I don't know nothing" is a *spoonerism*.

_____ 4. A *nemesis* is something like a jinx.

_____ 5. Going along with the majority is a *maverick's* way.

III. Find the Words

Somewhere in this box of letters, reading up, down, across, or diagonally, four vocabulary words that were taught in this lesson are hidden. As you locate each one, draw a circle around it.

W	L	P	T	G	W	P	N
H	I	R	A	Q	U	Y	E
I	X	O	S	M	R	R	M
C	G	T	L	D	O	R	E
R	Y	E	W	G	N	H	S
O	Z	A	S	L	A	I	I
S	T	N	A	B	E	C	S

IV. Extra Letters

In each of the vocabulary words below there is an extra letter. Put all the extra letters together and you will be able to spell out the title of a book.

lotharcio	procrustrean	quixtotic
parotean	maverbick	phailanderer
nemensis	sybaurite	tawldry
soltecism	philrippic	saturenine
jingoiste	spoonyerism	Pyrrhisc

V. Matching

Match the word in column A with its correct definition in column B by writing the letter of that definition in the space provided.

A	B
____ 1. jingoist	a. interchange of initial sounds
____ 2. lothario	b. changeable
____ 3. maverick	c. super-patriot
____ 4. nemesis	d. nonconformist

_____ 5. philanderer
_____ 6. philippic
_____ 7. procrustean
_____ 8. protean
_____ 9. Pyrrhic victory
_____ 10. quixotic
_____ 11. saturnine
_____ 12. solecism
_____ 13. spoonerism
_____ 14. sybarite
_____ 15. tawdry

e. impractical
f. language error
g. retribution
h. fond of high living
i. unfaithful lover
j. rake
k. gaudy
l. too costly
m. designed to secure conformity
n. bitter verbal attack
o. sluggish

Answers are on page 198.

Don Quixote = quixotic

Appearances And Attitudes (I)

What is the relationship of *bilious* to a body fluid?

Why might a *lachrymose* person have need of kleenex tissues?

Would you prefer a waiter who was *complaisant* or *churlish*?

Should we applaud or hiss *craven* actions?

Is it a good idea to submit your manuscript to a *captious* editor?

---

acidulous
baleful
bellicose
bilious
bumptious
captious
churlish
complaisant
contrite
convivial
craven
debonair
dyspeptic
lachrymose
neurasthenic

1. **acidulous** (ə-sij′-oo-ləs)—somewhat acid or sour.
   a. Joan's father took an *acidulous* view of her plans to get married.
   b. He is the kind of *acidulous* critic who hates every new book which is published.

2. **baleful** (bāl′-fəl)—deadly; sinister.
   a. I saw the *baleful* look on the gang leader's face, and I knew we were in for trouble.
   b. Overhead the *baleful* clouds were gathering.

3. **bellicose** (bel′-ə-kōs)—warlike; of a quarrelsome nature.
   a. Although our landlord sometimes sounds *bellicose,* he is actually very soft-hearted.
   b. Our ambassador often has to ignore *bellicose* statements from the prime minister.

4. **bilious** (bil′-yəs) bad-tempered; bitter. It comes from the French word *bilis* ("bile"), the fluid secreted by the liver.
   a. Twenty years in his company's complaint department gave Ted a *bilious* attitude toward the public.
   b. I overlooked Cynthia's *bilious* remarks because I know that she is bad-tempered until she has had her morning coffee.

5. **bumptious** (bump′-shəs)—arrogant; disagreeably conceited.
   a. My uncle's *bumptious* personality has caused him to be fired from several good jobs.
   b. In his *bumptious* fashion, Mario felt that every girl was madly in love with him.

6. **captious** (kap′-shəs)—critical; quick to find fault; quibbling.
   a. I don't mind criticism from Professor Torres, but his *captious* comments about my term paper did not endear him to me.
   b. The gardeners hate to work for Mrs. Lyons because of her *captious* eye.

7. **churlish** (churl′-ish)—boorish; surly. This adjective comes from "churl," the old word for a peasant.
   a. We were barred from the restaurant because some of our team members had behaved in a *churlish* fashion.
   b. Harry's allowance was cut off by his parents as punishment for his *churlish* table manners.

8. **complaisant** (kəm-plā´ z'nt)—willing to please; polite.
   a. Every employee at the state agency acts in an admirable, *complaisant* way.
   b. Uriah Heep adopted a *complaisant* pose as a cover-up for his hostility.

9. **contrite** (kən-trīt´)—crushed in spirit by a feeling of guilt.
   a. Because Judge Dooly believed that the prisoner was *contrite,* he gave him a light sentence.
   b. When the fraternity members realized the horror of their actions, they were truly *contrite.*

10. **convivial** (kən-viv´-ē-əl)—festive; sociable.
    a. All of the shoppers contributed to the *convivial* atmosphere at the mall.
    b. New Orleans at Mardi Gras time is world-famous for its *convivial* qualities.

11. **craven** (krā´-vən)—cowardly.
    a. Even the most *craven* animal will turn courageous when its young are threatened.
    b. Lieutenant Rader's *craven* behavior under fire resulted in his court-martial.

12. **debonair** (deb-ə-ner´)—genial; courteous. In Old French the words were *de bon aire* ("of a good race or breed").
    a. Fred Astaire, with his top hat at a jaunty angle, was the model of a *debonair* gentleman.
    b. Driving up in a sporty foreign car, my brother impressed the neighbors with his *debonair* appearance.

13. **dyspeptic** (dis-pep´-tik)—grouchy; gloomy; a person who suffers from dyspepsia or indigestion.
    a. Eric's *dyspeptic* analysis of our chances for success was discouraging.
    b. Our local newspaper features two columnists—one with a *dyspeptic* viewpoint, the other with an incurable optimism.

14. **lachrymose** (lak´-rə-mōs)—sad; mournful; inclined to shed many tears.
    a. Most television soap operas have *lachrymose* themes.
    b. The funniest Ringling Brothers Circus clown has a *lachrymose* expression painted on his face.

15. **neurasthenic** (noor-əs-thēn´-ik)—having emotional conflicts which lead to weakness and depression.
    a. Aunt Emily's *neurasthenic* complaints were solved when she won $50,000 in the lottery.
    b. My doctor said I was a *neurasthenic* type who would always wear myself out with worrying.

EXERCISES

I. Which Word Comes to Mind?

In each of the following, read the statement, then circle the word that comes to mind.

1. A defendant's attitude which impresses the jury

   (debonair,   contrite,   acidulous)

2. An ill-tempered waiter

   (complaisant,   craven,   churlish)

3. Physical ailments which stem from worry

(baleful,   neurasthenic,   bumptious)

4. A person suffering from indigestion

(dyspeptic,   bellicose,   captious)

5. An angry boss is insulting his workers

(lachrymose,   bilious,   convivial)

II. True or False?

In the space provided, indicate whether each statement is true or false.

_____ 1. A *craven* leader inspires respect in his followers.
_____ 2. Citizens are pleased to see a criminal who is *contrite*.
_____ 3. *Captious* people often split hairs.
_____ 4. It's difficult for a gawky 14-year-old to look *debonair*.
_____ 5. By displaying proper etiquette, one can expect to be praised for his *churlishness*.

III. Find the Words

Somewhere in this box of letters, reading up, down, across, or diagonally, three vocabulary words that were taught in this lesson are hidden. As you locate each one, draw a circle around it.

H	E	B	L	U	M	O	S
C	R	A	V	E	N	R	U
W	H	L	O	R	D	I	O
E	S	E	M	B	C	F	I
T	O	F	Y	A	R	M	L
E	X	U	P	H	S	O	I
Z	B	L	C	N	U	W	B

IV. Extra Letters

In each of the vocabulary words below there is an extra letter. Put all the extra letters together, and you will be able to spell out a word taught in a previous lesson. Its meaning is "cheap."

balefult   corntrite
bellidcose   laychrymose
caraven   neurawsthenic

V. Matching

Match the word in column A with its correct definition in column B by writing the letter of that definition in the space provided.

A	B
_____ 1. acidulous	a. arrogant
_____ 2. baleful	b. cowardly
_____ 3. bellicose	c. surly, boorish
_____ 4. bilious	d. sour
_____ 5. bumptious	e. weakened by emotional problems
_____ 6. captious	f. festive
_____ 7. churlish	g. grouchy
_____ 8. complaisant	h. sinister
_____ 9. contrite	i. sad
_____ 10. convivial	j. overwhelmed with guilt
_____ 11. craven	k. courteous
_____ 12. debonair	l. polite
_____ 13. dyspeptic	m. bad-tempered
_____ 14. lachrymose	n. critical
_____ 15. neurasthenic	o. warlike

Answers are on page 198.

Words About Groups

What does *genealogy* have to do with *Roots*?

Are we likely to find *esprit de corps* where there is *camaraderie*?

What is the connection between *liaison* and *ligature*?

Why wouldn't you publish the names of the members of your *cabal*?

Where are we more likely to find a *cortege*—at the florist's or at a funeral?

---

cabal
camaraderie
caste
cortege
detente
echelon
ecumenical
elite
esprit de corps
freemasonry
genealogy
hierarchy
hobnob
liaison
rapprochement

1. **cabal** (kə-bal′)—a clique; a small group joined in a secret intrigue; a conspiracy. This French word was formed from the initials of Charles II's ministers (Clifford, Arlington, Buckingham, Ashley, Lauderdale); *cabal* ultimately derives from the Hebrew word *qabbalah* which referred to a mystical interpretation of the Scriptures.
   a. The *cabal* met to formulate plans for the overthrow of the Bolivian government.
   b. When the Arab *cabal's* membership list was disclosed, it put an end to their activities.

2. **camaraderie** (käm′-ə-räd′-ər-ē)—comradeship; good fellowship. Two soldiers sharing the same room (in German, *kammer*) usually developed a loyal and warm friendship. The Communist Party adopted the word *comrade* to denote a fellow member.
   a. A beautiful *camaraderie* developed among the actors in the cast of *Chorus Line*.
   b. The good fellowship award was given to the beauty pageant contestant who contributed most to the *camaraderie* of all the girls.

3. **caste** (kast)—a distinct social class or system. Hindu society is traditionally divided into four major hereditary *castes,* each class separated from the others by restrictions in marriage and occupation.
   a. Satindra was a member of the untouchable *caste.*
   b. The union leader spoke angrily about a *caste* system at the factory.

4. **cortege** (kôr-tezh′)—a group of attendants accompanying a person; a ceremonial procession. It is not surprising that *cortege* is related to court, a place where followers and ceremonies abound.
   a. The funeral *cortege* of the Spanish dictator, Francisco Franco, stretched for two miles.
   b. Some actors never travel without a *cortege* of agents to publicize their every word and deed.

5. **detente** (dā-tänt′)—a relaxing or easing, especially of international tension. After the Cold War years following World War II, the U.S. embarked on a policy of closer ties with Russia; hence was born the policy of *detente*.
   a. The detractors of former Secretary of State, Henry Kissinger, claim that his efforts at *detente* with the Soviet Union weakened America's defenses.
   b. Even in our personal relationships, we can often accomplish more with *detente* than with obstinacy.

6. **echelon** (esh′-ə-län)—a level of command or authority or rank; a steplike formation of ships, troops, or planes. Coming to English through several languages, the word *echelon* has descended a ladder starting with the Latin word *scale,* which indeed means ladder, and explains why we still "scale a ladder."

a. The command *echelon* was unaware that the fighting troops were being attacked.

b. Starting at the lowest *echelon,* the dynamic Ms. Steinem worked her way to the top of her profession.

7. **ecumenical** (ek-yoo-men′-i-k′l)—universal; general; fostering Christian unity throughout the world. The idea of *ecumenism,* as well as the spirit of brotherhood, was fostered by the far-reaching policies of Pope John XXIII (1958–63).

a. The influence of Pope John's *ecumenical* pronouncements is still being felt today.

b. We must work not merely for our selfish interests but for the *ecumenical* welfare.

8. **elite** (i-lēt′)—the best or most skilled members of a given social group. The word is related to *elect* and suggests that some people are born with "a silver spoon in their mouth" or, at least, are entitled to special privileges.

a. The *elite* of the city teams vied for the honor of being chosen to travel to Cuba.

b. I attended an *elite* gathering of authors and was much impressed by the level of their language.

9. **esprit de corps** (es-prē′-də-kôr′)—a sense of union and of common interests and responsibilities. The French expression literally means "spirit of feeling as one body." It implies not only a camaraderie but a sense of pride or honor shared by those involved in an undertaking.

a. Coach Vince Lombardi established an *esprit de corps* that was powerful enough to catapult the team to the Rose Bowl.

b. Were it not for the amazing *esprit de corps* among the surviving members of the patrol, they would never have been able to accomplish their mission.

10. **freemasonry** (frē′-mās′n′-rē)—secret or tacit brotherhood; instinctive sympathy. The Freemasons is an international fraternity for the promotion of brotherly love among its members, as well as mutual assistance. It began in the Middle Ages as a class of skilled stoneworkers who possessed secret signs and passwords, a ritual that is still preserved today.

a. Count me among the *freemasonry* of those who thirst for knowledge.

b. The future of civilization rests with the *freemasonry* of people who believe in the humanity of each individual and share the dream of world peace.

11. **genealogy** (jē′-nē-äl′-ə-jē)—lineage; science of family descent. Though our hereditary character is transmitted through genes in our chromosomes, that does not assure us that our *genealogy* has provided us with the most desirable traits. Much can and does happen as the generations pass.

a. The young black man proudly displayed his *genealogical* chart, which linked him with African royalty.

b. Of course, if we trace our *genealogy* back far enough, we will find that we all share some common ancestors.

12. **hierarchy** (hī-ə-rär′-kē)—a group of persons or things arranged in order, rank, or grade; a system of church government by clergymen in graded ranks. The Greek word *hierarkhes* meant "high priest." From there it was a small step to the designation of the entire church leadership as a *hierarchy*. With the loss of temporal power by the church after the Middle Ages, the word now refers to any arrangement by authority or position.

a. The political *hierarchy* in our country begins with the voter in the polling booth.

b. To learn the operation of a newspaper, it is necessary to examine the entire *hierarchy* of jobs from copyboy to editor.

13. **hobnob** (häb'-näb')—to associate on very friendly terms. The title of the novel *To Have and Have Not* is an exact translation of the original meaning of *hobnob*. This word was formed by a combination of the Old English words *habban* ("to have") and *navban* ("not to have"). The modern meaning suggests the egalitarian idea of friendship not based on one's possessions.
   a. Juanita's vivacious temperament allowed her to *hobnob* with people in all walks of life.
   b. Calvin's parents refused to let him *hobnob* with the worst elements in the neighborhood.

14. **liaison** (lē'-ə-zän)—the contact maintained between military or naval units in order to undertake concerted action; a similar connection between the units of any organization; an illicit relationship between a man and a woman. This word is a cousin to *ligature*, a connection on the physical level similar to the connection made on an informational level by a *liaison*.
   a. The elected sophomore served as a *liaison* between the council and his class.
   b. Having been appointed chief *liaison* officer, Colonel Marks assumed responsibility for the flow of information.

15. **rapprochement** (ra-prōsh'-män)—a reestablishing of cordial relations. If there is to be an end to war, people and nations must learn to meet each other, to approach each other, on common grounds. That is what this word implies, a coming together in friendship and trust.
   a. After months of secret negotiations, a *rapprochement* was reached between the warring factions.
   b. Doctor Welby attempted to bring about a *rapprochement* between mother and son.

EXERCISES

I. Which Word Comes to Mind?

In each of the following, read the statement, then circle the word that comes to mind.

1. The superpowers agree to a mutual reduction of nuclear stockpiles

   (cabal,   echelon,   rapprochement)

2. A young man breaks the engagement because his fiance cannot afford a dowry

   (caste,   liaison,   hierarchy)

3. Firemen risk their lives to rescue a trapped buddy

   (cortege,   camaraderie,   genealogy)

4. He associates informally with the Cabots and the Lodges

   (detente,   freemasonry,   hobnob)

5. The sermon ended with a call for universal brotherhood and recognition of individual worth

   (ecumenical,   elite,   esprit de corps)

II. True or False?

In the space provided, indicate whether each statement is true or false.

_____ 1. The *cabal* holds a public forum to discuss the issue.
_____ 2. *Detente* involves risks and compromises by both sides.
_____ 3. A member of the *elite* feels that the world is his oyster.
_____ 4. *Esprit de corps* denotes a stronger bond than *camaraderie*.
_____ 5. A *liaison* serves a purpose similar to that of a go-between.

III. Find the Words

Somewhere in this box of letters, reading up, down, across, or diagonally, seven vocabulary words that were taught in this lesson are hidden. As you locate each one, draw a circle around it.

L	I	A	I	S	O	N	D
E	G	E	T	R	O	C	E
E	F	J	S	L	M	I	W
T	K	Y	E	T	S	A	C
I	T	H	M	X	F	Q	V
L	C	A	B	A	L	U	S
E	B	O	N	B	O	H	P

IV. Extra Letters

In each of the vocabulary words there is an extra letter. Put all the extra letters together and you will be able to spell out a vocabulary word taught in a previous lesson. Its meaning is "bad tempered."

cabbal
caiste
geneallogy
liaision

echoelon
camauraderie
eliste

V. Matching

Match the word in column A with its correct definition in column B by writing the letter of that definition in the space provided.

A	B
_____ 1. cabal	a. resumption of harmonious relations
_____ 2. camaraderie	b. arrangement by rank
_____ 3. caste	c. pal around
_____ 4. cortege	d. conspiracy
_____ 5. detente	e. family tree
_____ 6. echelon	f. worldwide
_____ 7. ecumenical	g. most qualified, best
_____ 8. elite	h. procession
_____ 9. esprit de corps	i. connection
_____ 10. freemasonry	j. steplike formation of troops
_____ 11. genealogy	k. secret brotherhood
_____ 12. hierarchy	l. class system
_____ 13. hobnob	m. relaxation of tension
_____ 14. liaison	n. group loyalty
_____ 15. rapprochement	o. friendship

Answers are on page 199.

Sounds Italian

Which is the fastest tempo—*andante, allegretto,* or *adagio?*

Is *fortissimo* a title given to a high-ranking officer?

Does *libretto* refer to the words or the music?

Which requires more than one note, a *crescendo* or an *arpeggio?*

Which indicates musical skill—*bravura, intaglio,* or *imbroglio?*

---

adagio
andante
arpeggio
bravura
contralto
crescendo
falsetto
fortissimo
imbroglio
intaglio
largo
libretto
salvo
staccato
vendetta

1. **adagio** (ə-dä′-jō)—slowly, in music. The plural, *adagios,* refers to a slow movement in music or a slow ballet dance requiring skillful balancing.
   a. The second movement of the symphony was played in *adagio* tempo.
   b. The ballerina executed the *adagios* in the pas de deux with exquisite grace and beauty.

2. **andante** (än-dän′-tä, än-dän′-tē)—moderate in tempo. This is a musical direction faster than *adagio* but slower than *allegretto.* A slightly faster tempo is given the diminutive *andantino.*
   a. The violin passage in the *andante* section was flawlessly performed.
   b. The smoothly flowing strains of the *andante* cantabile had me humming along from the first bar.

3. **arpeggio** (ärpej′-ē-ō, -pej′-ō)—the playing of the tones of a chord in rapid succession rather than simultaneously.
   a. The sound of the *arpeggio* simulates the music of a harp.
   b. The lively composition concluded with a series of crashing *arpeggios.*

4. **bravura** (brə–vyoor′-ə)—in music, a florid passage requiring great skill and spirit in the performer; a display of daring; a brilliant performance (used as a noun and as an adjective).
   a. Verdi is noted for his stunning *bravuras.*
   b. The more dangerous the stunts, the more the crowd cheered the *bravura* performances.

5. **contralto** (kən-träl′-tō)—the lowest female voice or part, between a soprano and a tenor; a woman having such a voice.
   a. The famous singer had a rich and powerful *contralto* voice.
   b. Though sopranos are the traditional prima donnas of the music world, many people prefer the fullness and melodiousness of the lower-pitched *contralto* voice.

6. **crescendo** (krə-shen′-dō, -sen′-dō)—a gradual increase in the volume or intensity of sound; a music passage played in *crescendo. Crescendo* is also used as a verb.
   a. The natives' chants *crescendoed* to a piercing frenzy.
   b. The gale reached its *crescendo* at dawn.

7. **falsetto** (fôl-set′-ō)—a typically male singing voice, the result of artificially produced tones in an upper register which go beyond the voice's normal range.
   a. The thief, speaking in *falsetto,* was able to convince the maid to open the door.
   b. The cantor's skill at a sustained *falsetto* won the admiration of the congregants.

8. **fortissimo** (fôr-tis'-ə-mō)—a very loud passage, sound or tone. The word is also used as an adverb.
    a. The "1812 Overture" ends with a *fortissimo* of crashing cymbals, rolling drums and roaring cannons.
    b. The deafening *fortissimo* of the storm's passage was followed by a silence broken only by the melancholy dripping of raindrops from the tree branches.

9. **imbroglio** (im-brōl'-yō)—a confused or difficult situation; a confused heap or tangle. The original Latin word describes the situation best—*in broglio* ("entangled in a bush").
    a. The derelict sat beside the *imbroglio* comprised of all his meager belongings.
    b. Accepting two dates for the same evening placed Nanette in an *imbroglio* she could not easily resolve.

10. **intaglio** (in-tal'-yō)—a figure or design cut beneath the surface of a hard metal or stone; the art of carving in this manner; a gemstone carved in *intaglio*. *Intaglio* is in contrast with cameo, where the design is raised and differs in color from the background.
    a. The archaeological discovery of an *intaglio* bracelet baffled the experts who had placed the origin of this process at a much later date.
    b. The *intaglio* design in jewelry is not as popular as the cameo.

11. **largo** (lär'-gō)—in a slow, solemn manner (a direction in music); a slow, broad movement (noun).
    a. The music depicting the army's retreat was played in *largo*.
    b. The *largo* movement began with the echoes of hope and ended in the anguished tones of despair.

12. **libretto** (li-bret'-ō)—the text of an opera or other dramatic musical work. It is the Italian diminutive of *libro* ("book").
    a. In the most famous team that produced light opera, Gilbert wrote the *librettos* and Sullivan the music.
    b. The *librettos* of many popular musicals would be quickly forgotten were it not for the memorable music they are wedded to.

13. **salvo** (sal'-vō)—a simultaneous discharge of firearms; a sudden outburst of cheers or the like. It is not surprising to find that words like *salutation, salutary, salve,* and *salvation* are related to *salvo* since the Latin *salve* ("hail"), and *salvus* ("safe or well"), form the ancestry of both strands of meaning.
    a. The new play received *salvos* of praise from the leading critics.
    b. The continuous *salvos* from the enemy artillery failed to dislodge the tenacious defenders from their mountaintop positions.

14. **staccato** (stə-kä'-tō)—music performed with a crisp, sharp attack to simulate rests between successive tones; composed of abrupt, distinct, emphatic parts or sounds. This word is from the Old French word *destachier* ("detach") and is contrasted with *legato*.
    a. From the distance, we heard the *staccato* beat of rain on a tin roof.
    b. The *staccato* click of Miss Benton's heels sounded on the tile floor as she hurried to answer the boss' summons.

15. **vendetta** (ven-det'-ə)—blood feud; a prolonged feud marked by bitter hostility. This is the Italian word for revenge and is related to *vindicate,* our meaning for which is "to avenge."
    a. The *vendetta* between the McCoys and the Hatfields became a tradition of American mountain folklore.
    b. The *vendetta* to defend the family honor has become outmoded with the loosening of family ties.

EXERCISES

I. Which Word Comes to Mind?

In each of the following, read the statement, then circle the word that comes to mind.

1. A musical direction

(largo,   falsetto,   contralto)

2. A volley of rockets

(salvo,   adagio,   andante)

3. An embarrassing situation

(fortissimo,   libretto,   imbroglio)

4. A bully trying to intimidate a scrawny boy

(vendetta,   bravura,   arpeggio)

5. Machine-gun fire

(crescendo,   intaglio,   staccato)

II. True or False?

In the space provided, indicate whether each statement is true or false.

___ 1. A *contralto* has a higher-pitched voice than a soprano.
___ 2. If the direction reads *andante*, the music should be played slowly.
___ 3. A man singing in *falsetto* has probably hit a wrong note.
___ 4. An *intaglio* design is cut below the surface.
___ 5. A participant in a *vendetta* tends to harbor unreasonable hatred.

III. Find the Words

Somewhere in this box of letters, reading up, down, across, or diagonally, five vocabulary words that were taught in this lesson are hidden. As you locate each one, draw a circle around it.

R	O	S	T	E	F	H	L
W	H	I	B	O	C	A	E
O	I	L	G	A	T	N	I
M	P	R	D	A	S	T	Q
Z	A	T	Y	I	D	X	U
L	B	S	O	V	L	A	S
O	I	G	G	E	P	R	A

IV. Extra Letters

In each of the vocabulary words below there is an extra or superfluous letter. Putting all the extra letters together, you will be able to spell out a word taught in a previous lesson. Its meaning is "critical."

arcpeggio   venidetta
fortaissimo   falosetto
largop   saulvo
staccatto   cresscendo

V. Matching

Match the word in column A with its correct definition in Column B by writing the letter of that definition in the space provided.

         A   *B*
___ 1. adagio   a. spirited or showy passage in music
___ 2. andante   b. predicament
___ 3. arpeggio   c. a mounting in intensity
___ 4. bravura   d. disconnected

—— 5. contralto

—— 6. crescendo

—— 7. falsetto

—— 8. fortissimo

—— 9. imbroglio

—— 10. intaglio

—— 11. largo

—— 12. libretto

—— 13. salvo

—— 14. staccato

—— 15. vendetta

e. opposite of cameo

f. slowly

g. slow and solemn

h. lower than soprano

i. salute

j. text of an opera

k. artificial tones

l. moderate, faster tempo than adagio

m. bitter quarrel

n. extremely loud

o. tones of a chord played in rapid succession

Answers are on page 199.

Jobs and Professions

Would you resent being sent to see an *alienist*?

Is a *lapidary* similar to a dromedary?

What's the proper name for an eye specialist?

Where would you go with a bad case of acne?

In what way does an *internist* differ from an intern?

---

alienist
amanuensis
beadle
cosmetologist
dermatologist
entomologist
farrier
graphologist
internist
lapidary
ophthalmologist
ornithologist
osteopath
pharyngologist
physiologist

1. **alienist** (āl′-yən-ist)—a doctor who specializes in mental disease. Alienation, referring to mental derangement or insanity, comes from the Latin word, *alienato* ("separation"). The question, "Have you taken leave of your senses?" shows the relationship to *alienist.*
   a. The defense lawyer hired an *alienist* to testify to his client's insanity.
   b. Dr. Fowler, an *alienist*, is annoyed with people who confuse his title with the word alien.

2. **amanuensis** (ə-man-yoo-wen′-sis)—secretary; one who copies something. It comes from the Latin *manus* ("hand") and *ensis* ("relating to"). In ancient times a scribe was known as an *amanuensis.*
   a. When illiteracy was widespread, people used the services of an *amanuensis* to write letters for them.
   b. My secretary likes to tease people by telling them she is a professional *amanuensis.*

3. **beadle** (bē′-d'l) minor official. *Beadle* comes from an Old French word which meant "messenger"—a man who preceded a procession. The functionary carrying a mace (symbolic club) at the head of a university procession is a *beadle.*
   a. Mr. Bumble in Dickens' *Oliver Twist* is the most famous *beadle* in literature.
   b. When the President arrived to address the joint meeting of Congress, he was ushered in by a pompous *beadle.*

4. **cosmetologist** (käz-mə-täl′-ə-jist)—an expert in cosmetics. When a woman applies cosmetics she is putting herself in order. The Latin word *cosmos* means order in the sense of an orderly universe. Since such order was equated with beauty, when a *cosmetologist* helps to apply makeup, she is maintaining the classical connection between the two.
   a. Our school hired a *cosmetologist* to teach the girls how to look beautiful.
   b. It was ironic that the least attractive woman in the room was a *cosmetologist.*

5. **dermatologist** (dur-mə-täl′-ə-jist)—a doctor who specializes in skin problems. From the Greek *derma* ("skin"). Your epidermis is your outer layer of skin.
   a. Dr. Zweben chose to be a *dermatologist* because patients rarely die of their skin ailments.
   b. Harold went to a *dermatologist* to investigate the strange discoloration on his arm.

6. **entomologist** (en-tə-mäl′-ə-jist)—a specialist in the study of insects. In Greek, *entomos* means "cut up." Insects' bodies appear to be divided into sections or "cut up."

a. My professor invited an *entomologist* to lecture on "Roaches I Have Known."

b. Eddie loved to play with insects when he was a kid, and interestingly enough, he grew up to be an *entomologist*.

7. **farrier** (far'-ē-ər) blacksmith; iron worker. The Latin word *ferrarius* means "of iron."

a. A *farrier* was summoned to the equine hospital to prepare a special horseshoe for the injured filly.

b. The *farriers* who worked on the skyscrapers had no fear of great heights.

8. **graphologist** (gra-fäl'-ə-jist)—a handwriting analyst. In Greek, *graphos* means "to write." *Graphologists* are often hired as entertainers today, analyzing the handwriting of guests at a party and describing their character traits and aptitudes.

a. Because my handwriting tends to slope upward, *graphologists* say I'm an optimist.

b. Even though Rachel's own handwriting is poor, it didn't stop her from becoming a *graphologist*.

9. **internist** (in-tur'-nist)—doctor who specializes in internal medicine. In Latin, *internus* means "inward." *Internists* are noted as diagnosticians, not surgeons.

a. The *internist* in our medical group is loath to prescribe drugs.

b. Charles consulted a Park Avenue *internist* who charged $100 for each visit.

10. **lapidary** (lap'-ə-der-ē)—an expert in precious stones. Julius Caesar used the word *lapis* when he meant stone. Lapidaries cut, polish, and engrave stones.

a. After the *lapidary* had washed the mud off the stone, he realized its true value.

b. "You've got rocks in your head," joked the *lapidary's* neighbor.

11. **ophthalmologist** (äf-thal-mäl'-ə-jist)—a doctor who treats eyes and their diseases. From the Greek *ophthalmos* ("eye"). Oculist is a synonym for *ophthalmologist*. An optometrist prescribes eyeglasses; an optician makes or sells eyeglasses.

a. It took an *ophthalmologist* to discover that Aunt Rose had a detached retina.

b. Ethel's *ophthalmologist* saved her from blindness by treating her glaucoma promptly.

12. **ornithologist** (ôr-nə-thäl'-ə-jist)—an expert in the branch of zoology dealing with birds. It is from the Greek *ornis* ("bird").

a. Audubon didn't have a degree as an *ornithologist*, but his paintings of birds displayed his vast knowledge of them.

b. The Museum of Natural History hired an *ornithologist* to supervise their bird displays.

13. **osteopath** (äs'-tē-ə-path)—one who treats ailments by placing pressure on bones and nerves. From the Greek *osteo* ("bone") and *pathos* ("suffering").

a. Uncle Henry always said that an *osteopath* was a respectable chiropractor.

b. By manipulating my son's bones, the *osteopath* was able to reduce his fever.

14. **pharyngologist** (far-in-gäl'-ə-jist)—a doctor who specializes in diseases of the pharynx, the cavity of the alimentary canal leading from the mouth and nasal passages to the larynx and esophagus.

    a. During a routine examination, the *pharyngologist* discovered that the heavy smoker had a possible mouth cancer.

    b. I laughingly accused the *pharyngologist* of putting his foot in his mou.h.

15. **physiologist** (fiz-ē-äl′-ə-jist)—a biologist who deals with the functions and vital processes of living organisms. It comes from the Greek *physis* ("nature") and *logos* ("discourse").

    a. Alvin, our school's Westinghouse Science Award winner, is planning to be a *physiologist.*

    b. After working with laboratory mice, I decided to become a *physiologist.*

EXERCISES

I. Which Word Comes to Mind?

In each of the following, read the statement, then circle the word that comes to mind.

1. You need treatment for a tennis elbow

(alienist, ophthalmologist, osteopath)

2. Someone may have forged your signature

(graphologist, cosmetologist, lapidary)

3. "Gnats to you!"

(entomologist, farrier, pharyngologist)

4. Teenagers frequently suffer from acne

(beadle, dermatologist, amanuensis)

5. "Hey, man, you're for the birds!"

(ornithologist, internist, physiologist)

II. True or False?

In the space provided, indicate whether each statement is true or false.

_____ 1. An *alienist* can give you an opinion about someone's emotional stability.

_____ 2. X-rays are usually employed by a competent *amanuensis.*

_____ 3. The *lapidary* knew that the opals would make a great necklace.

_____ 4. If you have blurred vision, you should consult an *ophthalmologist.*

_____ 5. Longfellow wrote, "The Village *Farrier.*"

III. Find the Words

Somewhere in this box of letters, reading up, down, across, or diagonally, three vocabulary words that were taught in this lesson are hidden. As you locate each one, draw a circle around it.

Y	R	A	D	I	P	A	L
A	H	T	B	G	N	R	A
D	S	W	E	F	J	Y	C
K	F	B	A	X	H	M	P
M	Z	N	D	I	O	Q	U
E	S	D	L	O	T	C	R
A	L	I	E	N	I	S	T

IV. Extra Letters

In each of the vocabulary words below there is an extra letter. Put all the extra letters together and you will be able to spell out a word taught in a previous lesson. Its meaning is "slowly."

cosmetoalogist

beaddle

lapaidary

aliegnist

graphiologist

enotomologist

V. Matching

Match the word in column A with its correct definition in column B by writing the letter of that definition in the space provided.

	A		B
____	1. alienist	a.	beauty expert
____	2. amanuensis	b.	blacksmith
____	3. beadle	c.	handwriting expert
____	4. cosmetologist	d.	psychiatrist
____	5. dermatologist	e.	stone cutter

_____ 6. entomologist
_____ 7. farrier
_____ 8. graphologist
_____ 9. internist
_____ 10. lapidary
_____ 11. ophthalmologist
_____ 12. ornithologist
_____ 13. osteopath
_____ 14. pharyngologist
_____ 15. physiologist

f. skin specialist
g. eye specialist
h. minor official
i. expert on birds
j. knows about insects
k. manipulates bones and nerves
l. doctor of internal medicine
m. biologist who studies vital functions
n. treats diseases of the pharynx
o. secretary

Answers are on page 200.

The Amanuensis Pool

Mythology (I)

Does a *Cassandra* speak the truth?

Is a *bacchanal* a wedding song or a riotous feast?

Why would one feel safe with a *palladium*?

What was *Narcissus'* undoing?

What color is *iridescent*?

Adonis
bacchanal
Cassandra
cornucopia
erotic
herculean
hermetic
hydra
hymeneal
iridescent
narcissism
odyssey
Olympian
palladium
phoenix

1. **Adonis** (ə-dän′-is)—an exceptionally handsome young man; a plant with solitary red or yellow flowers. Adonis was beloved by both Aphrodite, the goddess of love, and Persephone, the queen of the dead. He was killed by a boar in a hunting expedition and from his life's blood sprang up a crimson flower.
   a. Robert Redford is considered an *Adonis* of the film world.
   b. Though he was once the *Adonis* of the Broadway stage, Johnny found his popularity short-lived.

2. **bacchanal** (bak′-ə-n′l)—a follower of Bacchus (Greek, Dionysus), the god of wine; a drunken reveler; an orgy. Early Greek drama developed in connection with the festival honoring this god.
   a. The *bacchanal* lasted into the late hours of the night.
   b. The *bacchanalian* scene in the play was so realistic the audience began to wonder what was really in the wine glasses.

3. **Cassandra** (kə-san′-drə)—a daughter of King Priam and Queen Hecuba of Troy who had the gift of prophecy but was cursed by Apollo so that her prophecies, though true, were fated never to be believed; one who prophesies doom or disaster. The Trojans thought Cassandra was insane and disregarded her predictions. Among these were the revelation that Troy would be destroyed if Paris went to Sparta, and that there were armed Greeks in the Wooden Horse. If either of these prophecies had been heeded, Troy would have been saved.
   a. The general said, "If we remain militarily strong, we need not be concerned with the *Cassandras* who see only tragedy."
   b. Since Marge had ignored her work all term, it took no *Cassandra* to predict her inevitable failure.

4. **cornucopia** (kôr-ne-kō′-pē-ə)—abundance; horn of plenty. Named after the horn of the goat Amalthea that suckled the infant Zeus, the horn is always full of food and drink in endless supply.
   a. The people of the Third World still look for a *cornucopia* of riches that will end hunger and suffering in their lands.
   b. The spendthrift cannot expect a *cornucopia* of merchandise to cater to his fanciful tastes.

5. **erotic** (i-rät′-ik)—concerning sexual love and desire; amatory. Eros was the Greek god of love, identified by the Romans with Cupid and represented as a winged child. While *erotic* has retained the sexual connotation, *cupidity* has acquired the meaning of "greed."
   a. *Erotic* literature is no longer subject to the censor's pen.
   b. Genuine love between a man and a woman involves respect and regard for one another that go far beyond mere *erotic* sensations.

6. **herculean** (hur-kyə-lē′-ən, hur-kyōō′-lē-ən)—tremendously difficult and de-

25

manding; resembling Hercules in size, power or courage. Hercules was the son of Zeus and Alcmene who won immortality by performing Twelve Labors demanded by the jealous Hera.
   a.   Digging the tunnel was a *herculean* task.
   b.   With *herculean* courage, the wounded airman brought the crippled plane back to the safety of the carrier.

7.   **hermetic** (hur-met′-ik)—made airtight by fusion or sealing; insulated or cloistered; magical. Hermes (Latin, Mercury) was the messenger of the gods and the god of roads, commerce, invention, cunning and theft. A most versatile god, Hermes is identified with the caduceus, the golden staff with wings at the top and intertwined with serpents, which is the symbol of today's medical profession.
   a.   The sage spoke and then retreated to the *hermetic* confines of his room.
   b.   The food was preserved in *hermetically* sealed jars.

8.   **hydra** (hī′-drə)—the nine-headed serpent slain by Hercules; a persistent or many-sided problem that presents new obstacles as soon as old ones are solved. The *hydra* had to be slain by Hercules as one of his Twelve Labors. This monster grew two heads for each one cut off. Hercules finally destroyed the *hydra* by cauterizing the necks as he cut off the heads.
   a.   Economists are struggling to solve the *hydra*-headed problems of inflation without creating the evils of recession.
   b.   In a bizarre series of accidents that, *hydra*-like, seemed to grow one from the other, the team slipped from first to last place in the latter part of the season.

9.   **hymeneal** (hī-mə-nē′-əl)—pertaining to marriage; a wedding song or poem. Hymen, the god of marriage, was represented as a handsome youth holding a torch.
   a.   The *hymeneal* feast was attended by all the town's elite.
   b.   Playing a *hymeneal,* the musicians led the procession into the great hall for the wedding ceremony.

10.   **iridescent** (ir′-i-des′-ənt)—displaying lustrous colors like those of the rainbow. Iris was a messenger of the gods and regarded as the goddess of the rainbow.
   a.   The fashion show featured an *iridescent* display of color in the most modern styles.
   b.   The prelude was as *iridescent* as a prism in a morning room.

11.   **narcissism** (nar′-si-siz′-m)—excessive admiration of oneself; egocentrism. Narcissus was a youth who, having spurned the love of Echo, fell in love with his own image reflected in a pool, and after wasting away from unsatisfied desire was transformed into the flower that bears his name. The plant, incidentally, has narcotic effects (from the Greek *narke,* "numbness").
   a.   Psychoanalysts consider *narcissism* an infantile level of personality development.
   b.   Some people have such exaggerated opinions of themselves that they border on *narcissism.*

12.   **odyssey** (äd′-i-sē)—a long series of wanderings, especially when filled with notable experiences or hardships. *The Odyssey,* called "the greatest tale of all time," is the second epic of Homer. It recounts the wanderings and adventures of Odysseus after the fall of Troy, and his eventual return home to his faithful wife Penelope.
   a.   My travels last summer were so extensive and exciting I am thinking of writing my own *odyssey.*

b. The child's harrowing *odyssey* began with the outbreak of the war and did not end till he was reunited with the surviving members of his family many years later.

13. **Olympian** (ō-lim′pē-ən)—pertaining to the twelve gods of the ancient Greek pantheon whose abode was Mt. Olympus; majestic; incomparably superior; pertaining to the Olympic games. Olympus, the highest mountain in Greece, is located in northern Greece (Macedonia). It is sometimes used synonymously with "Heaven" or "the Sky."
    a. A turn of the road brought us to a landscape of *Olympian* beauty.
    b. An *Olympian* disregard for everyday matters does not become a person running for office.

14. **palladium** (pə-lā′-dē-əm)—anything believed to provide protection or safety; a safeguard or guarantee of the integrity of social institutions. Palladion was the fabled statue of Pallas Athena that assured the safety of Troy as long as it remained within the city.
    a. The Bill of Rights is the *palladium* of American civil liberties.
    b. After four successive championships, the coach began to regard the silver trophy as a *palladium* that guaranteed continued victories.

15. **phoenix** (fē′-niks)—a person or thing of peerless beauty or excellence; a person or thing that has become renewed or restored after suffering calamity or apparent annihilation. The phoenix was a mythical bird of great beauty, fabled to live 600 years in the Arabian desert, to burn itself on a funeral pyre, and to rise from its ashes to live through another cycle. It is an emblem of immortality.
    a. We seldom reflect upon our *phoenix*-like ability to wake each day refreshed and imbued with new energy.
    b. The fighter acquired the nickname *Phoenix* when he rallied after several knockdowns and virtual defeat to win the title.

EXERCISES

I. Which Word Comes to Mind?

In each of the following, read the statement, then circle the word that comes to mind.

1. Stung by Cupid's arrow

    (hydra,   Cassandra,   erotic)

2. A sumptuous feast

    (narcissism,   cornucopia,   odyssey)

3. Joseph's coat of many colors

    (iridescent,   hymeneal,   palladium)

4. Superhuman feats of strength

    (Adonis,   hermetic,   herculean)

5. Wine, women, and song

    (Olympian,   bacchanal,   phoenix)

II. True or False?

In the space provided, indicate whether each statement is true or false?

____ 1. *Phoenix* and *palladium* both suggest permanence.
____ 2. A stick-in-the-mud would be unlikely to engage in an *odyssey*.
____ 3. A *narcissist* is a lover of flowers.
____ 4. A *bacchanal* would likely attend every wedding feast but his own.
____ 5. *Cassandra's* song would probably be a top seller.

III. Find the Impostor

Find and circle the one word on each line which is not related to the other three.

1. Cassandra	dramatic	prophetic	doomsday
2. baccalaureate	revelry	bacchanal	dionysian
3. wisdom	metallic	palladium	safety
4. luxuriant	cornucopia	corpulent	plethora
5. erotic	wandering	digression	desultory

IV. Identification

With which god or hero is each of the following associated? Record your answer in the space provided.

1. bacchanal_____
2. hermetic_____
3. hydra_____
4. erotic_____
5. iridescent_____

V. Matching

Match the word in column A with its correct definition in column B by writing the letter of that definition in the space provided.

A	B
____ 1. Adonis	a. reveler
____ 2. bacchanal	b. nuptial
____ 3. Cassandra	c. adventurous journey
____ 4. cornucopia	d. superior
____ 5. erotic	e. a thing of beauty par excellence
____ 6. herculean	f. increasingly troublesome situation
____ 7. hermetic	g. profusion
____ 8. hydra	h. magical
____ 9. hymeneal	i. multi-colored
____ 10. iridescent	j. prophetess of doom
____ 11. narcissism	k. vanity
____ 12. odyssey	l. safeguard
____ 13. Olympian	m. extraordinarily handsome man
____ 14. palladium	n. filled with desire
____ 15. phoenix	o. mighty

Answers are on page 200.

Phoenix Making an Ash of Himself

Social Sciences

What does *anthropomorphism* have to do with Walt Disney?

Is an *archetype* similar to a prototype?

What do *demography* and *epidemiology* have in common?

Is there any connection between sublime and *subliminal*?

Why might you invite an *extrovert* to your party?

---

aberrant
anthropomorphism
archetype
authoritarian
catharsis
demography
epidemiology
euthanasia
extrovert
psychic
psychopath
psychotherapy
schizophrenia
subliminal
trauma

1. **aberrant** (a-ber'-ənt)—deviating from what is normal or typical. It comes from the Latin *aberrare* ("to go astray").
   a. For two months the prison psychologists studied Charles Manson's *aberrant* behavior.
   b. The L.A. Rams' *aberrant* performance in the football game worried their coach.

2. **anthropomorphism** (an-thrə-pə-môr'-fiz'm)—attributing human shape to gods, objects, animals. The Greek *anthropo* is a combining form which means "man" or "human."
   a. In a fit of *anthropomorphism*, the poet called his cat his bride.
   b. Movie cartoons frequently deal in *anthropomorphism,* wherein inanimate objects are given the power of speech.

3. **archetype** (är'-kə–tīp)—model; original pattern; prototype. One meaning of the Greek prefix *arch* is "main" or "chief."
   a. R. Buckminster Fuller's sketch became the *archetype* for future geodesic domes.
   b. The brothers hated Joseph because he was constantly being held up to them as the *archetype* of juvenile perfection.

4. **authoritarian** (ə-thôr-ə-ter'-i-ən)—characterized by unquestioning obedience to authority. An *authoritarian* figure is one who rejects individual freedom of judgment and action.
   a. The principal reason for Donna's anger was her father's *authoritarian* stance.
   b. One of the explanations for the tribe's survival was their acceptance of an *authoritarian* system.

5. **catharsis** (kə-thär'-sis)—the relieving of the emotions by art; the alleviation of fears by bringing them to consciousness. This Greek word has played an important role in theatre, as well as in psychiatry.
   a. The Aristotelian concept of tragic theater is that the audience is purified by means of the drama's *catharsis*.
   b. After the emotional *catharsis,* my psychiatrist felt that I was cured.

6. **demography** (di-mäg'-rə-fē)—the science of vital statistics, as of births, deaths, population, etc. It comes from the Greek root *demos* ("the people") and *graph* ("to write").
   a. We applied *demography* to help win our case with the Housing Commission.
   b. *Demographic* studies convinced the Board of Education that a desegregation attempt might be counter-productive at this time.

7. **epidemiology** (ep-ə-dē-mē-äl′-ə-jē)—the branch of medicine which investigates the causes and controls of epidemics. This word is composed of two Greek roots meaning "among the people."
   a. We turned to *epidemiology* to find the cause of Legionnaires' Disease.
   b. A professor of *epidemiology* at Baylor University isolated the cause of the sleeping sickness outbreak.

8. **euthanasia** (yōō-thə-nā′-zhə)—method of causing death painlessly; mercy killing. In Greek, it means 'happy death."
   a. I spoke against *euthanasia* in our classroom debate on mercy killing.
   b. After realizing that their daughter was incurably ill, the Reynolds family changed their minds about *euthanasia*.

9. **extrovert** (eks′-trə-vurt)—a person who is active and expressive; a person who is outgoing. The opposite is *introvert.*
   a. Following his psychoanalysis, my withdrawn, shy brother became an *extrovert.*
   b. It's strange, but in the presence of his mother the *extrovert* became an introvert.

10. **psychic** (sī′-kik)—of the psyche or mind; beyond natural or known physical processes. All of our words which begin with *psych* come from the Greek *psychikos* ("of the soul").
    a. The jury wanted hard facts, not so-called *psychic* evidence.
    b. In the science fiction film, *psychic* powers were stimulated in humans after they had drunk a special potion.

11. **psychopath** (sī′-kə-path)—a person afflicted with a mental disorder. The Greek root *path* means "suffering" or "disease."
    a. Our police force was searching for the homicidal *psychopath* who had slain six children.
    b. I was suspicious of Doctor Bonheim's claim that he could cure any *psychopath.*

12. **psychotherapy** (sī-kō-ther′-ə-pē)—using forms of mental treatment to cure nervous disorders. *Therapy* comes from the Greek *therapeia* ("one who serves or treats medically").
    a. The specialists decided that hypnosis was the form of *psychotherapy* which would help their patient.
    b. Some old-fashioned country doctors prefer aspirin to *psychotherapy.*

13. **schizophrenia** (skiz-ə-frē′-ni-ə)—a mental disorder characterized by delusions of persecution and omnipotence. Some victims of this disease are said to have a "split personality."
    a. Psychiatrists sometimes refer to Dr. Jekyll and Mr. Hyde when explaining *schizophrenic* behavior.
    b. It is now thought that *schizophrenia* may be the result of a chemical imbalance in the system.

14. **subliminal** (sub-lim′-ə-n′l)—below the threshold of apprehension; subconscious. *Limen* is a Latin word meaning "threshold."
    a. The *subliminal* effect of the rapidly-flashed pictures of popcorn was that the audience headed for the refreshment counter.
    b. In our art gallery, we rely on soft music and incense to create a *subliminal* appeal.

15. **trauma** (trô′-mə)—an emotional experience which has a lasting psychic effect. The Greek word *trauma* means "wound."

a. For weeks after the operation, Adele suffered from severe *trauma*.
b. The *trauma* caused by Eric's return to his old neighborhood was quite intense.

EXERCISES

I. Which Word Comes to Mind?

In each of the following, read the statement, then circle the word that comes to mind.

1. A nurse is suspected of having given an overdose of drugs to a cancer-ridden patient

(subliminal,   euthanasia,   anthropomorphism)

2. Researchers examine the tissues of the corpses

(epidemiology,   psychotherapy,   psychic)

3. Man bites dog

(aberrant,   authoritarian,   catharsis)

4. The government issues statistics on the ten fastest growing cities

(schizophrenia,   extrovert,   demography)

5. A citizen of Hiroshima continues to have nightmares

(archetype,   trauma,   psychopath)

II. True or False?

In the space provided, indicate whether each statement is true or false.

____ 1. *Psychotherapy* is used to treat muscles which have *atrophied*.
____ 2. *Aberrant* behavior is always welcomed by society.
____ 3. *Subliminal* suggestions tend to be subtle ones.
____ 4. *Psychopaths* and *schizophrenics* can be cured quickly today.
____ 5. Jupiter throwing his lightning bolts across the sky is an example of *anthropomorphism*.

III. Find the Words

Somewhere in this box of letters, reading up, down, across, or diagonally, three vocabulary words that were taught in this lesson are hidden. As you locate each one, draw a circle around it.

L	H	D	O	S	A	T	R
B	P	F	W	M	S	J	W
C	O	P	U	G	O	O	B
V	E	A	Z	I	K	S	E
A	R	L	I	N	D	X	G
T	N	A	R	R	E	B	A
C	I	H	C	Y	S	P	T

IV. Extra Letters

In each of the vocabulary words below there is an extra letter. Put all the extra letters together and you will be able to spell out a word taught in a previous lesson. Its meaning is "a series of wanderings."

anothropomorphism

cathardsis

archyetype

psychopasth

strauma

demeography

psychicy

V. Matching

Match the word in column A with its correct definition in column B by writing the letter of that definition in the space provided.

A

____ 1. aberrant

____ 2. anthropomorphism

____ 3. archetype

____ 4. authoritarian

B

a. medical research into epidemics

b. an outgoing person

c. attributing human shape to nonhumans

d. beyond natural processes

_____ 5. catharsis   e. use of mental treatment to cure disorders
_____ 6. demography   f. split personality
_____ 7. epidemiology   g. model
_____ 8. euthanasia   h. deviating from the normal
_____ 9. extrovert   i. emotional experience with a lasting effect
_____ 10. psychic   j. person with a severe mental disorder
_____ 11. psychopath   k. science of vital statistics
_____ 12. psychotherapy   l. subconscious
_____ 13. schizophrenia   m. mercy killing
_____ 14. subliminal   n. relieving of emotions
_____ 15. trauma   o. giving orders

Answers are on pages 200–201.

"Carrying anthropomorphism too far?"

From Sunny Spain

What would be your weakness if you had a *"mañana* complex"?

Where are you likely to see a *flotilla?*

Why is Don Quixote often called a *grandee?*

Who are the probable residents of the *barrio?*

Is a football stadium the right place for an *aficionado* of the sport?

---

aficionado
barrio
bonanza
bravado
desperado
flotilla
grandee
hacienda
lariat
machismo
mañana
palmetto
renegade
siesta
torero

1. **aficionado** (ə-fish-ə-nä'-dō)—a fan; devotee. Although this word originally described bull-fighting fans, it is now used to refer to devotees of all sports.
   a. Pablo used to be a bull-fighting *aficionado* but grew tired of the bloodshed.
   b. When I was an *aficionado* of baseball, I knew every player's batting average.

2. **barrio** (bär'-ē-ō)—part of the city where Spanish-speaking people live; ghetto.
   a. Even after he became rich, Jose would return to the *barrio* for a home-cooked meal.
   b. The two Spanish-speaking candidates campaigned actively for votes in the *barrio.*

3. **bonanza** (bə-nan'-zə)—rich pocket of ore; any source of wealth. In Spanish it means "fair weather at sea." A popular television program of the 1960's was entitled *"Bonanza."*
   a. The old mine turned out to be a *bonanza* for its owners.
   b. With this unexpected *bonanza,* Paul retired to the good life in Florida.

4. **bravado** (brə-vä'-dō)—pretended courage.
   a. In a display of *bravado,* the prisoner asked for a cigarette before being hanged.
   b. The poodle's *bravado* frightened the big dog away.

5. **desperado** (des-pə-rä'-dō)—bold outlaw; dangerous criminal. The relationship to our word "despair" is apparent. One who is without hope can be a dangerous criminal.
   a. The FBI men went into the woods to flush out the *desperado.*
   b. We were warned that the escaped *desperadoes* were heavily armed.

6. **flotilla** (flō-til'-ə)—a small fleet. The Spanish word *flota* means "fleet." *Flotilla,* then, is a diminutive form of *flota.*
   a. The colorful *flotilla* sailed out to meet the great ocean liner.
   b. Our slow vessel was swiftly overtaken by the pirate *flotilla.*

7. **grandee** (gran-dē')—a nobleman of the highest rank.
   a. A cocktail party was held in honor of the visiting *grandee* from Madrid.
   b. We were taken on a personal tour of his family's castle by the Spanish *grandee.*

8. **hacienda** (hä-sē-en´də)´—large estate; country house. The Old Spanish word *facienda* meant "estate." The change from *f* to *h* is apparent in many words.
   a. Expecting a broken down farm house, Edith was delighted to see the beautiful *hacienda.*
   b. At the end of the cattle round-up, we gathered at hacienda for a party.

9. **lariat** (lar'ē-it)—lasso; a rope used for tethering grazing horses. *Reata* is "rope" in Spanish.
   a. Will Rogers used to twirl his *lariat* in vaudeville shows.
   b. The rodeo star snaked his *lariat* over the calf's head and brought the animal to a halt.

10. **machismo** (mä-chēz'-mō)—manly self-assurance; masculine drive; virility.
    a. A male chauvinist harbors feelings of *machismo*.
    b. With a strong sense of *machismo*, Reynaldo refused to allow his wife to get a job.

11. **mañana** (mä-nya'-nä)—tomorrow; at some indefinite time in the future. There is a pejorative twist to *mañana*, suggesting laziness.
    a. Dorothy wanted the job done immediately, but *mañana* was good enough for her husband.
    b. If you keep waiting for *mañana*, you may find that it never comes.

12. **palmetto** (pal-met'-ō)—small palm tree.
    a. The terrible storm bent the *palmetto* almost to the ground.
    b. We hid in the *palmetto* grove where the others could not find us.

13. **renegade** (ren'-ə-gād)—deserter; turncoat; traitor. In Spanish, the word *renegado* means "to deny."
    a. One of the most notorious *renegades* in American history is Benedict Arnold.
    b. Angry at being humiliated, the soldier deserted and became a *renegade*.

14. **siesta** (sē-es'-tə)—midday nap. In Spanish and Latin American countries, businesses often close at midday to allow for *siesta* time.
    a. Following my afternoon *siesta*, I always feel refreshed.
    b. In Mexico we had to wait until the end of the *siesta* before we could resume our shopping.

15. **torero** (tə-rer'-ō)—bullfighter on foot. The *toreador* was a bullfighter on horseback, but that term is no longer used since all bullfighters today are *toreros*.
    a. The *torero's* beautiful costume is called "The Suit of Lights."
    b. After his great performance, the *torero* was awarded the ears and tail of the bull.

EXERCISES

I. Which Word Comes to Mind?

In each of the following, read the statement, then circle the word that comes to mind.

1. You go to see a performance of the opera "Carmen"

   (lariat,   flotilla,   torero)

2. The calendar pictures a man asleep under a tree next to a lawn mower

   (barrio,   bravado,   mañana)

3. A young man starts a fight to impress his girlfriend

   (machismo,   siesta,   renegade)

4. You win the lottery

(aficionado,   bonanza,   palmetto)

5. There is a wild police chase after the bank robber

(desperado,   grandee,   hacienda)

II. True or False?

In the space provided, indicate whether each statement is true or false.

1. A truly courageous person does not have to resort to *bravado*.
2. Feminists have contempt for those men who display *machismo*.
3. Ordinarily a *grandee* might take a *siesta* in his *hacienda*.
4. The Spanish Armada was too awesome to be described as a *flotilla*.
5. A *lariat* can be the high point of a Spanish meal when it is seasoned properly.

III. Find the Words

Somewhere in this box of letters, reading up, down, across, or diagonally, five vocabulary words that were taught in this lesson are hidden. As you locate each one, draw a circle around it.

O	R	E	R	O	T	D	S
G	R	A	N	D	E	E	K
T	B	N	I	A	V	T	F
A	S	A	C	V	G	J	X
N	G	N	P	A	Q	U	M
O	B	A	R	R	I	O	A
R	H	M	T	B	S	W	L

IV. Extra Letters

In each of the vocabulary words below there is an extra letter. Put all the extra letters together and you will be able to spell out a word taught in a previous lesson. Its meaning is "emotional experience."

siestta   lauriat
bornanza   barriom
floatilla   toarero

V. Matching

Match the word in column A with its correct definition in column B by writing the letter of that definition in the space provided.

	A		*B*
____	1. aficionado	a.	ghetto
____	2. barrio	b.	pretended courage
____	3. bonanza	c.	nobleman
____	4. bravado	d.	large estate
____	5. desperado	e.	midday nap
____	6. flotilla	f.	prosperity, source of wealth
____	7. grandee	g.	small palm tree
____	8. hacienda	h.	bullfighter
____	9. lariat	i.	deserter
____	10. machismo	j.	devotee
____	11. mañana	k.	virility
____	12. palmetto	l.	tomorrow
____	13. renegade	m.	small fleet
____	14. siesta	n.	lasso
____	15. torero	o.	bold outlaw

Answers are on page 201.

Time on Our Hands

How many years are there in a *score?* A *generation?*

With which war is *antebellum* usually associated?

If someone comes to you *anon* or *betimes* is he making haste?

How often do *biennial* publications appear?

What do family resemblances have to do with *atavism?*

---

anachronism
anon
antebellum
antediluvian
atavism
augury
betimes
biennial
diurnal
eon
ephemeral
epoch
generation
score
tercentenary

1. **anachronism** (ə-nak′-rə-niz′m)—anything that is out of place in time. It is formed by the combination of the Greek roots *ana* ("against") and *chronos* ("time").
   a. The author was guilty of an *anachronism* when he showed a frontier family with a washing machine.
   b. Paramount Pictures hired my uncle as a technical advisor to look out for *anachronisms.*

2. **anon** (ə-nän′)—soon; shortly. Used as an abbreviation, *anon.* means "anonymous."
   a. I'm busy right now but I'll come to see you *anon.*
   b. Peter promised to be here *anon* but he's a terrible liar.

3. **antebellum** (an′-ti-bel′-əm)—before the war; especially before the American Civil War. This word is formed from the Latin prefix *ante* ("before") and the root *bellum* ("war").
   a. *Gone With the Wind* shows us one version of the *antebellum* South.
   b. In *antebellum* Mississippi, slave auctions were widely attended.

4. **antediluvian** (an-ti-də-lōō′-vē-ən)—old-fashioned; before the flood. The Latin word for "flood" is *diluvium.*
   a. It is futile to try to change my grandmother's *antediluvian* ideas.
   b. Mitchell wore an *antediluvian* suit which caused the whole neighborhood to snicker.

5. **atavism** (at′-ə-viz′m)—reversion to a primitive type; resemblance to a remote ancestor. The Latin *atavus* means "father of a great-grandfather."
   a. The pictures of David and his grandfather, both at age 16, confirmed my belief in *atavism.*
   b. Sylvia was an *atavistic* throwback to her frugal ancestors.

6. **augury** (ô′-gyər-ē)—the art of prophecy; an omen. The original Latin word *augur* means "priest who presides at fertility rituals."
   a. If I had the power of *augury,* I would know which stocks are good investments.
   b. You might rely on *augury,* but I prefer to deal with facts.

7. **betimes** (bi-tīmz′)—early; promptly; before it is too late.
   a. Jesse leaves for work *betimes,* before the sun rises.
   b. After hearing a description of the symptoms, Dr. Salzer gave his diagnosis *betimes.*

8. **biennial** (bī-en′-ē-əl)—happening every two years. *Biennial* should not be confused with *biannual* which means "twice a year."

a. Since our annual meeting was so poorly attended, we plan to switch to a *biennial* one in the future.
b. A *biennial* plant lasts two years, producing flowers and seed the second year.

9. **diurnal** (dī-ur'-n'l)—daily; of the daytime. *Diurnal* is contrasted with *nocturnal*.
    a. My brother is a *diurnal* creature, usually in bed by 7:00 P.M.
    b. The custodian's *diurnal* chore was to raise the flag in front of the school.

10. **eon** (ē'-ən)—long, indefinite period of time; thousands of years.
    a. *Eons* ago, dinosaurs roamed this part of the country.
    b. You will have to wait an *eon* before they consent to your proposal.

11. **ephemeral** (i-fem'-ər-əl)—short-lived; transitory. *Ephemeros* is a Greek word meaning "for the day."
    a. "Fame is *ephemeral*," sighed the forgotten movie star.
    b. Steinbeck used to belittle his newspaper articles because of their *ephemeral* nature.

12. **epoch** (ep'-ək)—noteworthy period. It comes from a Greek word meaning "pause"—almost as if mankind takes time out before entering a new, important phase.
    a. We are living in the nuclear *epoch* when even tiny nations have the power to destroy.
    b. The Wright brothers' flight started an amazing *epoch* in the history of aviation.

13. **generation** (jen-ə-rā'-shən)—the period of time between the birth of one group and that of its off-spring. A *generation* is about 30 years.
    a. At our last family reunion, four *generations* were present.
    b. We find it very difficult to relate to the people of our grandparents' *generation*.

14. **score** (skôr)—twenty people or objects; twenty years. It comes from the Greek word for a "scratch" or "mark" used in keeping tallies.
    a. Mr. Schultz came to this country three *score* years ago.
    b. A *score* or more years ago, a trolley car used to run down this street.

15. **tercentenary** (tur-sen-ten'-ər-ē)—a period of 300 years. *Ter* is the Latin prefix for "three" and *centenary* means "hundred."
    a. In 1976 we celebrated the *tercentenary* of our town, founded in 1676.
    b. On the *tercentenary* of Shakespeare's birth, an enormous festival was held in London.

EXERCISES

I. Which Word Comes to Mind?

In each of the following, read the statement, then circle the word that comes to mind.

1. A woman wearing a style of dress which is completely out of date

(epoch,   antediluvian,   diurnal)

2. Julius Caesar looking at his wristwatch

(tercentenary,   ephemeral,   anachronism)

3. A young man following in his grandfather's footsteps

    (anon,   atavism,   score)

4. You meet your old classmates every two years at a reunion

    (antebellum,   betimes,   biennial)

5. Your fortune is told by a gypsy

    (augury,   generation,   eon)

II. True or False?

In the space provided, indicate whether each statement is true or false.

_____ 1. Abraham Lincoln's "Four*score* and seven" was 87 years.
_____ 2. *Ephemeral* is the opposite of "permanent."
_____ 3. Someone who comes to you *betimes* takes his time about it.
_____ 4. Cotton was the great crop of the *antebellum* South.
_____ 5. The U.S. will have its *tercentenary* celebration in 2076.

III. Find the Words

Somewhere in this box of letters, reading up, down, across, or diagonally, seven vocabulary words that were taught in this lesson are hidden. As you locate each one, draw a circle around it.

L	M	S	I	V	A	T	A
A	K	E	N	H	N	I	Y
N	L	E	R	O	C	S	R
R	X	P	E	P	N	Y	U
U	G	O	N	W	H	A	G
I	F	C	O	J	B	Z	U
D	B	H	M	S	I	P	A

IV. Extra Letters

In each of the vocabulary words below there is an extra letter. Put all the letters together and you will be able to spell out a word taught in a previous lesson. Its meaning is "ghetto."

abnon	bertimes	diurnial
epoach	augurry	anachoronism

V. Matching

Match the word in column A with its correct definition in Column B by writing the letter of that definition in the space provided.

A	B
____ 1. anachronism	a. short-lived
____ 2. anon	b. before the flood
____ 3. antebellum	c. twenty years
____ 4. antediluvian	d. reversion to an older type
____ 5. atavism	e. every two years
____ 6. augury	f. something misplaced in time
____ 7. betimes	g. period of 300 years
____ 8. biennial	h. soon, in a short while
____ 9. diurnal	i. thousands of years
____ 10. eon	j. thirty years
____ 11. ephemeral	k. daily
____ 12. epoch	l. before it is too late
____ 13. generation	m. noteworthy period
____ 14. score	n. before the war
____ 15. tercentenary	o. an omen

Answers are on pages 201–202.

Short but Challenging Words

With whom does one usually make a *tryst*?

Is *shunt* a contraction of two words?

Does *svelte* refer to a kind of material or a person's appearance?

What emotion is expressed by *quailing*?

Is *knell* a method of prayer or an evil omen?

---

bane
deign
eke
knell
mete
moot
mulct
plumb
quail
roil
ruck
shunt
svelte
thrall
tryst

1. **bane** (bān)—cause of death, ruin or distress. Obviously, you would avoid *baneful* herbs, like *baneberry,* and even shun *baneful* superstitions which could be equally harmful.
   a. Poor study habits were the *bane* of Walter's academic career.
   b. Gambling was the *bane* of Peter's existence.

2. **deign** (dān)—to think it beneath one's dignity; condescend; give. Related to the same Latin root, *dignitas,* as *deign* are *dignity, dignify, dignitary,* and *indignant,* all of which comment on one's worthiness.
   a. Charles would not *deign* to discuss his failure with us.
   b. I have applied for employment to several companies, but they have *deigned* not to reply.

3. **eke** (ēk)—to supplement; to manage to make a living with difficulty; to use frugally. *Eke* can be traced to the Latin *augere* and the Greek *auxanein,* which in turn give us words like *augment* and *auxiliary*.
   a. The sharecroppers *eked* out a living by farming a small piece of land.
   b. Mr. Hernandez *eked* out his income by working at night.

4. **knell** (nel)—to ring in a slow, solemn way; toll; to call or announce by a mournful ringing; an omen of death or failure. The opening line of Gray's famous elegy, "The curfew tolls the *knell* of parting day," sets the mournful, reflective mood of the poem.
   a. The President's veto meant the *knell* of all the valiant efforts to tighten gun controls.
   b. With bells *knelling* in farewell, the long funeral procession wound through the dusty town toward the cemetery.

5. **mete** (mēt)—to allot, distribute or apportion. Tennyson's famous line amply illustrates the sense of measuring out: "I *mete* and dole unequal laws unto a savage race."
   a. Some people *mete* out their friendship by the drop; others, by the cupful.
   b. The authorities *meted* out punishment to the instigators of the brawl.

6. **moot** (mōōt)—discussion or argument of a hypothetical law case; debatable; so hypothetical as to be meaningless. Law students sharpen their skills in a *moot* court where hypothetical cases are tried.
   a. The Supreme Court decision on capital punishment has made the deterrent effect of the death penalty a *moot* question.
   b. The class becomes impatient when Howard engages the teacher in discussing *moot* points.

7. **mulct** (mulkt)—to punish by a fine or by depriving of something; to extract by fraud or deceit. It is from the Latin *mulcta* ("a fine.").
    a. The petty official was suspected of having *mulcted* the treasury of thousands of dollars during his term of office.
    b. The judge *mulcted* the defendant with a heavy fine besides imposing a jail sentence for his part in the bank swindle.

8. **plumb** (plum)—perfectly vertical; directly; to test or sound with a *plumb* line (measure); to discover the facts of; to fathom, solve or understand. A lead weight (Latin *plumbum,* "lead") was used at the end of the *plumb* line. The chemical symbol for lead is Pb.
    a. It is not easy to *plumb* the intention of a fickle person.
    b. Shallow ideas should be *plumbed* and discarded.

9. **quail** (kwāl)—to draw back in fear; lose heart or courage; cower. A *quail* is also a partridge-like bird mentioned in the Bible as the source of the meat sent to the Israelites in the desert. The definition of the verb to *quail* is related to the Latin word *coagulare* ("coagulate"), describing what seems to happen physically when the blood "runs cold."
    a. The stout heart does not *quail* though the enemy be fierce and the battle unequal.
    b. The lone sailor *quailed* before the mighty waves roaring toward his flimsy raft.

10. **roil** (roil)—to make a liquid cloudy or muddy; to stir up or agitate; to make angry; rile. Some authorities believe the word comes from the Old French word for "rust" or "mud," or the Latin *ruber* ("red"). Others frankly admit the origin is unknown. But we can offer some interesting synonyms: *annoy, fret, ruffle, exasperate, provoke.*
    a. The delay in the announcement of the winner *roiled* the entire party.
    b. We watched the lake *roil* beneath the pounding rain.

11. **ruck** (ruk)—a heap or stack; a large quantity or crowd; mass of ordinary people or things; common run. Some words, like *queen* which once referred to anyone's wife, have moved up the social ladder; but *ruck* succeeded only in moving from things to humans. It still refers to people who are generally inferior.
    a. The *ruck* of humanity followed the rabble-rouser, intent only on plunder.
    b. Beneath the camouflage was hidden a *ruck* of food supplies sufficient to feed the city for a week in a crisis.

12. **shunt** (shunt)—to move or turn to one side; to shift or switch from one track to another. The word may be related to *shun,* which also has the sense of turning away.
    a. The surgeon *shunted* the blood circulation around the heart so that the rupture could be repaired.
    b. The freight train was *shunted* to another track just in time to avoid the hurtling passenger train.

13. **svelte** (svelt)—slender and graceful; suave; polished. The derivation from the Latin *evellare* ("to pull out"), implies that the *svelte* figure has been "drawn out" like a heated glass tube.
    a. Jennie maintained her *svelte* figure with a sensible diet, regular exercise, and, of course, a hereditary gift.
    b. Not every person with a *svelte* manner should be considered devious and dishonest.

14. **thrall** (thrôl)—a slave or bondman; a person under the moral or psychological

domination of something or someone; slavery. Performers who *enthrall* their audiences captivate their attention.

    a. Mr. Hyde was in the *thrall* of morbid fantasies that plagued his waking moments.

    b. The workers were held in *thrall* by the poor economic conditions that denied them upward mobility.

15. **tryst** (trist)—an appointment, as by lovers; to meet. In Scotland the word refers to a market, but the Old French *triste* ("hunting rendezvous") suggests that the Gallic hunters were not always after wild game.

    a. The *trysting* place at the college remained a guarded secret among the fraternity members.

    b. Martha came home very late from the *tryst,* bleary-eyed but happy.

EXERCISES

I. Which Word Comes to Mind?

In each of the following, read the statement, then circle the word that comes to mind.

1. The impoverished family barely survived the winter

(mulct,   moot,   eke)

2. To each according to his due

(thrall,   mete,   roil)

3. A house of terror for its inhabitants

(quail,   ruck,   deign)

4. Romeo and Juliet meet at the Friar's cell

(knell,   tryst,   shunt)

5. Drink was his undoing

(svelte,   plumb,   bane)

II. True or False?

In the space provided, indicate whether each statement is true or false.

_____ 1. One would normally be proud to be counted among the *ruck* of humanity.
_____ 2. The best time to appeal to someone for a favor is after he has been *roiled* up.
_____ 3. The *knelling* of bells has a somber, saddening effect.
_____ 4. Every girl is anxious to have a *svelte* figure.
_____ 5. A person found guilty of a serious crime in *moot* court must serve at least the minimum sentence.

III. Synonyms and Antonyms

Indicate whether the following pairs of words are the same, opposite, or unrelated in meaning by writing S, O, or U in the space provided.

_____ 1. thrall—master
_____ 2. moot—questionable
_____ 3. tryst—confidence

_____ 4. mete—assign
_____ 5. roil—soothe

IV. Anagrams

In four of the following, add or subtract a letter from the word, then rearrange the letters to form the new word whose meaning is given. In the last one, simply rearrange the given letters.

1. eke + one letter = timid_____
2. mete + one letter = rhythm_____
3. moot + one letter = power source_____
4. svelte − one letter = marker_____
5. bane = Israeli diplomat_____

V. Matching

Match the word in column A with its correct definition in column B by writing the letter of that definition in the space provided.

A	B
_____ 1. bane	a. agitate
_____ 2. deign	b. meeting
_____ 3. eke	c. toll
_____ 4. knell	d. curse
_____ 5. mete	e. fascination
_____ 6. moot	f. dole
_____ 7. mulct	g. willowy
_____ 8. plumb	h. condescend
_____ 9. quail	i. cheat
_____ 10. roil	j. barely survive
_____ 11. ruck	k. recoil
_____ 12. shunt	l. commonplace
_____ 13. svelte	m. test
_____ 14. thrall	n. switch to another track
_____ 15. tryst	o. debatable

Answers are on page 202.

Swollen to Svelte

Review

A. The Out-of-Place Word

In each of the following groups, find and circle the one vocabulary word that is out of place. You should be able to explain what the other three words have in common.

1. amanuensis, graphologist, nemesis, osteopath
2. antebellum, score, biennial, thrall
3. dyspeptic, philippic, neurasthenic, bilious
4. barrio, odyssey, grandee, flotilla
5. anachronism, bacchanal, narcissism, phoenix
6. farrier, trauma, extrovert, psychopath
7. philanderer, quixotic, solecism, echelon
8. adagio, salvo, vendetta, siesta
9. palladium, contrite, acidulous, craven
10. epidemiology, euthanasia, demography, lapidary

B. Rearranging Words

Rearrange the following groups of words using the first letter of each word to spell out one of the new words taught in this unit.

1. grandee, intaglio, tryst, jingoist, staccato, imbroglio, nemesis, Olympian

   _____

2. atavism, internist, odyssey, genealogy, detente, aberrant

   _____

3. roil, thrall, catharsis, ornithologist, graphologist, elite, erotic

   _____

4. torero, lapidary, Adonis, ruck, andante, imbroglio

   _____

5. osteopath, sybarite, crescendo, maverick, lachrymose, ecumenical, iridescent, subliminal

   _____

C. Getting Satisfaction

Where would you go with the following? Circle the correct answer.

1. A backache

   (cosmetologist, demographer, palladium, osteopath)

2. A desire to have your character analyzed

   (anthropomorphist, graphologist, freemason, narcissist)

3. Plans for a love affair

   (tryst, cortege, archetype, flotilla)

4. An idea to overthrow someone in power

(palmetto, cabal, catharsis, farrier)

5. A case of acne

(dermatologist, pharynologist, physiologist, amanuensis)

D. Making Pairs

From the group below, find the pairs of words that have something in common and record them in the spaces provided. You should be able to find ten such pairs and list them numerically. The first two have been done for you.

lothario ___1___	Cassandra ___2___	desperado _____	Olympian _____
augury ___2___	philanderer ___1___	dyspeptic _____	sybarite _____
renegade _____	acidulous _____	herculean _____	phoenix _____
protean _____	contralto _____	elite _____	ornithologist _____
libretto _____	esprit de corps _____	camaraderie _____	bacchanal _____

E. Cliché Time

Which of the words from this unit fit into the following familiar expressions? Choose the correct word from the choices given and record it in the space provided.

1. The _____ of my existence

(eon, bane, trauma, nemesis)

2. The noise reached a _____ .

(epoch, palladium, knell, crescendo)

3. We won but it was a _____ victory.

(Pyrrhic, baleful, hermetic, quixotic)

4. A _____ burst of machine gun fire

(moot, staccato, maverick, tawdry)

5. Where the _____ meet to eat

(saturnine, elite, svelte, contrite)

F. Find the Words

Somewhere in this box of letters, reading up, down, across, or diagonally, twenty vocabulary words that were taught in Unit 1 are hidden. As you locate each one, draw a circle around it.

T	N	A	R	R	E	B	A	A	C	S	W
A	B	O	M	O	O	T	N	K	A	F	H
V	I	M	E	T	E	A	Z	I	D	X	I
L	L	O	A	H	N	K	P	L	O	N	S
G	I	N	J	A	Y	O	Q	U	N	E	L
E	O	Y	M	I	C	S	E	D	I	M	L
N	U	F	A	U	T	N	U	H	S	E	A
E	S	O	N	E	L	A	G	Y	K	S	R
R	X	R	B	D	L	C	P	D	R	I	H
O	O	Z	U	M	E	S	T	R	Y	S	T
C	A	S	S	A	N	D	R	A	D	J	O
S	Q	U	I	E	K	E	H	C	O	P	E

Answers are on pages 202–203.

Medical Science

Why would anyone want a *cadaver*?

Is "Tarzan of the *Simians*" an appropriate movie title?

What do *mastectomy* and *vasectomy* have in common?

Is the army slang term, "gold brick," synonomous with any of the fifteen vocabulary words below?

Which of the medical terms below could a poet use to describe a hill?

---

abscess
aphasia
arteriosclerosis
biopsy
cadaver
carcinogen
comatose
etiology
malingerer
mastectomy
prosthesis
simian
therapeutic
tumescence
vasectomy

1. **abscess** (ab'-ses)—swollen, inflamed area of body tissues. It is from the Latin *abscessus* ("to go from"). It was originally thought that the humors (liquids) went from the body into the swelling.
    a. Dr. Harris discovered the *abscess* under my gum which had accounted for my pain.
    b. When Helen's *abscess* was lanced, she felt immediate relief.

2. **aphasia** (ə-fā'-zhə)—loss of the power to use or understand words, usually caused by brain disease or injury.
    a. Fortunately, Jeff's *aphasia* passed quickly, and by evening he was chattering away normally.
    b. The doctors believed that the *aphasia* which followed Justice Douglas' stroke would lead to his retirement.

3. **arteriosclerosis** (är-tir'-ē-ō-sklə-rō-sis)—a thickening and hardening of the walls of the arteries, as in old age.
    a. In my aunt's case, *arteriosclerosis* restricted the flow of blood to her brain, and she endured several strokes.
    b. Researchers at geriatric institutes are seeking ways to improve the blood flow in patients who suffer from *arteriosclerosis*.

4. **biopsy** (bī'-äp-sē)—the cutting out of a piece of tissue for diagnostic examination by microscope.
    a. While his surgeon awaited the results of the *biopsy*, the patient lay asleep on the operating table.
    b. June's family opened the champagne bottles for a celebration when the *biopsy* showed the tumor was benign.

5. **cadaver** (kə-dav'-ər)—dead body; corpse for dissection. It is from the Latin word *cadere* which means "to fall."
    a. Medical students used to pay grave robbers for the *cadavers* they stole.
    b. The unclaimed *cadaver* lay in the morgue for an entire month.

6. **carcinogen** (kär-sin'-ə-jən)—any substance that causes cancer.
    a. We were shocked to learn that Donny's pajamas were sprayed with a chemical suspected of being a *carcinogen*.
    b. The Evans family moved to the coast when it was reported that our community's drinking water was filled with *carcinogens*.

7. **comatose** (kom'-ə-tōs)—as if in a coma; lethargic. The Greek word *coma* means "deep sleep."
    a. Hal remained *comatose* after having been struck on the head.

    b. Trading was nonexistent on the Stock Exchange floor, and the business community seemed in a *comatose* state.

8. **etiology** (ēt-ē-äl′-ə-jē)—the science of the causes and origins of disease.
    a. Dr. James Parkinson spent many years tracing the *etiology* of palsy.
    b. Thanks to medical science, we now know a great deal about the *etiology* of feeblemindedness.

9. **malingerer** (ma-liŋ′-gər-ər)—one who fakes illness and pretends to be suffering.
    a. General Patton struck the alleged *malingerer* across the face.
    b. The doctors decided to frighten the *malingerer* back into good health.

10. **mastectomy** (mas-tek′-tə-mē)—the surgical removal of a breast.
    a. After viewing the special x-rays, the breast surgeon recommended an immediate *mastectomy.*
    b. Betty Ford, the former first lady, made a quick recovery after her *mastectomy.*

11. **prosthesis** (präs′-thə-sis)—replacement for a missing part of the body.
    a. Ethel's broken hip could not be pinned but would require a *prosthesis.*
    b. Learning to walk with the new *prosthesis* would only be successful if Sergeant Yates had motivation and will power.

12. **simian** (sim′-ē-ən)—of or like a monkey or an ape.
    a. Ira's long arms and body posture gave him a *simian* appearance.
    b. The *simian* experts at the zoo objected to the experimental surgery being performed on the apes.

13. **therapeutic** (ther-ə-pyo͞ot′-ik)—curative; serving to heal.
    a. A long vacation was the only *therapeutic* treatment prescribed for Myra.
    b. Scientists have found that aspirin has *therapeutic* possibilities which we had not appreciated.

14. **tumescence** (to͞o-meś-n's)—swelling.
    a. The obvious *tumescence* indicated that Roberta either needed to diet or was pregnant.
    b. Without actually probing the *tumescence,* we guessed that it was a swollen gland.

15. **vasectomy** (vas-ek′-tə-mē)—the surgical removal of the duct whch conveys the male sperm—the *vas deferens.*
    a. Both husband and wife agreed that a *vasectomy* would be their best form of contraception.
    b. A simple *vasectomy* can be performed in a physician's office without anaesthesia.

EXERCISES

I. Which Word Comes to Mind?

In each of the following, read the statement, then circle the word that comes to mind.

1. Eugene O'Neill's play, *The Hairy Ape*

      (vasectomy,   biopsy,   simian)

2. The Federal Drug Administration's report on harmful food additives

      (aphasia,   carcinogen,   prosthesis)

3. Breast surgery

(etiology,   malingerer,   mastectomy)

4. Days of anxious waiting for the unconscious patient to awaken

(abscess,   comatose,   therapeutic)

5. A disease of old age

(tumescense,   cadaver,   arteriosclerosis)

II. True or False?

In the space provided, indicate whether each statement is true or false.

_____ 1. Good news can serve as a *therapeutic* drug for many patients.
_____ 2. Speech therapy is prescribed for many people who suffer from *aphasia*.
_____ 3. When the government suspects the presence of a *carcinogen* in a food, it increases sales and distribution.
_____ 4. A wooden leg was a common *prosthesis* years ago.
_____ 5. Most motion picture horror stories have at least one *cadaver* to boast about.

III. Find the Words

Somewhere in this box of letters, reading up, down, across, or diagonally, four vocabulary words that were taught in this lesson are hidden. As you locate each one, draw a circle around it.

A	L	B	R	A	K	R	Y
S	P	O	M	W	E	H	S
J	U	H	X	V	Z	Y	P
B	L	P	A	O	K	T	O
X	G	D	E	S	S	W	I
D	A	F	T	G	I	N	B
C	E	S	I	M	I	A	N

IV.   Extra Letters

In each of the vocabulary words below there is an extra letter. Put all of the extra letters together, and you will be able to spell out two words taught in a previous lesson; their meanings are "cause of distress" and "to manage with difficulty."

combatose   proesthesis
siamian   vasecktomy
tumenscence   carecinogen
abescess

V.   Matching

Match the word in column A with its correct definition in column B by writing the letter of that definition in the space provided.

A

_____ 1. abscess
_____ 2. aphasia
_____ 3. ateriosclerosis
_____ 4. biopsy
_____ 5. cadaver
_____ 6. carcinogen
_____ 7. comatose
_____ 8. etiology
_____ 9. malingerer
_____ 10. mastectomy
_____ 11. prosthesis
_____ 12. simian
_____ 13. therapeutic
_____ 14. tumescence
_____ 15. vasectomy

B

a. replacement for a part of the body
b. one who pretends to be ill
c. contraceptive surgery
d. curative
e. examination of body tissue
f. hardening of the arteries
g. swelling
h. science of the causes and origins of disease
i. removal of a breast by surgery
j. cancer-causing substance
k. illness affecting speech and understanding
l. dead body
m. ape-like
n. inflamed area in body tissues
o. unconscious

Answers are on page 203.

Animal World

Is an elephant a *saurian,* an *ursine,* or neither?

What do *felines* and *vulpines* have in common?

Which denotes the animal with the worst "table manners"—*lupine, vulpine,* or *porcupine?*

To which animal is a *vixenish* woman compared?

Would a racing fan best be described as a *saurian,* an *equine,* or a *piscine* fancier?

---

bovine
equine
feline
hircine
leonine
lupine
ophidian
ovine
piscine
porcine
saurian
taurine
ursine
vixen
vulpine

1. **bovine** (bō′-vīn,-vin,-vēn)—an ox, cow, or related animal; having oxlike qualities; slow, dull, stupid, or stolid.
   a. People with *bovine* temperaments may be dependable but they are not exciting company.
   b. Because of their easygoing nature, *bovine* creatures have been domesticated to serve mankind faithfully.

2. **equine** (é-kwīn, ek′-wīn)—a horse; of, like, or characteristic of a horse.
   a. The zebra belongs to the *equine* group.
   b. Although the glory of the *equines* in the development of the West has ended, horses still play an important part in the world of sports.

3. **feline** (fē′-līn)—a member of the family which includes lions, tigers, jaguars, and wild and domestic cats; resembling or suggestive of a cat, as in suppleness, slyness, treachery, or stealthiness.
   a. When Maria heard herself described as *feline,* she did not know if the speaker referred to her sleekness or her tendency to gossip.
   b. She walked with a *feline* grace that was a pleasure to behold.

4. **hircine** (hur′-sīn,-sīn)—of or characteristic of a goat, especially in strong odor or lustfulness. Pan, the god of woods, fields, and flocks, had a human torso with goat's legs, horns, and ears. He is often represented as frightening the nymphs in the forest.
   a. An unpleasant *hircine* odor emanated from the hunter's clothing.
   b. There was a *hircine* lasciviousness in Glen's leers and innuendoes that the girls at the party quickly grew to despise.

5. **leonine** (lē′-ə-nīn)—of, pertaining to, or characteristic of a lion. Like Felix the cat and Bossie the cow, Leo the lion takes his name from the original Latin.
   a. Flagrant injustice always evoked a *leonine* rage in the senator.
   b. Emitting a huge *leonine* sigh, old Mr. Carew shuffled back to his seat.

6. **lupine** (loo′-pīn)—wolflike; rapacious or ravenous.
   a. Stories like *The Call of the Wild* remind us that dogs are *lupine* creatures.
   b. The crash victims ate their first meal with *lupine* voracity.

7. **ophidian** (ō-fid′-ē-ən)—snakelike; a snake or serpent.
   a. The *ophidian* exhibit at the museum shows the lizards and serpents in their natural habitat.
   b. With *ophidian* guile, Linda set out to demolish the competition and win the starring role for herself.

8. **ovine** (ō'-vīn)—designating sheep or sheeplike; an ovine animal.
   a. It is unrealistic to expect the workers to agree, like *ovines,* to any paltry offer made by the management.
   b. Coach Donahue demanded unquestioning obedience from the men, but on the field you could not accuse them of *ovine* behavior.

9. **piscine** (pī'-sēn, pis'-īn)—of, pertaining to, or typical of a fish or fishes. Pisces, the twelfth sign of the zodiac, is also called "the fish."
   a. Nellie had been taught to swim at such an early age, she felt a *piscine* comfort in the water.
   b. Scientists could not agree whether the few bones belonged to a *piscine* or a land creature.

10. **porcine** (pôr'-sīn)—of or pertaining to swine or pigs; piglike. The cartoon character Porky the Pig derives his name from the Latin *porcus,* pig.
    a. A bald, *porcine* old man sat on the bench greedily eating a huge lunch.
    b. Reverend Tolliver's sermon stressed the point that *porcine* pleasures ill become the nobility of the soul.

11. **saurian** (sôr'-ē-ən)—of or having the characteristics of lizards; a lizard. The names of the prehistoric animals, like the dinosaur and the brontosaur, used combining forms with the Greek root *saurios* ("lizard").
    a. The flesh-eating *saurians* walked on their hind legs, the planteaters on all fours.
    b. *Saurians* include a wide range of reptiles from the gentle chameleon to the ferocious crocodile.

12. **taurine** (tôr'-ēn)—of or resembling a bull. The second sign of the zodiac is Taurus the Bull.
    a. Not many Americans take to the *taurine* sport of bullfighting.
    b. It is not the color red that enrages the bull but rather it is the waving and goading gestures that arouse the *taurine* instinct.

13. **ursine** (ur'-sīn)—of or characteristic of a bear. The constellations Ursa Major and Ursa Minor, popularly called the Big Dipper and the Little Dipper, appeared to the ancients to have the outlines of a "Great Bear" and a "Little Bear."
    a. Contrary to popular belief, the *ursine* habit of hibernating is interrupted several times by periods of wakefulness.
    b. Using the *ursine* appetite for sweets as an incentive, trainers have taught bears to appear to be "reading" as they turn pages looking for honey.

14. **vixen** (vik'-sən)—a female fox; a quarrelsome, shrewish, or malicious woman. Vixen may also be used as an adjective.
    a. Petruchio knew the secret of turning a *vixen* into an obedient and loving housewife.
    b. Margot's *vixen* temperament shows in her refusal to yield to even the most reasonable suggestion to end the quarrel.

15. **vulpine** (vul'-pīn, -pin)—of, resembling, or characteristic of a fox; clever, devious, or cunning. The famous play *Volpone, or The Fox,* was an early seventeenth-century drama by Ben Jonson.
    a. Sherlock Holmes, as a successful detective, possessed certain *vulpine* qualities that gave him the edge over his adversaries.
    b. Fables sometimes represent *vulpine* characters as coming out second best in spite of their cunning.

EXERCISES

I. Which Word Comes to Mind?

In each of the following, read the statement, then circle the word that comes to mind.

1. Carmen sings to her lover before he enters the arena

(bovine,   saurian,   taurine)

2. The sour-grapes fable

(equine,   vulpine,   leonine)

3. Little Bo Peep

(vixen,   ovine,   feline)

4. A lady-killer

(lupine,   ophidian,   porcine)

5. A costly error in a World Series game

(ursine,   piscine,   hircine)

II. True or False?

In the space provided, indicate whether each statement is true or false.

_____ 1. *Ophidians* and *saurians* have much in common.
_____ 2. Both lions and tigers can be described as *leonine*.
_____ 3. Horse racing would be impossible without *equines*.
_____ 4. An aquarium would house many *ursine* creatures.
_____ 5. A *bovine* and *taurine* animal make a natural pair.

III. Find the Impostor

Find and circle the one word on each line which is not related to the other three.

1. equity	equine	equerry	equestrian
2. ephemeral	fleeting	folino	transient
3. shrew	vexing	virago	vixen
4. bullish	matador	terrain	taurine
5. angler	finny	piscine	angular

IV. Anagrams

In each of the following, subtract one or more letters from the word, then rearrange the letters to form the new word whose meaning is given.

1. ursine – one letter = awakened_____
2. vixen – two letters = disallow_____
3. bovine – two letters = skeleton component_____
4. hircine – three letters = part of the face_____
5. saurian – two letters = a plastic wrap_____

V. Matching

Match the word in column A with its correct definition in column B by writing the letter of that definition in the space provided.

A

____	1. bovine
____	2. equine
____	3. feline
____	4. hircine
____	5. leonine
____	6. lupine
____	7. ophidian
____	8. ovine
____	9. piscine
____	10. porcine
____	11. saurian
____	12. taurine
____	13. ursine
____	14. vixen
____	15. vulpine

B

a. lionlike
b. relating to swine
c. snakelike
d. bearlike
e. resembling a cat
f. ill-tempered woman
g. fishlike
h. pertaining to a horse
i. lizard
j. rapacious
k. relating to a bull
l. devious
m. sluggish
n. sheeplike
o. goatlike

Answers are on pages 203–204.

Identity crisis

Countdown—Words With Numbers

Is a *millennium* the same as, more than, or less than a million?

In what profession is it important to follow *protocol*?

Is *bicameral* a double-strength lens or a legislative system?

In what way is the word *decimate* linked to a mutiny?

What is the *penultimate* letter of a word?

---

atonement
bicameral
Decalogue
decimate
dichotomy
double-think
millennium
nihilism
penultimate
primeval
protocol
quatrain
quintessence
tessellated
untrammeled

1. **atonement** (ə-tōn′-mənt)—amends for wrong-doing; expiation. The theological use of this word can be readily understood if it is interpreted to mean "being at one" with God, taking the proper action to correct an injury or repair a relationship.
   a. The Day of *Atonement*, the holiest day of the Jewish year, is observed by fasting and prayer.
   b. How, ask the environmentalists, can man make *atonement* for the crime of poisoning the atmosphere?

2. **bicameral** (bī-kam′-ə-rəl)—composed of two houses, chambers or branches. It is easy to identify the prefix *bi*, which we find in *bicentennial, biceps,* and *binomial*. The second part, obviously related to *camera*, tells us that photography, like the legislature, requires a chamber in which to function.
   a. The *bicameral* system of government in the U.S. arose as a compromise between the advocates of a strong national government and the supporters of states rights.
   b. The House of Lords in England, though nominally making Parliament *bicameral*, does not wield the same power as the House of Commons.

3. **Decalogue** (dek′-ə-lôg)—the Ten Commandments. The precepts spoken by God to Israel on Mt. Sinai are the basis of Mosaic Law.
   a. The *Decalogue* remains the most sublime declaration of man's relationship with his Creator and his fellow men.
   b. Some believe that modern society has paved the way for its own destruction by transgressing the sacred *Decalogue*.

4. **decimate** (des′-ə-māt)—to destroy a great number or proportion of. The word is traceable to the cruel punishment for mutiny—selecting by lot and killing one in every ten people. The same Latin root, *decem* ("ten"), gives us *decimals, decade*, and even *December* (the tenth month if you begin, as the Romans did, with March).
   a. Besides causing enormous destruction of property, the violent earthquake *decimated* the city's population.
   b. The ecological imbalance has *decimated* many species of animal life and brought some to the brink of extinction.

5. **dichotomy** (dī-kōt′-ə-mē)—division into two usually contradictory parts or opinions. The Greek root means something cut in two. In modern usage the word has special significance in logic (a division into mutually exclusive groups) and in botany (a branching into two equal subdivisions).
   a. There is a clear *dichotomy* of opinion on the subject of abortion.

b. Dolores and Irv's *dichotomy* of viewpoints on mercy killing has caused many a heated battle.

6. **double-think** (dub'-əl-think)—the belief in two contradictory ideas at the same time. This, as well as other forms of Newspeak, was formulated by George Orwell in his novel, *1984*.
   a. "War is peace" is an example of *double-think*.
   b. Is *double-think* self-deception or ignorance?

7. **millennium** (mə-len'-ē-əm)—a span of a thousand years; a period of general righteousness and happiness, especially in the indefinite future.
   a. The last fifty years of this *millennium* have wrought the greatest changes in the history of civilization.
   b. Our pastor said that we can bring the *millennium* in our lifetime if we treat each other with a spirit of generosity and forgiveness.

8. **nihilism** (nī'-ə-liz'm)—total rejection of established laws and institutions; total destructiveness toward the world and oneself. The *nihilist* adopts the extreme position that nothing exists or can be communicated; hence, he lives in a lonely, empty world.
   a. Since Max has turned toward *nihilism,* we are afraid that he will do something antisocial.
   b. We must counter the folly of *nihilism* by improving the quality of life without yielding to despair because of our slow progress.

9. **penultimate** (pi-nul'-tə-mit)—next to the last. The Latin *paene* ("almost") and *ultimus* ("last") combine to form this word.
   a. *Y* is the *penultimate* letter of our alphabet.
   b. The *penultimate* scene of the play had the audience sitting on the edge of their seats.

10. **primeval** (prī-mē' vəl)—original; belonging to the first or earliest ages. It is important to differentiate between primeval and its synonyms; *prime* "first in numerical order" and *primitive* "suggesting the simplicity of original things." Other synonyms are *pristine* and *primordial*.
    a. Longfellow's "Hiawatha" begins with the sonorous tones of "This is the forest *primeval*."
    b. Many characteristics of the *primeval* forms of life have been gradually shed to produce the most adaptable creatures.

11. **protocol** (prō'-tə-kôl)—forms of ceremony and etiquette observed by diplomats and heads of states; the first copy of a treaty or document. The Greek roots refer to the first leaf glued to the front of the manuscript and containing the notes of the contents.
    a. Upon his arrival, Ambassador Lefton presented his credentials to the monarch, as *protocol* demanded.
    b. "Forget about *protocol*," said the hostess, urging us to take any seat.

12. **quatrain** (kwôt'-rān)—a stanza or poem of four lines, usually with alternate rhymes.
    a. "The Rubaiyat of Omar Khayyam" is the famous Fitzgerald translation of a group of *quatrains* by a Persian poet.
    b. The Shakespearean sonnet is composed of three *quatrains* followed by a couplet that summarizes or epitomizes the major point.

13. **quintessence** (kwin-tes'-ns)—the most perfect embodiment of something; the purest or most typical instance. In ancient philosophy, the fifth and highest

essence *quinta essentia* ("ether"), was supposed to be the constituent matter of the heavenly bodies, the others being earth, air, fire, and water.
    a. Prejudice is the *quintessence* of falsehood.
    b. The *quintessential* characteristic of Shakespeare is his profound understanding of human nature.

14. **tessellated** (tes'-ə-lā-tid)—like a mosaic; checkered. A variety of the Latin *tessera* ("four"), the word finds its most practical application in art, architecture, and the building trades.
    a. Archaeologists have marveled at the intricate *tessellated* design of the floor in the ancient palace.
    b. The common checkerboard, both in the game and in the field of clothing, demonstrates the use of *tessellated* designs by different craftsmen.

15. **untrammeled** (un-tram'l'd)—unhampered; unrestrained. The fishermen of the Middle Ages made a three-layered net *(tres macula)* of varying degrees of coarseness so that the fish would be entangled in one or more of the meshes.
    a. It was Bobby's ardent desire to feel *untrammeled* in his choice of a career.
    b. Chicago was said to be *untrammeled* by the financial woes that have plagued major cities.

EXERCISES

I. Which Word Comes to Mind?

In each of the following, read the statement, then circle the word that comes to mind.

1. Negotiations to settle a strike are broken off

(atonement,   dichotomy,   double-think)

2. A young lady practices curtsying for hours in preparation for meeting royalty

(quatrain,   tessellated,   protocol)

3. A Golden Age is just around the corner

(quintessence,   millennium,   bicameral)

4. A baseball game's eighth inning

(penultimate,   decimate,   untrammeled)

5. The radicals' weapons were terrorism, rioting, and subversion

(primeval,   nihilism,   Decalogue)

II. True or False?

In the space provided, indicate whether each statement is true or false.

_____ 1. *Double-think* suggests a careful analysis of both sides of a problem.
_____ 2. A *tessellated* floor and a *quatrain* of poetry are both related to the same number.
_____ 3. The *Decalogue* is a play with ten speaking parts.
_____ 4. A prisoner being released from jail feels *untrammeled*.
_____ 5. *Dichotomy* and *bicameral* have prefixes with the same meaning.

III. Find the Words

Somewhere in this box of letters, reading up, down, across, or diagonally, five vocabulary words that were taught in this lesson are hidden. As you locate each one, draw a circle around it.

L	O	C	O	T	O	R	P
N	I	H	I	L	I	S	M
A	C	T	O	F	S	G	Y
D	E	C	I	M	A	T	E
B	T	D	K	R	W	S	H
P	R	I	M	E	V	A	L
N	I	A	R	T	A	U	Q

IV. Extra Letters

In each of the vocabulary words below there is an extra letter. Put all the extra letters together and you will be able to spell out a word taught in a previous lesson. Its meaning is "Suggestive of a cat."

aftonement

quatraine

protocoll

primevail

millenniumn

bicamereal

V. Matching

Match the word in column A with its correct definition in Column B by writing the letter of that definition in the space provided.

	A		B
____	1. atonement	a.	Mosaic Code
____	2. bicameral	b.	annihilate
____	3. Decalogue	c.	proper behavior
____	4. decimate	d.	next to last

——— 5. dichotomy
——— 6. double-think
——— 7. millennium
——— 8. nihilism
——— 9. penultimate
——— 10. primeval
——— 11. protocol
——— 12. quatrain
——— 13. quintessence
——— 14. tessellated
——— 15. untrammeled

e. perfection
f. belief in contradictory ideas
g. checkered
h. rejection of any purpose in existence
i. a thousand years
j. congressional, composed of two houses
k. the act of making amends
l. division of opinion
m. earliest
n. four-line stanza
o. freed

Answers are on page 204.

Countdown

Legal Language (I)

Is a *tort* a kind of pastry?

Does an *intestate* person require the services of a physician?

Are three judges necessary to form a *tribunal*?

Can a case be started in an *appellate* court?

What do you do to a body when you *exhume* it?

---

adjudicate
appellate
collusion
deposition
equity
exhume
incommunicado
intestate
ipso facto
lien
litigation
perjury
pettifogger
tort
tribunal

1. **adjudicate** (ə-jōō′də-kāt)—to hear and settle a case by judicial procedure. As a transitive verb, *adjudicate* means to settle the rights of the parties in a court case. As an intransitive verb, it means simply to act as a judge.
   a. The court *adjudicated* the case for months before deciding on the offshore drilling rights of the states.
   b. It takes patience and common sense to *adjudicate* in a dispute between friends and reach a fair decision.

2. **appellate** (ə-pel′-it)—having the power to hear appeals and to reverse lower court decisions. An *appellant* is the one who appeals from a judicial decision or decree. An *appellee* is one against whom an appeal is taken.
   a. The *appellate* court upheld the verdict of the lower court in the celebrated trial involving the student who received a diploma without learning to read.
   b. An *appellate* decision by the state court can be overturned by the Supreme Court.

3. **collusion** (kə-lōō′-zhən)—a secret agreement for a deceitful or fraudulent purpose; conspiracy. Though the word has a serious connotation today, it is derived from the Latin *ludere* ("to play"), and *ludus* ("game"). A *collusion* often implies an attempt to defraud a person of his rights by the forms of law.
   a. The captain of the Zaire forces defending Mutshatsha was accused of acting in *collusion* with the enemy in the surrender of the city.
   b. The senator felt that there was *collusion* on the part of his committee to deny him the chairmanship.

4. **deposition** (dep′-ə-zish′ən)—testimony under oath, especially a written statement by a witness for use in court in his absence. In ordinary usage, *deposition* refers to the act of depriving of authority, or the placing or laying down, as of sediment or precipitation.
   a. In the *deposition* made to the police at the scene of the crime, the accused dope smuggler appeared vindictive and unrepentant.
   b. The forcible *deposition* of the Lebanese president by the Syrian army was intended to bring an end to almost two years of civil war.

5. **equity** (ek′-wə-tē)—something that is just, impartial and fair; the value of a business or property in excess of any claim against it; justice applied in circumstances not covered by law.
   a. *Equity* demands that the solution to the energy crisis does not bring undue hardship to one group and windfall profits to another.
   b. The family *equity* in the estate after all obligations had been paid amounted to ten thousand dollars.

6. **exhume** (iks-hyōōm′)—to dig out of the earth; disinter; reveal. From the Latin *humus* ("ground").

    a.   The district attorney, suspecting foul play, got a court order to *exhume* the body.

    b.   It took ten years of digging in the library to *exhume* the material which she needed for her exposé of corruption.

7.   **incommunicado** (in-kə-my$\overline{oo}$′-nə-kä-dō)—without the means or right of communication with others, as one held in solitary confinement.

    a.   In order to avoid offending voters, it is sometimes expedient for a political candidate to be *incommunicado* on sensitive issues.

    b.   Patty Hearst was advised by her lawyers to remain *incommunicado* until the charges against her were made public.

8.   **intestate** (in-tes′-tāt)—having made no valid will; one who dies without a legal will.

    a.   The media at first reported that the millionaire Howard Hughes had died *intestate.*

    b.   The administration of property left by an *intestate* is a complicated matter that usually ends with the government receiving the lion's share.

9.   **ipso facto** (ip′-sō fak′-tō)—by the fact itself; by that very fact.

    a.   Though an alien, *ipso facto,* has no right to a U.S. passport, the administration does not plan to press charges against the eight million who entered the country illegally.

    b.   Training in speech is *ipso facto* training in personality.

10.   **lien** (lēn)—the right to take and hold or sell the property of a debtor as security or payment for a debt; mortgage. The word is related to the Latin *ligare* ("to bind"), indicating that certain possessions are bound or tied to the payment of a debt.

    a.   A *lien* was placed against the Russian vessel that had violated the newly-declared U.S. fishing territorial waters.

    b.   Before you purchase that house, check to see if it is free of any *liens* against the present owner.

11.   **litigation** (lit-ə-gā′-shən)—legal action or process. A person who will sue at the drop of a hat, a handkerchief, or a word is said to be *litigious.*

    a.   The *litigation* over the closing of the child care centers dragged on for months.

    b.   After years of *litigation,* only the lawyers made any money from the case.

12.   **perjury** (pur′-jer-ē)—the deliberate, wilful giving of false, misleading, or incomplete testimony by a witness under oath in a criminal proceeding.

    a.   Shakespeare tells us, "At lovers' *perjuries,* Jove laughs."

    b.   As the guest left, he thanked the hostess with as much enthusiasm as he could muster without actually *perjuring* himself.

13.   **pettifogger** (pet′-ē-fäg-ər)—a petty, quibbling, unscrupulous lawyer; a shyster. *Shyster* comes from the American lawyer Scheuster, who in 1840 was rebuked in court for his objectionable practices. *Pettifogger,* similarly, is derived from the pettiness of the Fuggers, a 16th-century German family of financiers and merchants.

    a.   The attorney's underhanded and disreputable methods earned him a reputation as a *pettifogger.*

    b.   The editorial attacked the cautious *pettifoggers,* who could only agree on what could not be done in dealing with the energy crisis.

14.   **tort** (tôrt)—any wrongful act not involving breach of contract for which a civil

suit can be brought. The Latin *tortum* ("twisted"), is related to *torque,* a twisting force, and *torture.*

  a. The lawyer claimed the injury done to his client was wilful and subject to the laws of *tort.*
  b. It was difficult to prove the defendant guilty of a *tort* as his intentions could not be clearly established.

15. **tribunal** (tri-by$\overline{oo}$′-nəl)—a seat or court of justice. The tribune was the Roman official chosen by the plebeians (commoners) to protect their rights against the patricians (wealthy class).

  a. The Supreme Court, the highest *tribunal* of our nation, refused to review the convictions of the Watergate defendants.
  b. An honest man is answerable to no *tribunal* but his own judgment.

EXERCISES

I. Which Word Comes to Mind?

In each of the following, read the statement, then circle the word that comes to mind.

1. No evidence of a will was found

(equity,   intestate,   litigation)

2. Any statement made now can be held against you

(deposition,   tort,   ipso facto)

3. If we do not get satisfaction here, we will take this case to a higher court

(collusion,   tribunal,   appellate)

4. The witness has told only half the story in court

(adjudicate,   perjury,   exhume)

5. Lie low till the furor subsides

(incommunicado,   pettifogger,   lien)

II. Extra Letters

In each of the vocabulary words below there is an extra letter. Put all the extra letters together and you will be able to spell out a word taught in a previous lesson. Its meaning is "changeable."

habeas corppus

plargiarism

proobation

arsont

bearrister

amicaus curiae

litingious

II. True or False?

In the space provided, indicate whether each statement is true or false.

_____ 1. A *collusion* is an intellectual clash between two strong lawyers.

_____ 2. An *adjudicated* settlement is one made out of court.

—— 3. *Torts* involve an injury or damage done without breach of contract.
—— 4. A *pettifogger* is overly concerned with trifles.
—— 5. *Ipso facto* refers to facts, like axioms, that are universally accepted.

IV. Matching

Match the word in column A with its correct definition in column B by writing the letter of that definition in the space provided.

—— 1. adjudicate
—— 2. appellate
—— 3. collusion
—— 4. deposition
—— 5. equity
—— 6. exhume
—— 7. incommunicado
—— 8. intestate
—— 9. ipso facto
—— 10. lien
—— 11. litigation
—— 12. perjury
—— 13. pettifogger
—— 14. tort
—— 15. tribunal

a. testimony under oath
b. claim against property
c. a wrongful act
d. act as a judge
e. one harping on insignificant matters
f. court of law
g. by that very fact
h. dig out of the earth
i. conspiracy
j. impartiality
k. able to uphold or reverse previous decisions
l. isolated
m. lying under oath
n. not having a will
o. legal action

V. Hidden Words

The winding letters below form three words from this lesson. The letters of each word are separated according to a simple formula. Find the words and the formula.

CLOI   LTRU   UINO
  ELN   ISB   ALN

Answers are on page 204.

Deposition

Appearances and Attitudes (II)

What is the relationship of *florid* to Florida?

Why might you send a *flaccid* person to a body-building spa?

Would Telly Savalas (Kojak) object to being called *glabrous*?

Do we expect judges to behave in a *dispassionate* manner?

Why must a spy be *circumspect*?

---

circumspect
demure
dispassionate
dolorous
edacious
effete
feisty
flaccid
flippant
florid
glabrous
imperious
ingenious
intractable
intransigent

1. **circumspect** (sur'-kəm-spekt)—careful; cautious; prudent. The original meaning of this word was "to look about." A person who "looks about" is cautious—hence, *circumspect*.
   a. The killer was *circumspect* about leaving any clues which would tie him to the victim.
   b. We complimented the lawyer for his *circumspect* handling of the embarrassing matter.

2. **demure** (di-myŏŏr')—modest; shy. It comes from a Latin word which means "mature" or "proper."
   a. Shakespeare's advice to a *demure* young maiden is: "Say nay but take it."
   b. Even when she was in her thirties, the actress was still being cast as a *demure* high school girl.

3. **dispassionate** (dis-pash'-ən-it)—fair; impartial; calm.
   a. As a *dispassionate* observer, I agreed to settle the dispute.
   b. It's easy to be *dispassionate* about international problems which do not appear to affect us directly.

4. **dolorous** (dō'-lər-əs)—painful; mournful.
   a. Merchants whose stores had been looted during the blackout wore *dolorous* expressions.
   b. Nearing the funeral, we were greeted by a *dolorous* chant from the church choir.

5. **edacious** (i-dā'-shəs)—devouring; consuming. It comes from the Latin *edere* ("to eat").
   a. The *edacious* forest fire destroyed everything in its path.
   b. Betty Ann enjoys buffet luncheons because she has an *edacious* appetite.

6. **effete** (e-fēt')—worn out; spent and sterile. The Latin word *effetus* means "that which has brought forth offspring."
   a. After years of intermarriage, the royal family line was *effete* and exhausted.
   b. Long service in the coal mines left Hal Fletcher *effete* and tubercular.

7. **feisty** (fīs'-tē)—touchy; excitable; quarrelsome.
   a. The *feisty* boxer was sensitive about his height and ready to fight with any taller person.
   b. It took an hour to settle Sara's *feisty* boyfriend dow   ter he thought he had been insulted.

8. **flaccid** (flak'-sid)—weak; feeble; flabby.
   a. Because she had been confined to her bed for three weeks after surgery, Mrs. Leslie's muscles were *flaccid*.
   b. Senator Dwyer's *flaccid* response to the accusations was highlighted by the media.

9. **flippant** (flip'-ent)—disrespectful; saucy, impertinent.
   a. A sure way to get under Mr. Tarranto's skin is to give *flippant* answers to his serious questions.
   b. Marjorie's *flippant* attitude toward her grandmother's illness led to a bitter family argument.

10. **florid** (flôr'-id)—ruddy; rosy; ornate. *Florid* also means "highly-colored," which reveals its connection with the Latin word for flower, *floris*.
    a. After living outdoors all summer, Myra had a *florid* glow in her cheeks.
    b. Our mayor is fond of using *florid,* overblown language in his campaign speeches.

11. **glabrous** (glā'-brəs)—bald; smooth.
    a. Yul Brynner's *glabrous* scalp is his trademark in show business.
    b. As I meditate, I find it restful to run my fingertips over the surface of a *glabrous* stone.

12. **imperious** (im-pir'-ē-əs)—overbearing; arrogant; domineering. It is easy to see the relationship of this word to *emperor.*
    a. We were turned off by the official's *imperious* manner.
    b. In an *imperious* tone, my grandfather ordered the sheriff off his property.

13. **ingenious** (in-jēn'-yəs)—clever; original; inventive; resourceful.
    a. Rube Goldberg, the cartoonist, was famous for his wildly *ingenious* mechanical devices.
    b. The *ingenious* solution to the city's transportation problems was to cut the fares in half.

14. **intractable** (in trak' to b'l)   hard to manage; unruly; stubborn.
    a. The union chief was willing to compromise on wages but he was *intractable* when it came to working conditions.
    b. Mrs. Finkel usually sent her *intractable* pupils directly to the principal's office.

15. **intransigent** (in-tran'-si-jənt)—uncompromising; refusing to come to an agreement.
    a. Owners of baseball teams used to hire top-notch lawyers to bring *intransigent* players to terms.
    b. Charles Bronson took an *intransigent* position when he refused to star in any more cowboy movies.

EXERCISES

I. Which Word Comes to Mind?

In each of the following, read the statement, then circle the word that comes to mind.

1. A married man takes his secretary to a dark restaurant

   (florid,   circumspect,   intransigent)

2. My father is the absolute boss in our house

   (dispassionate,   glabrous,   imperious)

3. An argument is in progress; neither side wants to give in

                              (intractable,   flaccid,   edacious)

4. The night club comedian upset his conservative audience

                                    (flippant,   dolorous,   effete)

5. A blush stole over the teenager's cheek

                                    (feisty,   ingenious,   demure)

II. True or False?

In the space provided, indicate whether each statement is true or false.

_____ 1. *Intransigent* people are definitely *intractable*.
_____ 2. A *glabrous* person is usually vain about his attractive hair.
_____ 3. The winner's headquarters was filled with *dolorous* sounds when the victory was announced.
_____ 4. Julius Caesar's *imperious* manner befitted his position as a dictator.
_____ 5. Clark Kent's *effete* appearance was a way of disguising his true identity as Superman.

III. Find the Words

Somewhere in this box of letters, reading up, down, across, or diagonally, five vocabulary words that were taught in this lesson are hidden. As you locate each one, draw a circle around it.

B	D	I	C	C	A	L	F
K	F	E	I	S	T	Y	F
P	A	M	R	L	G	I	L
U	F	K	Q	U	A	B	O
H	V	B	J	I	M	C	R
L	E	F	F	E	T	E	I
A	C	T	O	X	L	W	D

IV. Extra Letters

In each of the vocabulary words below there is an extra letter. Put all the extra letters together and you will be able to spell out a word taught in a previous lesson. Its meaning is "high-ranking nobleman."

flogrid   doldorous
irmperious   felaccid
circumaspect   glaberous
feinsty

V. Matching

Match the word in column A with its correct definition in column B by writing the letter of that definition in the space provided.

A	B
____ 1. circumspect	a. modest
____ 2. demure	b. arrogant
____ 3. dispassionate	c. worn out
____ 4. dolorous	d. mournful
____ 5. edacious	e. quarrelsome
____ 6. effete	f. cautious
____ 7. feisty	g. clever
____ 8. flaccid	h. disrespectful
____ 9. flippant	i. stubborn
____ 10. florid	j. rosy
____ 11. glabrous	k. consuming
____ 12. imperious	l. uncompromising
____ 13. ingenious	m. bald
____ 14. intractable	n. flabby
____ 15. intransigent	o. impartial

Answers are on pages 204–205.

Mystery and the Occult

Do you have to join a spa to *exorcise*?

Is *alchemy* a respected branch of chemistry?

Should Julius Caesar have heeded the *soothsayer*?

What happens if you fail your *polygraph* test?

Can "The Lady or the Tiger?" story be called a *conundrum*?

---

alchemy
arcane
conundrum
demonology
exorcise
inscrutable
pallor
phenomenology
polygraph
purloin
ritual
shamus
soothsayer
thaumaturgy
warlock

1. **alchemy** (al'-kə-mē)—a method of miraculous change of one thing into another. In the Middle Ages, the chief aim of honest and dishonest experimenters was to change base metals into gold and to discover the elixir of eternal youth.
    a. Even though the charlatan was practicing 15th century *alchemy*, some fools believed him.
    b. Through some incredible *alchemy*, the ugly frog was changed into a handsome prince.

2. **arcane** (är-kān')—beyond comprehension; mysterious; secret. The Latin word *arcanus* means "shut up" or "hidden."
    a. I find much modern poetry to be *arcane*, totally beyond my grasp.
    b. Teddy offered an *arcane* explanation for his whereabouts which confused us even further.

3. **conundrum** (kə-nun'-drəm)—a riddle; any puzzling question or problem.
    a. The most famous literary *conundrum* can be found in Sophocles' play, *Oedipus Rex*.
    b. Anyone who could solve the *conundrum* of the three caskets would win the hand of the beautiful Portia.

4. **demonology** (dē-mə-näl'-ə-jē)—the study of demons or of beliefs about them.
    a. Seeing the books on *demonology* in their apartment confirmed Rosemary's suspicions about her neighbors.
    b. Before making the movie about witches, the director steeped himself in the lore of *demonology*.

5. **exorcise** (ek'-sôr-sīz)—to drive away an evil spirit by charms or incantations.
    a. The distraught parents asked the Vatican to help *exorcise* the spirit which they believed was tormenting their child.
    b. In the stage play, the priest used a crucifix and a Bible to *exorcise* the demons.

6. **inscrutable** (in-skrōō'-tə-b'l)—mysterious; completely obscure; unfathomable.
    a. Since many Chinese are expert at keeping a straight face, we have developed the cliche about the "*inscrutable* Orientals."
    b. Sam Spade kept the suspects in the dark with his *inscrutable* expression.

7. **pallor** (pal'-ər)—lack of color; unnatural paleness.
    a. Having remained indoors for years, Aunt Sabina had an unhealthy *pallor*.
    b. When we saw Miriam exit from the haunted house we were frightened by her *pallor*.

8. **phenomenology** (fi-näm-ə-näl'-ə-jē)—the science which classifies and describes unusual happenings.

a. A student of *phenomenology* could provide you with many stories about unidentified flying objects.

b. *Phenomenology* tells us about "supernatural" happenings without attempting to explain them.

9. **polygraph** (păl'-i-graf)—an instrument which records changes in blood pressure, respiration, pulse rate, etc; a lie detector.

a. *Playboy* ran a feature story on the *polygraph* test administered to the murderer of Martin Luther King.

b. In the hands of a specialist, the *polygraph* is almost infallible in getting at the truth.

10. **purloin** (pur-loin')—to steal.

a. To profit from his insurance, Chris arranged to *purloin* his own jewelry.

b. Edgar Allan Poe's story, "The *Purloined* Letter," is an international classic.

11. **ritual** (rich'-ōō-wal)—a system of rites, religious or otherwise; a prescribed form or procedure; ceremony.

a. Dr. Lister went through an involved *ritual* of cleansing his hands before every operation.

b. The devil worshippers opened every meeting with the *ritual* of their eerie chant.

12. **shamus** (shā'-mis)—private detective. The caretaker of a synagogue is also called a *shamus* (shä´mis).

a. In all the detective stories I have read, the *shamus* was a hard-drinking woman-chaser.

b. Philip Marlowe preferred the title of Private Investigator to *shamus*.

13. **soothsayer** (sōōth'-sā-er)—one who predicts the future. *Sooth* is an Anglo-Saxon word meaning "true"; hence, a *soothsayer* is a "sayer of truth."

a. The emperor was warned by the *soothsayer* not to go to the temple.

b. No *soothsayer* could have predicted the bizarre ending of this real-life mystery.

14. **thaumaturgy** (thô'-me-tur-jē)—magic; the supposed working of miracles.

a. Through an act of sheer *thaumaturgy* the elephant was made to disappear in front of our eyes.

b. In the time of King Arthur, Merlin was the acknowledged master of *thaumaturgy*.

15. **warlock** (wôr'-läk)—sorcerer; conjurer; male witch. From the Anglo-Saxon word for traitor or liar. A *warlock* was supposed to be able to cast a magic spell because of a compact he made with the Devil.

a. Witches and *warlocks* are expected to "do their thing" on October 31st.

b. The Salem Puritans suspected many people of being *warlocks,* in cahoots with Lucifer.

EXERCISES

I. Which Word Comes to Mind?

In each of the following, read the statement, then circle the word that comes to mind.

1. The last page of the murder mystery, with all the guests in the living room

(thaumaturgy,   demonology,   shamus)

2. "As I gaze into my crystal ball . . ."

(warlock,   soothsayer,   arcane)

3. "Man, your face is as white as a ghost's"

(*pallor,   conundrum,   inscrutable*)

4. A pickpocket's nimble fingers

(*purloin,   alchemy,   ritual*)

5. "Would you be willing to take a test to prove your innocence?"

(*exorcise,   phenomenology,   polygraph*)

II. True or False?

In the space provided, indicate whether each statement is true or false.

_____ 1. A *warlock* has military responsibilities.
_____ 2. To wear your heart on your sleeve is to have an *inscrutable* expression.
_____ 3. A cattle rustler is one who would *purloin* a sirloin.
_____ 4. When we say, "It's Greek to me," we are referring to something which is *arcane*.
_____ 5. Abracadabra is the start of a familiar *ritual*.

III. Find the Words

Somewhere in this box of letters, reading up, down, across, or diagonally, four vocabulary words that were taught in this lesson are hidden. As you locate each one, draw a circle around it.

P	H	I	L	E	A	T	A
U	R	M	O	C	R	L	E
R	F	Q	S	K	C	A	N
L	P	U	S	H	A	U	K
O	X	Y	E	D	N	T	W
I	J	M	C	A	E	I	O
N	Y	S	Z	L	D	R	G

IV. Extra Letters

In each of the vocabulary words below there is an extra letter. Put all of the extra letters together and you will be able to spell out a word taught in a previous lesson. Its meaning is "a minor official."

purbloin   arcaned
shameus   allchemy
thaumataurgy   riteual

V. Matching

Match the word in column A with its correct definition in column B by writing the letter of that definition in the space provided.

A	B
____ 1. alchemy	a. beyond comprehension
____ 2. arcane	b. ceremony
____ 3. conundrum	c. sorcerer
____ 4. demonology	d. riddle
____ 5. exorcise	e. to steal
____ 6. inscrutable	f. the study of demons
____ 7. pallor	g. changing one thing into another
____ 8. phenomenology	h. to drive away an evil spirit
____ 9. polygraph	i. lack of color
____ 10. purloin	j. private eye
____ 11. ritual	k. unfathomable
____ 12. shamus	l. one who predicts the future
____ 13. soothsayer	m. classification of unusual happenings
____ 14. thaumaturgy	n. supposed working of miracles
____ 15. warlock	o. lie detector

Answers are on page 205.

Warlock—80m. to the gallon

Size and Shape (I)

Can *infinitesimal* units be measured?

Who discovered *Lilliput*?

Is *megalopolis* a disease?

Does *palatial* refer to a place or to a part of the body?

How would you feel if someone referred to your *peccadillos*?

---

amplitude
elfin
infinitesimal
Lilliputian
megalopolis
minimize
minutiae
palatial
peccadillo
picayune
simulacrum
soupçon
teeming
titanic
vista

1. **amplitude** (am′-plə-tōōd)—greatness of size; fullness; breadth of range. The nature of this word has made it extremely useful in specialized fields such as physics, electronics, astronomy, and mathematics. All the technical definitions, however, are related to the idea of a maximum size.
   a. The *amplitude* of the professor's knowledge amazed the audience.
   b. It takes a heart of wisdom to appreciate the *amplitude* of our blessings even in difficult times.

2. **elfin** (el′-fin)—fairylike; delicate; small and charmingly merry or mischievous. In folklore, an elf was a tiny, often prankish fairy who lived in the woods and possessed magical powers, like Shakespeare's Puck.
   a. The *elfin* world of the poet's imagination was peopled by gnomes and leprechauns and other creatures of fantasy.
   b. Despite Perry's appearance of innocence, his *elfin* smile tells me I had better beware.

3. **infinitesimal** (in-fin-ə-tes′-ə-m′l)—too small to be measured. Mathematicians, philosophers and photographers are accustomed to dealing in concepts that range from the infinite (too large to be measured) to the infinitesimal.
   a. Messages are carried to the brain through the *infinitesimal* vessels of the nervous system.
   b. Martin may boast a lot, but his contribution to the team effort is *infinitesimal*.

4. **Lilliputian** (lil-ə-pyōō′-shən)—very small; tiny, narrow-minded; petty. In Swift's *Gulliver's Travels,* the hero was shipwrecked on the island of Lilliput, the inhabitants of which stood six inches tall.
   a. No wonder we can't solve our problems if our outlook remains *Lilliputian*.
   b. Standing next to the basketball team's center at the athletic awards assembly, I felt like a *Lilliputian*.

5. **megalopolis** (meg′-ə-läp′-ə-lis)—an extensive, heavily populated, continuously urban area, including any number of cities. This is larger than a metropolis since it includes an inner city, suburbia, exurbia, and any adjacent towns.
   a. The area from Baltimore to Washington is so densely populated that the entire stretch can be considered one *megalopolis.*
   b. If the population explosion continues unchecked, the entire country will gradually be transformed into one gigantic *megalopolis* after another, separated only by farms, rivers or mountains.

6. **minimize** (min′-ə-mīz)—to reduce to a minimum; decrease to the least possible amount or degree; belittle. Again we meet a synonym for "small," *minim,* this time combined with the suffix *ize,* "to make," and denoting as in the definition for infinitesimal, making something appear to be of the least possible amount, value, or importance.

a. After the accident, Mr. Jenkins tried in vain to *minimize* the effect that the liquor had on his driving.
b. By careful attention to our inventory and orders, we can *minimize* our losses and maximize our profits.

7. **minutiae** (mi-nōō'-shē-ē)—small or trivial details; trifling matters. The word is not restricted in meaning to unimportant details since a seemingly minor point can prove to be of major significance.
a. The defense attorney poured over the *minutiae* of the case, looking for a crack in the prosecution's argument.
b. A thorough knowledge of the *minutiae* of his craft earned the artist an international reputation.

8. **palatial** (pa-lā'-shəl)—like a palace; large and ornate. A closely related word derived from the same Latin root *palatine* ("palace"), refers to royal privileges, a high official, a Roman soldier as well as to the chief of the seven hills upon which Rome was built.
a. The duchess fell upon hard times and had to open her *palatial* estate to tourists.
b. The *palatial* tapestry on display at the Cloisters was the highlight of our visit.

9. **peccadillo** (pek-ə-dil'-ō)—a small sin or fault. We admire the person who dresses impeccably, "without fault"; perhaps are tolerant to the *peccadillos* of our friends; and probably forgive the person who offers his *peccavi* ("confessions," or literally "I have sinned").
a. What human being, no matter how upright, has not committed some *peccadillo*?
b. We can overlook Melanie's *peccadillos* but not her brazen impudence.

10. **picayune** (pik-ə-yūn')—of little value or account; petty or prejudiced. Originally, this meant a coin of small value. Inevitably, the meaning was transferred to a person of low esteem because of his criticism or bias.
a. George remained silent after the beating the team suffered, not wishing to seem *picayune* by criticizing anyone.
b. Bentley is notorious for raising the most *picayune* objections.

11. **simulacrum** (sim-yōō-lā'-krəm)—a slight, unreal, or superficial likeness or semblance; an image or representation of something.
a. After weeks of interviewing witnesses, the police artist produced a sketch that he hoped was at least a *simulacrum* of the criminal who had terrorized the city.
b. Whatever *simulacrum* the vase bore to a work of art was covered by centuries of dust.

12. **soupçon** (sōōp-sōn')—suspicion; a slight trace or flavor; a very small amount. The first definition, derived from the French, is the original meaning. The others are extensions of the same idea, a common phenomenon of language development.
a. There was merely a *soupçon* of tartar sauce in the delicate concoction.
b. Ned spoke with a *soupçon* of arrogance that did not go unnoticed by the interviewer and cost him the job.

13. **teeming** (tē'-miŋ)—swarming; prolific or fertile. The Old English word *teman* meant "to produce offspring." Indeed, an obsolete meaning of teeming was "to become pregnant to produce offspring." What is perhaps more interesting is that our word *team* also comes from the Old English *team,* which meant "childbearing" or "brood." What would the Jets says to that?

a. The poem by Emma Lazarus, inscribed on the base of the Statue of Liberty, welcomes the *teeming* masses, yearning to be free.

b. Doris' mind is always *teeming* with a thousand projects.

14. **titanic** (tī-tan'-ik)—of enormous size, strength, or power. In classical mythology the *Titans* were a race of giants who ruled the world before the gods and goddesses. Cronus, perhaps the most famous (think of our word *chronology*), swallowed all his children in an attempt to avert a prophecy of doom; but one son, Jupiter (Zeus), survived and eventually overthrew his father.

a. The quarterback led his team in a *titanic* effort to erase the six-point lead caused by his unfortunate fumble.

b. The airport was constructed in *titanic* proportions to allow for the anticipated expansion of the city.

15. **vista** (vis'-tə)—a far-reaching intellectual view; a view or prospect, especially one seen through a long, narrow avenue or passage; a mental view extending over a long period of time or embracing many remembrances or experiences.

a. Before us stretches an infinite *vista* of human improvement.

b. The *vistas* of one's youth are often recalled with pleasure and nostalgia.

EXERCISES

I. Which Word Comes to Mind?

In each of the following, read the statement, then circle the word that comes to mind.

1. The myriad molecules on the head of a pin

(infinitesimal, vista, picayune)

2. The two cities have grown so quickly you can hardly tell where one ends and the other begins

(megalopolis, Lilliputian, palatial)

3. Most of their points were scored when our best man was in the penalty box

(amplitude, elfin, minimize)

4. Mac stumbled once over his lines but otherwise his performance was perfect

(minutiae, peccadillo, simulacrum)

5. This is the biggest rocket in our arsenal

(soupçon, titanic, teeming)

II. True or False?

In the space provided, indicate whether each statement is true or false.

_____ 1. An *elfin* creature is huge and lumbering.
_____ 2. *Soupçon* is the call to dinner.
_____ 3. You should feel complimented if your mental powers are called *Lilliputian.*
_____ 4. *Vistaed* galleries are so called because they attract many visitors.
_____ 5. A *teeming* street is dilapidated and deserted.

III. Synonyms and Antonyms

Find and circle two words on each line which are either synonyms or antonyms.

1. infinitesimal	titanic	pompous	hopeful
2. swarming	cooperative	teeming	moderate
3. economy	amplitude	pettiness	range
4. picayune	searching	serviceable	unbiased
5. exaggerate	imitate	minimize	assemble

IV. Hidden Words

The lines of letters below form seven words from this lesson. The letters of each word are arranged according to a simple formula. Find the words and the formula.

```
P   M   P   M   T   T   S               _____

    A   I   I   I   I   E   O           _____

L   N   C   N   T   E   U               _____

    A   I   A   U   A   M   P           _____

T   M   Y   T   N   I   C               _____

    I   I   U   I   I   N   O           _____

A   Z   N   A   C   G   N               _____

    L   E   E   E
```

V. Matching

Match the word in column A with its correct definition in Column B by writing the letter of that definition in the space provided.

	A		*B*
____	1. amplitude	a.	imitation
____	2. elfin	b.	make less
____	3. infinitesimal	o.	fullness
____	4. Lilliputian	d.	unimportant details
____	5. megalopolis	e.	trace
____	6. minimize	f.	narrow-minded
____	7. minutiae	g.	fertile
____	8. palatial	h.	enormous
____	9. peccadillo	i.	delicate
____	10. picayune	j.	extended city
____	11. simulacrum	k.	ornate
____	12. soupçon	l.	petty
____	13. teeming	m.	minor sin
____	14. titanic	n.	extended view
____	15. vista	o.	immeasurably small

Answers are on pages 205–206.

Words With Tales Attached

Why would prisoners welcome *gossamer* bars for their cells?

Technically, why is an open-air *conclave* a paradox?

Does *junket* make you think of a trip, scrap metal, or a Chinese ship?

Would you prefer *draconian* or *epicurean* treatment?

Is a *juggernaut* something to fear, to drink, or to wear?

---

accolade
conclave
dirge
draconian
epicurean
gossamer
immolate
juggernaut
junket
ostracism
proletariat
rigmarole
rubric
Socratic
sycophant

1. **accolade** (ak'-ə-lād)—praise or approval; an embrace of greeting or salutation. When French generals kiss the cheeks of the men being honored, they are continuing a custom of the early French kings who placed their arms around the neck (Latin *ad* "to" and *colum* "neck") of the new knight in order to kiss him. William the Conqueror used his fist to confer knighthood. Later a gentle stroke with the flat of the sword on the side of the neck became the accepted method.
   a. In their lavish *accolades*, the critics have compared this play with the finest dramas ever written.
   b. "*Accolades*," observed Mr. Raritan, "are reserved not merely for good intentions but for superior performances."

2. **conclave** (kän'-klāv)—a private or secret meeting; an assembly or gathering, especially one with authority, power, and influence. When a pope is to be elected, the College of Cardinals meets in a room locked on the inside and outside. No one is permitted to leave until a new pope has been chosen. From Latin, then, a *conclave* is a meeting in a room locked with *(con)* a key *(clavis)*. You can recognize the same root in *clef, clavicle,* and *conclude.*
   a. At the annual *conclave,* the delegates proposed a sweeping revision of the charter.
   b. A *conclave* of political leaders was held to name the next mayor.

3. **dirge** (durj)—a funeral hymn; a slow, sad song, poem, or musical composition; a lament. *Dirge* is a contraction of the first word of a Latin funeral service which begins, "Dirige, Domine. . . . " ("O Lord, direct my way in Thy sight"). This in turn is based on the words of a Psalm (" . . . Make Thy way straight before my face").
   a. The widow, moved by the solemn music of the *dirge,* broke into uncontrollable sobs.
   b. The autumn wind sang the *dirge* of summer.

4. **draconian** (drā-kō'-nē-ən)—harsh or vigorous; a law or code of extreme severity. Draco was an Athenian lawgiver whose code or laws, established in 621 B.C., called for the most severe penalties for the smallest offense.
   a. The student editorial labeled the new security system a *draconian* measure which violated individual rights.
   b. To balance the budget, the mayor was forced to adopt *draconian* regulations that further reduced services to the city residents.

5. **epicurean** (ep-ə-kyŏŏr'-ē-ən)—devoted to the pursuit of pleasure; fond of good food, comfort, and ease. The followers of Epicurus are associated with the pursuit of pleasure, so that *epicureanism* has become synonymous with luxurious living. The early *Epicureans* were contrasted with the Stoics, followers

of Zeno, who taught that the wise man should be free from passion and submissive to natural law. The Stoic today is one who endures the hardships of life without complaint.

a. The banquet tables were laden with *epicurean* delicacies that we had never seen before.

b. The *epicurean* way of life holds little attraction to the person who is committed to the nobler ideals of improving society.

6. **gossamer** (gos'-ə-mer)—soft, sheer, gauzy fabric; fine film of cobwebs seen in autumn; anything delicate, light or insubstantial. Lexicographers theorize that this word, derived from Middle English *goose* and *somer,* was first used as a name for Indian summer, when geese were in season.

a. The *gossamer*-thin wire was part of the electronic gear transmitting secret information from the foreign embassy.

b. The merry company, the sparkling conversation, the *gossamer* trees conspired to make Sharon feel heady and romantic.

7. **immolate** (im'-ə-lāt)—to kill, as a sacrifice; to destroy or renounce for the sake of something else. Ground grain or meal (Latin *mola*) was sprinkled by the Roman priest on the head of an animal before it was sacrificed. Later, this preparatory act of sprinkling, *immolation,* came to mean the sacrifice itself.

a. As a protest against universal indifference to human suffering, the bearded stranger tried to *immolate* himself on the U.N. plaza.

b. We value each life too highly to risk the *immolation* of so many young men for the sake of maintaining a puppet dictator in power.

8. **juggernaut** (jug'-ər-nôt)—anything that exacts blind devotion or terrible sacrifice; any terrible, irresistible force. *Juggernaut* is the Hindu god whose idol is dragged in a religious procession on an enormous car. Devotees are sometimes crushed under the wheels of the advancing car. The word today is applied to any large, overpowering, destructive force or object such as war, a giant battleship or a powerful football team.

a. The Nazi *juggernaut* rolled over the Maginot Line and quickly subdued Western Europe at the outset of World War II.

b. The formidable Crimson *juggernaut* pushed the defending champions down the field until a fumble, a long pass, and a field goal turned the tide.

9. **junket** (jun'-kit)—a party, banquet, or outing; a trip taken by an official and paid for with public funds. *Junket* began as a Latin word *juncus* ("a twig"), and referred to a basket made of rushes and twigs. Soon the word was applied to delicacies, especially cream and cheese preparations, served in these baskets. Finally, it became the feast served out of doors, a picnic. The political slant to *junket* probably stems from the clambakes or beer-and-pretzels feasts once offered by political clubs to their followers. After moving into the political sphere, the word acquired its modern meaning of an official trip underwritten by the taxpayer—a long way from the twigs and cheese.

a. The editor received many letters critical of the congressional *junkets* to the Far East.

b. The opening gun of the campaign was a *junket* attended by every aspiring politico in the district.

10. **ostracism** (äs'-trə-siz'm)—a rejection or exclusion from a group or society by general consent. In ancient Athens, if the assembly decided a person was endangering the public welfare or liberty, a vote was taken to send the guilty one into exile. A potsherd or oyster shell (from the Greek *ostra*) on which was written the name of the person to be *ostracized* was dropped into an urn. The modern blackballing of members from organizations closely follows this method.

a. I called attention to Carol's unselfishness and loyalty and urged the group not to *ostracize* her for one small slip of the tongue.
b. Roger's attempt to win the game all by himself led to his *ostracism*.

11. **proletariat** (prō-lə-tar′-ē-ət)—the working class; the unpropertied class. *Proles,* a Latin word for "offspring," is the source of *proletariat* or the poor class, who, because they were prolific, served the state only by producing offspring.
a. Over the years, the *proletariat* has made tremendous strides in improving the conditions of life for those formerly deprived.
b. In a democratic society, the line between the *proletariat* and the landowners is not so rigid, for people move freely from one to the other.

12. **rigmarole** (rig′-mə-rōl)—confused, incoherent, foolish talk; a complicated and petty procedure. *Rigmarole* is an alteration of *ragman roll,* a series of documents in which the Scottish noblemen acknowledged their allegiance to Edward I of England.
a. How Mr. Sykes hated to go through the *rigmarole* of a formal dinner.
b. In order to join the fraternity, Bob found he had to go through the *rigmarole* of secret handshakes, greetings, and passwords.

13. **rubric** (rōō′-brik)—a title, heading, or direction in a book, written or printed in red or otherwise distinguished from the rest of the text; an established custom or rule of procedure; a short commentary or explanation covering a broad subject. In the monasteries, the monks who copied the works of the ancient authors often adorned their manuscripts with beautiful decorations. For headings, they followed the Roman practice of using red ink (Latin, *ruber*). Thus *rubric* came to mean not only the initial ornamental letters but also the directive or rule of conduct which was often part of the heading.
a. Professor Morand ended his lecture with a *rubric* designed to summarize his principal ideas.
b. Following the *rubric* regarding the election of a president, each state continues to send its representatives to the Electoral College.

14. **Socratic** (sō-krat′-ik)—pertaining to Socrates or his philosophical method of repeated questioning to elicit truths implicit in all rational beings. Socrates, a Greek philosopher and the chief speaker in Plato's *Dialogues,* developed his ideas by constantly asking questions or forcing admissions from his opponents. Condemned to death for irreverence to the gods and corrupting the youth, Socrates is now remembered as a seeker after truth and a man who taught his disciples how to think.
a. The *Socratic* method of inquiry is ideally suited to a discussion of motives in a play or novel.
b. "There is no need," said Mr. Holmes, "to enter into all this *Socratic* dialogue when the case is so elementary."

15. **sycophant** (sik′-ə-fənt)—a self-seeking, servile flatterer; fawning parasite; one who attempts to win favor or advance himself by flattering persons of influence. Since the Greek roots mean "showing figs," two possible explanations have been offered for the story behind *sycophant.* One is that the gesture of a fig was used to denounce a criminal, making a *sycophant* an informer. The other is more literal. It was unlawful to export figs and one who reported such an act was called a *sycophant,* or fig-shower. The modern meaning derives from the informer's cringing and servile manner.
a. Tom's laughing at all the teacher's jokes and volunteering for every task were looked upon as *sycophancy* by his classmates.
b. I do not envy the *sycophant* who has advanced himself at the expense of his self-respect.

EXERCISES

I. Which Word Comes to Mind?

In each of the following, read the statement, then circle the word that comes to mind.

1. They are the backbone of our industrial power

(rubric,   proletariat,   juggernaut)

2. The silent treatment

(conclave,   dirge,   ostracism)

3. In some underdeveloped countries, a thief is punished by having his hand cut off

(Socratic,   draconian,   junket)

4. Eat, drink, and be merry

(epicurean,   immolate,   sycophant)

5. This play deserves the Drama Critics' Award

(accolade,   rigmarole,   gossamer)

II. True or False?

In the space provided, indicate whether each statement is true or false.

_____ 1. A *sycophant* speaks with sincerity.
_____ 2. A *dirge* would be inappropriate at a wedding.
_____ 3. A *rigmarole* is a tall-masted sailing ship.
_____ 4. A *rubric* has to be written in red.
_____ 5. A model sailing ship in a bottle is a good example of a *juggernaut*.

III. Synonyms and Antonyms

Indicate whether the following pairs of words are the same, opposite, or unrelated in meaning by writing S, O, or U in the space provided.

_____ 1. ostracism—acceptance
_____ 2. accolade—encomium
_____ 3. immolate—soften
_____ 4. rigmarole—fabrication
_____ 5. epicurean—pleasure-bound

IV. Extra Letters

In each of the vocabulary words below there is an extra letter. Put all the extra letters together and you will be able to spell out a word taught in a previous lesson. Its meaning is "an omen of death."

1. rubrick
2. syncophant
3. rigemarole
4. immollate
5. prolletariat

V. Matching

Match the word in column A with its correct definition in column B by writing the letter of that definition in the space provided.

A	B
_____ 1. accolade	a. peasantry
_____ 2. conclave	b. lament
_____ 3. dirge	c. cabal
_____ 4. draconian	d. established procedure
_____ 5. epicurean	e. rigorous and severe
_____ 6. gossamer	f. foolish talk
_____ 7. immolate	g. overwhelming force
_____ 8. juggernaut	h. excursion
_____ 9. junket	i. sensualist
_____ 10. ostracism	j. blackballing
_____ 11. proletariat	k. delicate
_____ 12. rigmarole	l. in the manner of questions and answers
_____ 13. rubric	m. obsequious flatterer
_____ 14. Socratic	n. commendation, praise
_____ 15. sycophant	o. kill for sacrifice

Answers are on page 206.

Words with tails attached

Of Loves and Fears and Hates

What does a *philatelist* collect?

Is the opposite of a *misogynist* a *philologist* or a *philogynist*?

Would a person who thinks he is Napoleon be considered a *paranoid* or a *Francophile*?

Is *claustrophobia* a condition that is best handled by a beautician, a psychologist, or a banker?

Where is the most fearful place for a *Russophobe*?

---

acrophobia
bibliophile
claustrophobia
Francophile
hydrophobia
misanthropy
misogyny
paranoid
philately
Philistine
philogyny
philology
Russophobia
triskaidekaphobia
xenophobia

1. **acrophobia** (ak-rə-fō′-bē-ə)—abnormally intense fear of being in high places.
   a. Standing on the swaying bridge high above the swirling waters was enough to give me a case of *acrophobia* for quite a time.
   b. In his speech accepting the medal for bravery, the veteran fireman told how he was almost disqualified as a trainee because of his *acrophobia*.

2. **bibliophile** (bib′-lē-ō-fīl)—one who loves books; a book collector. The opposite is a *biblioclast*.
   a. The *bibliophile's* eyes were aglow with his new acquisition, a rare variorum edition of Shakespeare's *The Tempest*.
   b. The discovery of hundreds of library books in Mr. Gerard's home led police to conclude that he was a biblioklept as well as a *bibliophile*.

3. **claustrophobia** (klôs-trə-fō′-bē-ə)—an abnormal dread of being in closed or narrow spaces. One who has a fear of open spaces suffers from *agoraphobia.*
   a. The patient displayed *claustrophobic* tendencies in his insistence that his door remain open at all times.
   b. In pioneer days, *claustrophobia,* if it existed at all, was an individual's problem; in modern times, it is societal.

4. **Francophile** (fraŋ′-kə-fīl)—an admirer of France, its people, and its customs. It may also be used as an adjective.
   a. As with other vogues and fads, the day of the *Francophile* has come to an end.
   b. When Bob began to call himself Rober, accenting the first syllable and rolling the *r*'s in a guttural sound, we knew he was entering the *Francophile* stage of his hallucinations.

5. **hydrophobia** (hī-drə-fō′-bē-ə)—fear of water; rabies. One of the symptoms of the disease caused by the bite of a rabid animal is an inability to swallow; hence, the name *hydrophobia* for the disease itself.
   a. Fearing the child might develop *hydrophobia* from the dog bite, the anguished parents broadcast an appeal to locate the animal and have it tested for rabies.
   b. Little Alex's difficulty in swallowing after his tonsillectomy brought on a spell of *hydrophobia.*

6. **misanthropy** (mis-an′-thrō-pē)—hatred of or distrust of mankind. The *misanthropist* has his opposite in the *philanthropist,* that is, one who loves mankind—and has the means to support worthy causes.

a. Moral corruption, so rampant in our society, has turned some people into *misanthropes,* others into reformers.

b. Silas Marner, the classic example of the *misanthrope,* was brought out of the darkness of his existence by the love of a little child.

7. **misogyny** (mis-äj'-ə-nē)—hatred of women.
    a. The portrait of Lucy Manette balances Dickens' *misogynic* representation of women like Madame DeFarge.
    b. In a society where polygamy was practiced, the *misogynist* would be out of place.

8. **paranoid** (par'-ə-noid)—showing unreasonable distrust, suspicion, or an exaggerated sense of one's own importance. Paranoia is usually a chronic condition characterized by delusions of persecution or of grandeur that the afflicted strenuously defends with apparent logic and reason.
    a. Stanley became *paranoid* on the subject of his accident, claiming that the police and the witnesses were conspiring against him.
    b. Our civilization can ill afford the luxury of a *paranoid* attitude toward nuclear proliferation, for even a small misstep could spell doomsday.

9. **philately** (fi-lat'-ə-lē)—the collection and study of postage stamps, postmarks, and related materials. The derivation, from the Greek *philo* ("loving"), and *ateles* ("without charge"), reminds us that the original stamp indicated a tax-free shipment.
    a. The *philatelic* public was delighted by the early announcement of commemorative stamps for the Bicentennial.
    b. Though there is much information and pleasure to be gained from *philately,* the primary motive for some collectors is cash value.

10. **Philistine** (fi-lis'-tīn, -tēn; fil'-i-stēn)—a smug, ignorant, especially middle-class person who is held to be indifferent or antagonistic to artistic and cultural values; boorish or barbarous; an ignoramus or outsider.
    a. Oscar Wilde said, "It is only the *Philistine* who seeks to estimate a personality by the vulgar test of production."
    b. Cynics often act the part of the misunderstood genius at war with *Philistine* society.

11. **philogyny** (fi-läj'-ə-nē)—love of or fondness for women.
    a. Casanova, the Italian adventurer, cultivated a reputation for *philogyny* through his many love affairs.
    b. One who flirts with many women is not necessarily a *philogynist* and may, indeed, be quite the opposite.

12. **philology** (fi-läl'-ə-jē)—historical and comparative linguistics; the study of human speech, especially as the vehicle of literature; literary or classical learning. The *philologist* is known by other related labels, the *philologer* and the *philologue.*
    a. The dating of the rare manuscript in the fifth century was based chiefly on *philological* evidence.
    b. *Philology* has been able to recreate the original Indo-European and other proto-historic languages, though no record survives from the time they were spoken.

13. **Russophobia** (rus-ə-fō'-bē-ə)—dislike or fear of Russia or its policies.
    a. World War II was followed by a long period of *Russophobia* that has only recently been modified by detente.
    b. *Russophobia,* as indeed the fear of anything, can best be dealt with by knowledge and strength.

14. **triskaidekaphobia** (tris-kī-dek-ə-fō'-bē-ə)—fear of the number 13. Though the word is long, the arithmetic etymology from Greek is simple: *treis* ("three"), *kai* ("and"), and *deka* ("ten").
   a. *Triskaidekaphobia* has been carried to ridiculous extremes as in the case of hotels that do not have a floor numbered 13.
   b. Among the Jewish people, *triskaidekaphobia* has not made any headway for a family joyfully celebrates the thirteenth birthday of a young man as he assumes his religious duties and obligations.

15. **xenophobia** (zen-ə-fō'-bē-ə)—an unusual fear or contempt of strangers or foreigners, especially as reflected in one's political or cultural views.
   a. Insecurity may often lead an American traveling abroad to exhibit *xenophobic* tendencies.
   b. The "One World" philosophy, aided by the advances in mass media, will one day make *xenophobia* extinct.

EXERCISES

I. Which Word Comes to Mind?

In each of the following, read the statement, then circle the word that comes to mind.

1. Bats and beavers are prone to this

   (claustrophobia,   hydrophobia,   philogyny)

2. No member of the famous trapeze artists, The Flying Valencias, ever had this

   (Francophilism,   misanthropy,   acrophobia)

3. Jack the Ripper must have been one

   (misogynist,   philatelist,   philologist)

4. Beware of Friday the 13th

   (bibliophile,   triskaidekaphobia,   Philistine)

5. The U.S. citizen likes anything that is American and detests everything else

   (xenophobe,   Russophobe,   paranoid)

II. True or False?

In the space provided, indicate whether each statement is true or false.

____ 1. A *bibliophile* is a file clerk in a library.
____ 2. A *Francophile* would feel quite at home in Philadelphia.
____ 3. You can assume that a hermit is a *misanthrope*.
____ 4. Some men dream of having a harem, but not the *misogynist*.
____ 5. A *Philistine* would be a frequent visitor to the museums.

III. Creating New Words

Using the following roots and affixes from this lesson, form a new word for each definition given.

phil, philia   xeno   acro   biblio
anthropo   triskaideka   phobia

1. love of strangers_____
2. love of mankind_____
3. fear of books_____
4. love of heights_____
5. love of 13 Frenchmen_____

IV. Finding Roots

Find and circle the four roots in the box below that can be combined with —*phobia* or —*phile* to form words from this lesson.

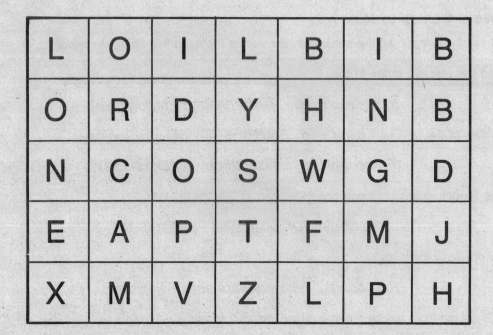

L	O	I	L	B	I	B
O	R	D	Y	H	N	B
N	C	O	S	W	G	D
E	A	P	T	F	M	J
X	M	V	Z	L	P	H

V. Matching

Match the word in column A with its correct definition in column B by writing the letter of that definition in the space provided.

A

____ 1. acrophobia
____ 2. bibliophile
____ 3. claustrophobia
____ 4. Francophile
____ 5. hydrophobia
____ 6. misanthropy
____ 7. misogyny
____ 8. paranoid
____ 9. philately

B

a. lover of Gallic customs
b. love of women
c. rabies
d. materialist
e. lover of books
f. fear of the number 13
g. distrust of everyone
h. distrust of women
i. study of languages of the world

_____ 10. Philistine   j. fear of high places
_____ 11. philogyny   k. fear of foreigners
_____ 12. philology   l. stamp-collecting
_____ 13. Russophobia   m. dislike of the USSR
_____ 14. triskaidekaphobia   n. one with delusions of grandeur
_____ 15. xenophobia   o. fear of being shut in

Answers are on page 206.

Hydrophobia

Science—"Ology" Words

Did *rhinology* originate on the Rhine River?

Is *speleology* a game, a science, or a disease?

Which is the study of women's diseases: *gynecology* or *endocrinology*?

If a psychologist treats psychoses, does a *neurologist* treat neuroses?

Does *morphology* involve medical research, linguistics, or both?

archaeology
cardiology
ecology
endocrinology
gerontology
gynecology
morphology
necrology
neurology
paleontology
pathology
rhinology
seismology
speleology
toxicology

1. **archaeology** (är-kē-äl'-ə-jē)—the systematic recovery by scientific methods of material evidence remaining from man's life and culture in past ages, and the detailed study of this evidence.
   a. Recent *archaeological* discoveries of potsherds near Tel Aviv, Israel, should shed light on the origins of our written alphabet.
   b. *Archaeology* has attracted many young enthusiasts who see in the patient digging and sorting of artifacts an exciting adventure that combines history, science, and detective work.

2. **cardiology** (kär-dē-äl'-ə-jē)—the medical study of the diseases and functioning of the heart. Emphasis on prevention and treatment of heart disease has made most people familiar with cardiographs, the curve that traces the mechanical movements of the heart.
   a. Many young doctors, inspired by the desire to eradicate heart disease, the nation's number one killer, are entering the field of *cardiology.*
   b. *Cardiology* has made giant strides with open-heart surgery and nuclear-powered pacemakers, but heart transplants remain stymied by the tendency of the body to reject foreign tissue.

3. **ecology** (i-käl'-ə-jē)—the science of the relationships between organisms and their environments. This field is also called bionomics.
   a. *Ecology*-minded groups are a new element in society, acting as a brake to the ruthless exploitation and contamination of the world's natural resources.
   b. A compromise is being sought between the indiscriminate development of new energy sources and *ecological* safeguards to protect the world from disasters.

4. **endocrinology** (en-dō-kri-näl'-ə-jē, -krī–näl'-ə-jē)—the physiology of the ductless glands, such as the thyroid or adrenal, whose secretions pass directly into the blood stream from the cells of the gland.
   a. Tim's abnormal growth pattern was investigated by the *endocrinologist* as a possible dysfunction of the thyroid glands.
   b. *Endocrinology* is a vast field encompassing the complex interrelationship of basic body functions such as renal activity, reproduction, smooth muscle contraction, and normal growth and development.

5. **gerontology** (jer-ən-täl'-ə-jē)—the scientific study of the physiological and pathological phenomena associated with aging. The Greek stem *geront* ("old"), explains the source of the names of such popular medicines as Geritol.
   a. The conquest and control of many diseases in modern times has led to the prolongation of life and opened the new field of *gerontology* to the medical and business world.
   b. *Gerontologists* insist that old age should not be a period of life filled with fear, misery, and loneliness.

6. **gynecology** (gī-nə-käl′-ə-jē)—a branch of medicine that deals with women, their diseases, hygiene, and medical care.
   a. Many doctors specialize in both *gynecology* and obstetrics.
   b. The ovarian infection required *gynecological* surgery.

7. **morphology** (môr-fäl′-ə-jē)—the biological study of the form and structure, rather than the functioning of living organisms. In linguistics, *morphology* denotes the study of word formations, including the origin and function of inflections and derivations.
   a. Evidence points to a number of common genetic factors in the *morphology* of gamblers.
   b. Modern English has freely adapted foreign elements, whereas Old English, or Anglo-Saxon, had a *morphology* that tended to build new words by varying combinations of its native stock.

8. **necrology** (nə-kräl′-ə-jē)—a list or record of people who have died, especially in the recent past.
   a. The publication carried a *necrology* of contributors who had died during the past year.
   b. During our visit to the newspaper plant, we were surprised to learn that the *necrology* of most famous living people had already been prepared and was constantly being updated.

9. **neurology** (noo-räl′-ə-jē, nyoo-)—the medical science of the nervous system and its disorders.
   a. A *neurological* examination suggested the root of the patient's problem was nothing more than excessive fatigue resulting from overwork.
   b. Despite exhaustive interviews and tests, the *neurologist* was unable to determine the cause of Ernie's paralysis and recommended psychological investigation.

10. **paleontology** (pāl-ē-ən-täl′-ə-jē)—the study of fossils and ancient life forms. *Paleo* is a combining form indicating "ancient" or "prehistoric."
    a. The findings of *paleontology* shed light on the evolution and relationships of modern animals and plants as well as on the chronology of the history of the earth.
    b. *Paleontological* discoveries tend to place the origins of our earth farther back in time than had been hitherto believed.

11. **pathology** (pə-thäl′-ə-jē)—the scientific study of the nature of disease, its causes, processes, development, and consequences; the anatomic or functional manifestations of disease.
    a. The stories Jane concocted were so bizarre we suspected she had become a *pathological* liar.
    b. No symptom was ignored, no detail overlooked as Philadelphia mobilized its scientific resources to track the *pathology* of the strange disease that had mysteriously killed 27 people.

12. **rhinology** (rī-näl′-ə-jē)—the anatomy, physiology and pathology of the nose. The Greek root *rhinokeros* ("nose-horned"), explains how the rhinoceros got its name.
    a. Cyrano or Pinnochio would have been a *rhinologist's* delight.
    b. The congestion in his lungs, according to the *rhinologist*, could be traced to the absence of the follicles that filter the air as it enters the nasal passage.

13. **seismology** (sīz-mäl′-ə-jē, sīs-)—the geophysical science of earthquakes and of the mechanical properties of the earth.
    a. *Seismologists*, like meteorologists, can merely predict or measure great natural disturbances but they can do little to prevent them.

b. The recent earthquake reported by *seismologists* in the Peking area measured an intensity of 8 on the Richter scale.

14. **speleology** (spē-lē-ăl'-ə-jē)—the scientific study or systematic exploration of caves.
    a. Many a spelunker, or amateur cave explorer, has developed her hobby into the specialty of *speleology*.
    b. The *speleologist* explained that stalactites, or drippings of crystalline calcium carbonate hanging from the roof of a cave, often combined with stalagmites, or drippings of similar crystals on the floor, to form complete columns.

15. **toxicology** (tăk-si-kăl'-ə-jē)—the study of the nature, effects, and detection of poisons and the treatment of poisoning.
    a. Early *toxicologists* used a mixture of toxin and its antitoxin as a vaccine against diphtheria.
    b. *Toxicology* must deal not only with the effect of poisons on living organisms but with those substances otherwise harmless that prove toxic under peculiar conditions, and with the industrial or legal ramifications of this.

EXERCISES

I. Which Word Comes to Mind?

In each of the following, read the statement, then circle the word that comes to mind.

1. Fears that the Alaskan pipeline will destroy the delicate balance of animal life in the region

    (neurology,   archaeology,   ecology)

2. A special panel on diseases of the aged

    (endocrinology,   gerontology,   rhinology)

3. The honored list of soldiers who made the supreme sacrifice

    (necrology,   gynecology,   toxicology)

4. The monster left an impression of his footprint in the rock

    (paleontology,   morphology,   seismology)

5. The Dead Sea Scrolls were hidden for centuries in the Qumran cave

    (cardiology,   speleology,   pathology)

II. True or False?

In the space provided, indicate whether each statement is true or false.

_____ 1. *Archaeology* and *paleontology* could be dealing with the same material.
_____ 2. Mr. Rohas opened the door to the *gynecologist's* office, gulped, and realized he was in the wrong place.
_____ 3. Every *cardiologist* must have a repertoire to demonstrate his dexterity with a deck of cards.
_____ 4. *Morphology* is concerned with finding pain killers.
_____ 5. *Pathologists* work closely with engineers to construct safe, durable roadways.

III. Putting the Scientists in the Proper Place

For each of the following pairs indicate *yes* in the space provided if the scientist is correctly paired with the "tools of his/her trade" and *no* if not.

_____ 1. archaeologist—arches
_____ 2. gerontologist—aged people
_____ 3. morphologist—drugs
_____ 4. seismologist—Richter scale
_____ 5. pathologist—charts and maps
_____ 6. paleontologist—fossils
_____ 7. speleologist—caves
_____ 8. toxicologist—serums
_____ 9. rhinologist—zoo animals
_____ 10. necrologist—old coins

IV. Find the Words

Somewhere in this box of letters, reading up, down, across, or diagonally, the roots of seven vocabulary words that were taught in this lesson are hidden. As you locate each one, draw a circle around it.

E	N	N	C	E	T
O	D	E	R	N	O
S	E	C	O	I	X
M	O	R	P	H	I
N	E	U	R	R	C
G	Y	N	E	C	D

V. Matching

Match the word in column A with its correct definition in column B by writing the letter of that definition in the space provided.

A

_____ 1. archaeology
_____ 2. cardiology
_____ 3. ecology

B

a. environmentalism
b. obituary
c. study of antiquities

—— 4. endocrinology
—— 5. gerontology
—— 6. gynecology
—— 7. morphology
—— 8. necrology
—— 9. neurology
—— 10. paleontology
—— 11. pathology
—— 12. rhinology
—— 13. seismology
—— 14. speleology
—— 15. toxicology

d. study of afflictions of the nervous system
e. something abnormal
f. study of diseases of the heart
g. study of earthquakes
h. study of aging
i. cave exploration
j. pathology of ductless glands
k. science of the nose
l. study of prehistoric fossils
m. study of women's diseases
n. study of poisons
o. form and structure

Answers are on pages 206–207.

Studying scientists

Review

A. The Out-of-Place Word

In each of the following groups, find and circle the one vocabulary word that is out of place. You should be able to explain what the other three words have in common.

1. pettifogger, quatrain, litigation, deposition
2. mastectomy, biopsy, vasectomy, equity
3. philately, alchemy, bibliophile, xenophobia
4. hircine, draconian, Lilliputian, Socratic
5. warlock, demonology, exorcise, etiology
6. cardiology, toxicology, gynecology, phenomenology
7. titanic, picayune, vulpine, infinitesimal
8. vixen, purloin, bovine, leonine
9. amplitude, Decalogue, quintessence, dichotomy
10. equine, ophidian, ursine, elfin

B. Rearranging Words

Rearrange the following groups of words using the first letter of each word to spell out one of the new words taught in this unit.

1. cardiology, cadaver, ostracism, neurology, endocrinology, litigation, abscess, vixen

   _____

2. ursine, Lilliputian, imperious, paleontology, exorcise, nihilism

   _____

3. thaumaturgy, collusion, ophidian, ovine, millenium, etiology, aphasia, shamus

   _____

4. conundrum, tort, tribunal, ingenious, immolate, acrophobia, necrology

   _____

5. dirge, claustrophobia, morphology, epicurean, inscrutable, equine, atonement, triskaidekaphobia

   _____

C. On Location

What would you expect to find in the following places? Circle the correct answer.

1. The morgue

   (collusion, cadaver, ritual, aphasia)

2. A courtroom

   (equity, rubric, rhinology, nihilism)

3. A gypsy tea room

   (shamus, warlock, soothsayer, pettifogger)

4. The library

(bibliophile,   Philistine,   sycophant,   proletariat)

5. A medical supply house

(conundrum,   prosthesis,   tort,   Decalogue)

D. Making Pairs

From the group below, find the pairs of words that have something in common and record them in the spaces provided. You should be able to find ten such pairs. List them numerically, using the same number for each pair.

circumspect _____	Francophile _____	decimate _____	amplitude _____
peccadillo _____	titanic _____	Russophobe _____	adjudicate _____
intractable _____	Decalogue _____	misogyny _____	tumescence _____
tort _____	tribunal _____	abscess _____	demure _____
picayune _____	litigation _____	intransigent _____	philogyny _____

E. Cliché Time

Which of the words from this unit fit into the following familiar expressions? Choose the correct word from the choices given and record it in the space provided.

1. The sick man had a ghostly _____ .

(dirge,   pallor,   lien,   vista)

2. Charlie Chan was called an _____ Oriental.

(hircine,   intestate,   inscrutable,   epicurean)

3. The prisoner was held _____ .

(incommunicado,   comatose,   glabrous,   immolate)

4. A _____ mass of humanity

(demure, tessellated, lupine, teeming)

5. A Congressional _____ .

(Philistine,   junket,   peccadillo,   protocol)

F. Find the Words

Somewhere in this box of letters, reading up, down, across, or diagonally, twenty-one vocabulary words that were taught in Unit 2 are hidden. As you locate each one, draw a circle around it.

A	B	R	H	V	I	S	T	A	S	A	C
W	P	A	L	L	O	R	M	O	T	I	B
E	R	N	I	F	L	E	T	C	R	F	E
Y	S	E	A	R	N	E	A	B	E	T	M
G	N	E	N	I	V	O	U	H	R	B	K
O	L	A	U	T	I	R	R	G	U	N	C
L	E	Q	U	I	T	Y	I	D	M	A	O
O	E	N	I	V	O	B	N	I	E	I	L
R	E	N	I	L	E	F	E	R	D	M	R
C	H	X	E	N	O	P	H	O	B	I	A
E	E	G	R	I	D	O	M	L	I	S	W
N	T	D	I	C	C	A	L	F	O	T	E

Answers are on page 207.

Appearances and Attitudes (III)

Is there any merit in being *meretricious*?

What is the relationship between *mutable* and mutation?

Why did Shakespeare call Romeo's *mercurial* friend Mercutio?

Does one need a license to be *licentious*?

How should you feel if your creative writing is described as *jejune*?

---

jejune
libidinous
licentious
mercurial
meretricious
minatory
mutable
niggardly
nonchalant
noxious
obdurate
obtuse
officious
omniscient
pusillanimous

1. **jejune** (ji-jōōn')—barren; flat; dull. The Latin word *jejunus* means "empty."
   a. Sad to say, he took an exciting theme and turned it into a *jejune* story which put us all to sleep.
   b. Blanche was raised on a *jejune* diet of soap operas which did nothing to develop her mind.

2. **libidinous** (li-bid'-nəs)—characterized by lust; lewd; lascivious. In psychoanalytic theory, the *libido* is the driving force behind all human action.
   a. The comic's *libidinous* patter was censored by the cautious sponsor before it ever got on the air.
   b. Much material of a *libidinous* nature is available only in certain areas of the city.

3. **licentious** (li-sen'-shəs)—morally unrestrained; lascivious. This is derived from an Old French word which meant "license" and referred to an abuse of liberty or undisciplined freedom.
   a. The Broadway play was picketed by a civic group on the grounds that it was *licentious.*
   b. Having spent the preceding twenty years of his life in a *licentious* manner, Clive decided to join a monastery.

4. **mercurial** (mər-kyoor'-ē-əl)—changeable; volatile. These adjectives are characteristic of the heavy, silver-white metallic element mercury. In Roman mythology the swift messenger of the gods, Mercury, was volatile, quick-witted, eloquent, and manually skillful.
   a. Since my boss is a man of *mercurial* moods, we never know what to expect from him.
   b. Shakespeare's Mercutio in *Romeo and Juliet* was aptly named because he had a *mercurial* temperament.

5. **meretricious** (mer'-ə-trish'-əs)—flashy; tawdry; falsely alluring. It is from the Latin word *meretricius* ("prostitute").
   a. Marilyn Monroe projected a *meretricious* quality which distressed her.
   b. The clever defense lawyer changed his client's garb from *meretricious* to prim.

6. **minatory** (min'-ə-tôr-ē)—menacing; threatening.
   a. Our flight attendant assured the obnoxious passenger that he could be arrested for his *minatory* remarks.
   b. President Carter said that he would never knuckle under to *minatory* gestures from foreign leaders.

7. **mutable** (myo͞ot'-ə-b'l)—inconstant; fickle; tending to frequent change. In biology, a *mutation* is a change in some inheritable characteristic.
   a. She swore by the moon but her lover pointed out how *mutable* that was.
   b. As politicians often find out, the electorate can be most *mutable*.

8. **niggardly** (nig'-ərd-lē)—stingy; miserly. *Niggardly* comes from a Norman French word meaning "to rub" or "to pinch." A pennypincher is *niggardly*.
   a. Although Father could be *niggardly* when it came to our allowances, he was most generous with his gifts and presents.
   b. In doling out praise, there is no one so *niggardly* as our baseball coach.

9. **nonchalant** (nän-shə-länt,'-lənt)—cool; indifferent; without warmth or animation. It comes from a French root, *chaloir* ("to care for").
   a. Julio's seemingly *nonchalant* manner is actually a cover-up for his nervousness.
   b. Detective Gates sauntered toward the suspect in a *nonchalant* way, trying not to arouse his suspicions.

10. **noxious** (näk'-shəs)—unwholesome; harmful to health. The Latin *nocere* means "to hurt."
    a. The firemen began to gasp as they got a whiff of the *noxious* gas.
    b. Automobile manufacturers have been given a deadline for eliminating most of their cars' *noxious* fumes.

11. **obdurate** (äb'-door-ət,-dyoor)—hardhearted; inflexible; not easily moved to pity.
    a. Shylock remained *obdurate* when Antonio asked for mercy.
    b. Judge Lenihan had an undeserved reputation for being obstinate and *obdurate*.

12. **obtuse** (əb-to͞os')—slow to understand; dull.
    a. Her husband's *obtuse* behavior proved a constant embarrassment to Lillian.
    b. "How can one person be so *obtuse*!" Nurse Stevens shouted as she prepared to explain the treatment to her new aide for the fifth time that morning.

13. **officious** (ə-fish'-əs)—meddlesome; offering unnecessary and unwanted advice.
    a. The room was filled with *officious* bureaucrats who were doing their best to frustrate the public.
    b. I don't mind working for a competent supervisor but I hate to get involved with an *officious* foreman.

14. **omniscient** (äm-nish'-ənt)—having infinite knowledge; knowing all things.
    a. When we are young we pester our parents with questions because we believe they are *omniscient*.
    b. Judy went into the exam with an *omniscient* attitude but came out feeling like a moron.

15. **pusillanimous** (pū-s'l-an'-ə-məs)—cowardly; fainthearted. In Latin, "tiny mind."
    a. General Patton could not tolerate *pusillanimous* performance in battle.
    b. The Danish patriots warned their government against *pusillanimous* arrangements with the Nazis in 1940.

EXERCISES

I. Which Word Comes to Mind?

In each of the following, read the statement, then circle the word that comes to mind.

1. A Chinese fortune cookie accurately predicts your future

(jejune,   omniscient,   licentious)

2. Eight poker players puffing on cigars in your living room

(noxious,   officious,   niggardly)

3. You receive an anonymous letter hinting at violence

(libidinous,   minatory,   nonchalant)

4. Your father absolutely refuses to let you borrow his car

(meretricious,   obtuse,   obdurate)

5. The Lion in *The Wizard of Oz*

(pusillanimous,   mercurial,   mutable)

II. True or False?

In the space provided, indicate whether each statement is true or false.

——— 1. The conservative congregation was quite pleased with the minister's *libidinous* position.
——— 2. One of our most coveted military awards, the Purple Heart, is given to those who have distinguished themselves by *pusillanimous* actions in combat.
——— 3. An *officious* bank manager can make his tellers uneasy.
——— 4. Putting a $50 bill in the church collection plate was a *niggardly* gesture.
——— 5. Interior decorators generally abhor *meretricious* furniture.

III. Find the Words

Somewhere in this box of letters, reading up, down, across, or diagonally, three vocabulary words that were taught in this lesson are hidden. As you locate each one, draw a circle around it.

B	R	E	W	P	I	N	K
J	E	J	U	N	E	O	T
D	R	I	S	S	M	X	A
L	E	Q	U	D	A	I	H
A	Z	T	O	P	T	O	C
W	B	J	G	Y	Z	U	R
O	G	E	A	F	W	S	B

IV. Extra Letters

In each of the vocabulary words below there is an extra letter. Put all of the extra letters together and you will be able to spell out a word taught in a previous lesson. Its meaning is "worn out."

jejeune

merfcurial

muftable

obdureate

minattory

libidineous

V. Matching

Match the word in column A with its correct definition in Column B by writing the letter of that definition in the space provided.

A

____ 1. jejeune

____ 2. libidinous

____ 3. licentious

____ 4. mercurial

____ 5. meretricious

B

a. morally unrestrained

b. threatening

c. volatile

d. unwholesome

e. indifferent

—— 6. minatory
—— 7. mutable
—— 8. niggardly
—— 9. nonchalant
——10. noxious
——11. obdurate
——12. obtuse
——13. officious
——14. omniscient
——15. pusillanimous

f. cowardly
g. uninteresting, dull
h. stingy
i. slow to understand
j. hardhearted
k. flashy; cheap
l. meddlesome
m. knowing all things
n. inconstant
o. lewd

Answers are on page 208.

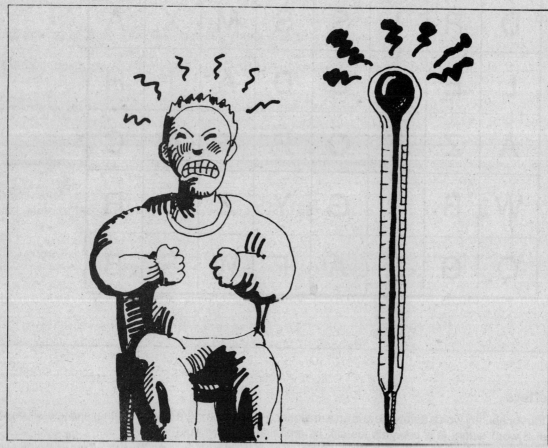

Mercurial

Legal Language (II)

Why do prison reformers advocate *indeterminate* sentences?

What does a lawyer mean when he labels a question as *immaterial*?

Should our *extradition* treaties with other countries be of interest to a criminal?

Why is a *litigious* person likely to be found in court?

When is a lawyer a *barrister*?

---

amicus curiae
arson
barrister
embezzle
extradition
habeas corpus
immaterial
incarcerate
indeterminate
larceny
litigious
miscreant
perpetrator
plagiarism
probation

1. **amicus curiae** (ə-mī′-kəs-kyoor′-ī-ē)—a friend of the court; a lawyer or layman who advises the court on a legal matter.
    a. Our law professor is frequently called to serve as *amicus curiae* on difficult cases.
    b. I offered my help as *amicus curiae* in the family squabble but both sides rejected it.

2. **arson** (är′-s′n)—the crime of setting fire to property in order to collect insurance.
    a. The Fire Marshall characterized the case as an *arson*.
    b. A pyromaniac has a compulsion to start fires; an *arsonist* does it for money.

3. **barrister** (bar′-is-tər, ber′-) lawyer in England. A *barrister* practices at the *bar*, or court of justice.
    a. Lord Dorset called upon the finest *barrister* in London to defend him.
    b. It's always amusing for tourists to see the British *barristers* wearing their court wigs.

4. **embezzle** (im-bez′′l)—to steal money which was entrusted to your care.
    a. The treasurer of our union tried to *embezzle* pension funds but he was caught.
    b. Aunt Anna thought every banker was trying to *embezzle* her savings.

5. **extradition** (eks-trə-dish′-ən)—turning over a fugitive from one jurisdiction to another. The root of the word is the Latin *trachtio* ("the act of handing over").
    a. Armed with the *extradition* papers, Sheriff Bates flew to Italy.
    b. Until we sign an *extradition* treaty with Costa Rica, some criminals will continue to flee there.

6. **habeas corpus** (hā′-bi-əs   kôr′-pəs)—a court order requiring that a prisoner be produced to determine the legality of his imprisonment; a procedure which lawyers use to get clients out of illegal detention. In Latin it means "to have the body."
    a. When F. Lee Bailey produced a writ of *habeas corpus,* the police were forced to release their suspect.
    b. Captain Gordon was demoted because he failed to obey a *habeas corpus* order.

7. **immaterial** (im̃-ə-tir′-ē-əl)—without substance; unimportant.
    a. Lawyers are fond of calling a question "*immaterial*, irrelevant, and inconsequential."
    b. What seemed to be serious charges turned out to be quite *immaterial*.

8. **incarcerate** (in-kär′-sə-rāt)—to jail; confine.
    a. Judge Miller threatened to *incarcerate* anyone who disturbed his court.
    b. King Edward *incarcerated* his brother, Clarence, in the Tower of London.

9. **indeterminate** (in-di-tur'-mi-nit)—having inexact limits; indefinite.
   a. If a prisoner is given an *indeterminate* sentence of 2–20 years, he can be freed early if he behaves well in jail.
   b. "Scarface" Kelly had to serve the full fifteen years of his *indeterminate* sentence because of his numerous attempts to escape.

10. **larceny** (lär'-sə-nē)—theft. *Grand larceny* involves theft in excess of a fixed sum, whereas *petty larceny* refers to a less consequential theft.
    a. Since this is George's fourth conviction for grand *larceny*, he will go to jail for life.
    b. My partner was promoted to detective after making an important *larceny* arrest.

11. **litigious** (li-tij'-əs)—quarrelsome; given to carrying on lawsuits.
    a. Uncle Charlie, our *litigious* relative, is currently involved in three cases.
    b. A litigant is a *litigious* person engaged in a litigation.

12. **miscreant** (mis'-kri-ənt)—villain; criminal; evil person. The original meaning was "unbeliever" or "heretic." From there it was an easy jump to "villain."
    a. The *miscreant's* tears had no effect on Judge Safian.
    b. We were not taken in by the *miscreant's* vow to turn over a new leaf.

13. **perpetrator** (pur'-pə-trā-tər)—a person who commits an offense.
    a. Policemen are careful to use the term "alleged *perpetrator*" when describing a suspect.
    b. Although Roy was the *perpetrator* of the cruel hoax, he escaped serious punishment.

14. **plagiarism** (plā'-jə-riz'm)—passing off someone else's writings or ideas as your own. The Latin word for kidnaper is *plagiarius.*
    a. We were saddened to learn that Henry was found guilty of *plagiarism* in the poetry contest.
    b. My English teacher tolerates almost any mistake but she detests *plagiarism.*

15. **probation** (prō-bā-'shən)—a period of testing or trial. This refers to a suspension of sentence on the condition that the convicted person demonstrates good behavior in order to stay out of jail.
    a. After his release from prison, Vincent was required to report to his *probation* officer every month.
    b. Before getting permanent status, the young policeman had to undergo a six month period of *probation.*

EXERCISES

I. Which Word Comes to Mind?

In each of the following, read the statement, then circle the word that comes to mind.

1. A prominent psychiatrist offers to help out in a court case

(*perpetrator,   larceny,   amicus curiae*)

2. The fire marshall suspects foul play

(*probation,   arson,   immaterial*)

3. Detectives fly across the border to bring back a suspect

(*indeterminate,   extradition,   habeas corpus*)

4. A scholar suggests that Shakespeare was not especially original

(plagiarism,   incarcerate,   miscreant)

5. The crooked bank manager fears the day when his books will be audited

(litigious,   embezzle,   barrister)

II. True or False?

In the space provided, indicate whether each statement is true or false.

____ 1. Burning down a building is an act of *larceny*.
____ 2. *Litigious* people provide a good income for lawyers.
____ 3. An alert lawyer can use a writ of *habeas corpus* to keep his client out of jail before charges are brought against him.
____ 4. When you *embezzle* funds you misuse money which has been entrusted to you.
____ 5. That which is *immaterial* is usually critical in any court case.

III. Find the Words

Somewhere in this box of letters, reading up, down, across, or diagonally, three vocabulary words that were taught in this lesson are hidden. As you locate each one, draw a circle around it.

C	Y	N	E	C	R	A	L
H	B	G	P	N	O	M	F
I	Z	R	O	K	W	T	S
L	Y	S	A	M	S	W	K
M	R	I	G	N	Q	U	O
A	D	L	X	O	C	I	B
E	M	B	E	Z	Z	L	E

IV.   Extra Letters

In each of the vocabulary words below there is an extra letter. Put all the extra letters together and you will be able to spell out a word taught in a previous lesson. Its meaning is "trip taken by an official and financed with public funds."

perjjury   ipso fackto
tourt   pettiefogger
tribunnal   littigation

V.   Matching

Match the word in column A with its correct definition in column B by writing the letter of that definition in the space provided.

	A		B
——	1. amicus curiae		a. court order for a prisoner's appearance
——	2. arson		b. misappropriate money
——	3. barrister		c. unimportant
——	4. embezzle		d. villain
——	5. extradition		e. friend of the court
——	6. habeas corpus		f. one who commits an offense
——	7. immaterial		g. quarrelsome
——	8. incarcerate		h. British lawyer
——	9. indeterminate		i. false claim of authorship
——	10. larceny		j. indefinite
——	11. litigious		k. period of testing
——	12. miscreant		l. transfer of a fugitive
——	13. perpetrator		m. place in jail
——	14. plagiarism		n. crime of setting fire
——	15. probation		o. theft

Answers are on page 208.

Foreign Terms (I)

Is a *junta* a tasty dessert?

What foreign expression means "end of the century"?

What does a firing squad have to do with *coup de grace*?

How does *laissez-faire* differ from *savior faire*?

Why does Emily Post frown upon behavior that is *gauche*?

---

avant-garde
bête noire
bon mot
coup de grace
cul-de-sac
deus ex machina
fait accompli
fin de siècle
gauche
junta
laissez-faire
mot juste
non compos mentis
non sequitur
sine qua non

1. **avant-garde** (ä-vänt-gärd′)—the leaders of a movement; vanguard. *Avant-garde* people are generally regarded as reformers, people with new ideas who are somewhat ahead of their time.
   a. Lord Keynes was an *avant-garde* economist in the period before World War I.
   b. The painter once belonged to an *avant-garde* movement but is considered a conservative today.

2. **bête noire** (bāt nwär′)—someone or something which is feared or disliked. In French, the two words mean "black beast." A black sheep was an eyesore in the flock—its wool was less valuable. If something is your *bête noire,* you do your best to avoid it; it is a thorn in your side.
   a. Although I was good in math, geometry proved to be my *bête noire.*
   b. The regional primaries were later seen as the incumbent's *bête noire.*

3. **bon mot** (bôn′ mō′)—a bright saying; witticism. In French, *bon* means "good," and *mot* means "word." A clever remark or ad lib is often labeled a *bon mot.*
   a. Groucho Marx was applauded for his *bon mot* on the talk show.
   b. I tried all evening to come up with a sparkling *bon mot* but my wit had deserted me.

4. **coup de grace** (kōō-də-gräs′)—the shot or blow which brings death; the finishing stroke. The actual French meaning is "blow of mercy." The officer in charge of a firing squad administers the *coup de grace* by firing a bullet into the victim's head after his men have shot.
   a. Tom's foul shot in the last second of the game was the *coup de grace* for our opponents.
   b. After the prisoner confessed, his torturers administered the *coup de grace.*

5. **cul-de-sac** (kul′-də-sak′)—a passage or street with only one outlet; a situation from which there is no escape; an argument which leads nowhere. In French it means "bottom of the sack."
   a. We chose to build in a *cul-de-sac* because there would be little traffic on our block.
   b. Although we disagree on busing, that topic always proves to be a *cul-de-sac* in our family.

6. **deus ex machina** (dē′-əs eks mak′-i-ne)—someone who intervenes unexpectedly to solve a dilemma. The literal Latin meaning is "god out of the machine." In the ancient theater the first few acts laid out the problems facing the characters and when no solution was apparent, a "god" was lowered onto the stage and helped to resolve the issues.
   a. When things were mighty bleak, Jerry's rich uncle arrived from Canada and turned out to be the family's *deus ex machina.*

    b. His plays often end with a *deus ex machina* that the critics call a far-fetched coincidence.

7. **fait accompli** (fe'-tä-kōn-plē')—something that is already done so that there is no use in debating it. In French, "an accomplished fact."
    a. Dad brought home a Buick, and that *fait accompli* put an end to our discussion as to what kind of car we should buy.
    b. There was nothing democratic about the general's way of running the army because he relied upon the technique of *fait accompli*.

8. **fin de siècle** (fan-də-sye'-kl)—referring to the last years of the 19th century; decadent. The French meaning is "end of the century."
    a. The art gallery staged a showing of *fin de siècle* paintings.
    b. We accused our grandfather of having *fin de siècle* ideas.

9. **gauche** (gōsh)—awkward; lacking grace; without tact. It is French for "left-handed." Lefties were thought to be clumsy (*sinister* in Latin). Another French meaning is "warped."
    a. Following his *gauche* behavior, Arthur was ordered to leave the room.
    b. Harriet's *gauche* remark was unforgivable, and she deserved to have egg on her face.

10. **junta** (hoon'-tə, jun'-)—a political group which seeks to control a government; a faction or cabal. In Spanish this word originally meant "to join." In Spain, a *junta* was a legislative assembly; the word was corrupted to *junto* which meant "clique" or "faction." Today, we use the original word with its changed meaning.
    a. The air force *junta* was arrested before it could overthrow the dictator.
    b. After seizing power, the three-man *junta* held a press conference.

11. **laissez-faire** (les-ā-fer')—hands-off policy; letting business operate without government interference. There was a mid-18th century school of French economists whose motto was *laissez-faire, laissez-passer* ("let us alone, let us have free passage for our goods").
    a. My parents were very progressive, and followed a *laissez-faire* policy in bringing us up.
    b. The South American government adopted a *laissez-faire* attitude in order to attract foreign investment.

12. **mot juste** (mō zhüst')—the right word; exact phrase.
    a. You can always rely upon Shakespeare to come up with the *mot juste*.
    b. I was searching for the *mot juste* but my mind was a blank.

13. **non compos mentis** (nän-käm'-pəs-men'-tis)—incapable of handling one's own affairs; insane. In Latin, "not of sound mind." This could be said of someone who has lost his memory and understanding by reason of disease or accident.
    a. The judge declared Mrs. Elkins *non compos mentis* and appointed a lawyer to handle her estate.
    b. After three martinis, I am definitely *non compos mentis*.

14. **non sequitur** (nän' sek'-wi-tər)—in logic this is a conclusion which does not follow from the evidence; a remark which seems out of place. The Latin meaning is "it does not follow."
    a. When she does not pay attention to our conversation, Betty comes up with one *non sequitur* after another.
    b. I said that Albert is near-sighted, and Phyllis, with a typical *non sequitur*, said, "Yes, he's hard of hearing."

15. **sine qua non** (sin'-ā kwä nōn')—an essential condition; that which is indispensable. The Latin meaning is "without which not."
   a.   Money is the *sine qua non* in our society.
   b.   The *sine qua non* for admission to our club is a sense of humor.

EXERCISES

I. Which Word Comes to Mind?

In each of the following, read the statement, then circle the word that comes to mind.

1. A murderer who pleads temporary insanity

   (laissez-faire,   non compos mentis,   cul-de-sac)

2. An ailing horse is being put out of his misery

   (coup de grace,   mot juste,   gauche)

3. Several schemers plan a take-over

   (fait accompli,   junta,   sine qua non)

4. You ask for her age and she says, "I'm five feet tall"

   (bête noire,   fin de siècle,   non sequitur)

5. Alban Berg was a composer who experimented with atonalities

   (avant-garde,   bon mot,   deus ex machina)

II. True or False?

In the space provided, indicate whether each statement is true or false.

_____ 1. Being born in this country is a *sine qua non* for anyone running for the presidency.
_____ 2. If you are in the *avant-garde,* you are inclined to conservatism.
_____ 3. Someone who always seems to get the better of you is your *bête noire.*
_____ 4. It is considered *gauche* to sip your coffee from the saucer.
_____ 5. "Open sesame" was the *mot juste.*

III. Find the Words

Somewhere in this box of letters, reading up, down, across, or diagonally, four vocabulary words that were taught in this lesson are hidden. As you locate each one, draw a circle around it.

B	A	L	Y	H	R	O	D
M	O	T	J	U	S	T	E
T	Z	N	G	I	M	W	M
F	A	X	M	C	R	S	O
B	Q	U	E	O	N	X	P
K	C	J	U	N	T	A	S
C	A	S	E	D	L	U	C

IV. Extra Letters

In each of the vocabulary words below there is an extra letter. Put all the extra letters together and you will be able to spell out a word taught in a previous lesson. Its meaning is "theft."

gaulche

moat juste

born mot

juncta

fine de siècle

avant-garden

nony compos mentis

V. Matching

Match the word in column A with its correct definition in column B by writing the letter of that definition in the space provided.

A	B
___ 1. avant-garde	a. one who changes the course of events
___ 2. bête noire	b. end of the century
___ 3. bon mot	c. clumsy
___ 4. coup de grace	d. political faction

_____ 5. cul-de-sac
_____ 6. deus ex machina
_____ 7. fait accompli
_____ 8. fin de siècle
_____ 9. gauche
_____ 10. junta
_____ 11. laissez-faire
_____ 12. mot juste
_____ 13. non compos mentis
_____ 14. non sequitur
_____ 15. sine qua non

e. something hateful
f. hands off
g. insane
h. bright saying
i. out of place remark
j. absolute requirement
k. blind alley
l. vanguard
m. right word
n. completed deed
o. finishing stroke

Answers are on pages 208–209.

C'est Français

Where would you go if you took a *tour de force?*

Could the operator of a penny lemonade stand be called an *entrepreneur?*

Why does the word *impasse* often occur in labor-management relations?

Is an *éclat* likely to be found in a pastry shop?

Would you like to be complimented for your *repartee?*

coiffure
demarche
denouement
éclat
élan
entrepreneur
impasse
ingenue
malaise
mélange
repartee
sangfroid
tête-à-tête
tour de force
vignette

1. **coiffure** (kwä-fyoor′)—a style of hair arrangement.
    a. Mrs. Dupont's elegant *coiffure* was admired by all the ladies.
    b. The dampness in the air ruined the model's expensive *coiffure*.

2. **demarche** (dā-märsh′)—a line of action; change of policy. *Demarche* comes from the French *marcher* ("to walk").
    a. After a strategy conference, the State Department's suggested *demarche* was communicated to the President.
    b. The two diplomats initiated the necessary *demarches* in the enemy's capital to begin the peace talks.

3. **denouement** (dā-nōō′-män)—the outcome of a plot. The French meaning is "the untying of a knot."
    a. The *denouement* of the play was so unrealistic that the audience booed loudly.
    b. At the time of the lengthy opera's *denouement,* we were fast asleep.

4. **éclat** (ā-klä′)—acclaim; brilliant success. The French word *éclater* means "to burst out."
    a. The novelist's *éclat* brought him a host of relatives seeking loans and gifts.
    b. Farah Fawcett feared that her *éclat* would vanish with the onset of old age.

5. **élan** (ā-län′)—enthusiasm; ardor; vigor. Its original meaning was "to throw a lance."
    a. At the age of 80, Bernard Shaw was still admired for his *élan.*
    b. With uncharacteristic *élan,* Cynthia devoted herself to making a success of her third marriage.

6. **entrepreneur** (än-trə-prə-nur′)—one who organizes and manages a business undertaking.
    a. Sol Hurok, the great *entrepreneur,* first brought the Russian Bolshoi Theatre to this country.
    b. A shrewd *entrepreneur* made a fortune in sponsoring teenage beauty contests throughout the U.S.

7. **impasse** (im′-pas)—difficulty without a solution; stalemate; blind alley.
    a. When both sides reached an *impasse,* a mediator was called to settle the dispute.
    b. After struggling for 24 hours, the exhausted chess players acknowledged the *impasse* and adjourned the game.

8. **ingenue** (an-zhə-nōō′)—actress playing an innocent, inexperienced young woman.
    a. Sheila told the producer that she was sick of playing *ingenue* roles.

   b. It was ridiculous for the 50-year-old actress to undertake the part of the *ingenue*.

9. **malaise** (ma-lāz')—a feeling of discomfort or uneasiness. In French, *mal* means "bad" and *aise* means "ease."
   a. I had a sense of *malaise* about the investment and should have paid attention to my intuition.
   b. The heart attack started with a mild *malaise* and then graduated to severe chest pains.

10. **mélange** (mã-länzh')—mixture; hodgepodge. The French verb *mêler* means "to mix."
   a. Sloan decorated the woman's room with a *mélange* of exciting colors.
   b. A *mélange* of sounds greeted our ears as we entered the dark nightclub.

11. **repartee** (rep-ər-tē')—quick, witty reply; wit. The French meaning is "the quick return of a thrust or blow."
   a. Dorothy Parker, the author, was noted for her brilliant *repartee*.
   b. We expected sparkling *repartee* at our party, but it turned out to be a dull evening.

12. **sangfroid** (saŋ-frwä')—composure; equanimity. In French it means "cold blood."
   a. To be "cool" today means to be possessed of *sangfroid*.
   b. Ellis was suspicious of Irene's *sangfroid* because she was normally quite emotional.

13. **tête-à-tête** (tāt'-ə-tāt')—intimate conversation between two people. The literal meaning is "head-to-head."
   a. At the rear of the restaurant, Lorraine and Jules were engaged in a heated *tête-à-tête*.
   b. After a brief *tête-à-tête*, Leslie saw it my way.

14. **tour de force** (toor-də-fôrs')—a feat of strength or skill.
   a. Alec Guinness played eight roles in the motion picture and was applauded for his *tour de force*.
   b. Winning his seventh gold medal in the 1972 Olympics was the high point of Mark Spitz's *tour de force*.

15. **vignette** (vin-yet')—an anecdote; a brief literary composition.
   a. Television reporters fanned out on the convention floor in search of *vignettes* with human interest.
   b. Blossom sent a humorous *vignette* about her kindergarden class to *Readers Digest,* and they published it.

EXERCISES

I. Which Word Comes to Mind?

In each of the following, read the statement, then circle the word that comes to mind.

1. A cold-blooded killer

(vignette, sangfroid, mélange)

2. There is loud applause for the star of *Hamlet*

(tour de force, demarche, malaise)

3. You get together with your brother for a serious conversation

(*denouement,   entrepreneur,   tête-à-tête*)

4. Two rival hostesses emerge abashed after some sharp word play

(*repartee,   coiffure,   éclat*)

5. A producer advertises his search for a 14-year-old Juliet

(*élan,   impasse,   ingenue*)

II.   True or False?

In the space provided, indicate whether each statement is true or false.

_____ 1. The *denouement* of a mystery story should satisfy every one of the readers' questions.
_____ 2. In order for success in most projects, a certain degree of *élan* is required.
_____ 3. The bargainers reached an *impasse,* and everyone went home satisfied with the way the strike had been concluded.
_____ 4. A man with *sangfroid* could stare a gunman in the eye and not show his fear.
_____ 5. Madame de Pompadour was noted for her *coiffure.*

III.   Find the Words

Somewhere in this box of letters, reading up, down, across, or diagonally, five vocabulary words that were taught in this lesson are hidden. As you locate each one, draw a circle around it.

E	E	T	R	A	P	E	R
E	S	S	A	P	M	I	H
A	G	I	K	N	X	S	L
F	V	T	A	L	C	E	K
T	M	L	B	L	S	A	D
U	E	J	Y	D	A	O	P
C	N	W	H	Z	R	M	X

IV. Extra Letters

In each of the vocabulary words below there is an extra letter. Put all the extra letters together and you will be able to spell out a word taught in a previous lesson. Its meaning is "awkward."

élang	decmarche
vaignette	échlat
tour de fource	mealaise

V. Matching

Match the word in column A with its correct definition in column B by writing the letter of that definition in the space provided.

A	B
____ 1. coiffure	a. organizer and manager
____ 2. demarche	b. outcome of a story
____ 3. denouement	c. feeling of uneasiness
____ 4. éclat	d. deadlock, stalemate
____ 5. élan	e. composure
____ 6. entrepreneur	f. actress playing unsophisticated roles
____ 7. impasse	g. conversation for two
____ 8. ingenue	h. line of action
____ 9. malaise	i. skillful performance
____ 10. mélange	j. brilliant success
____ 11. repartee	k. vigor
____ 12. sangfroid	l. colorful anecdote
____ 13. tête-à-tête	m. mixture
____ 14. tour de force	n. hairdo
____ 15. vignette	o. wit

Answers are on page 209.

Tete-a-tete?

Crossword Puzzle Words

Was Bernard Shaw's play called "*Alms* and the Man"?

What would you see if you spied a *bevy* of chorines?

Which of the vocabulary words below might be used to describe a tycoon?

Why might a "peeping Tom" be near an *aperture?*

What does *careen* tell you about the control of a moving vehicle?

---

acrid
addle
ado
alms
amulet
aperture
askew
bauble
bevy
bilk
blithe
careen
chary
nabob
onus

1. **acrid** (ak'-rid)—bitter; sharp; irritating to taste or smell.
    a. *Acrid* smoke arising from the burning couch awakened the family dog.
    b. Visitors are always amused by the *acrid* level of debate in Parliament.

2. **addle** (ad'-l)—to muddle; confuse. This word is often used in compounds such as *addlebrained.*
    a. The rookie became *addled* when he had to reassemble the many parts of the machine gun.
    b. One government report indicated that you can *addle* your brain through excessive use of marijuana.

3. **ado** (ə-do͞o')—fuss; trouble; bother.
    a. When all the excitement died down, we could see that it had been much *ado* over nothing.
    b. In order to spare his parents any further *ado*, Daniel packed his bags and left town.

4. **alms** (ämz)—money, food, or clothing given to poor people. Note the connection with *eleemosynary* which means "charitable."
    a. Each morning the Buddhist monks go into Bangkok seeking *alms.*
    b. "Call it the dole, welfare, *alms*—I'm in favor of helping people who cannot help themselves."

5. **amulet** (am'-yə-lit)—something worn around the neck as a protection against bad luck; a charm.
    a. The most precious object found in the tomb was a golden *amulet* which had been worn by the Egyptian princess.
    b. Lester treasured his *amulet*—a family heirloom which brought him good luck.

6. **aperture** (ap'-ər-chər)—opening; hole; gap.
    a. Rodents had a field day, leaping through the *aperture* in our kitchen wall.
    b. By staring into the cave's dark *aperture*, we could see the dim light of the miner's helmet.

7. **askew** (ə-sky o͞o')—on one side; crooked.
    a. Mr. Cronkite's tie was *askew* but he straightened it just before the show went on the air.
    b. Every picture in my apartment is *askew* when the cleaning woman leaves.

8. **bauble** (bô'-b'l)—trinket; toy; showy but worthless thing. The Old French word *baubel* meant "toy."
    a. My little niece is fascinated by *baubles*, bangles, and beads.
    b. "Just a little *bauble* for your birthday," said Mr. Astor, proudly displaying the emerald bracelet.

9.   **bevy** (bev'-ē)—group; flock. *Bevy* comes from an Old French word which meant "drinking group."
  a.   The hunters' guns were poised as everyone waited for the *bevy* of quail to be flushed out of the tall grass.
  b.   As the *bevy* of cheerleaders swept by, Timmy shouted, "Give me a J!"

10.   **bilk** (bilk)—deceive; swindle; cheat. This word may be a corruption of *balk,* a term used in the card game of cribbage.
  a.   The real estate agent protested that he never intended to *bilk* us out of our investment.
  b.   Many students who did not pay back their government loans have, in effect, *bilked* the taxpayers.

11.   **blithe** (blīth)—light-hearted; joyful; cheerful. The Anglo-Saxon word *blithia* was used to describe a bright sky.
  a.   Because Eloise was always so cheerful in the mornings, her husband called her his "*blithe* spirit."
  b.   Noel had a *blithe* way of treating the most depressing facts.

12.   **careen** (kə-rēn')—to cause to lean sideways; to lurch or toss from side to side. The Latin word *carina* means "side of a ship."
  a.   We watched the tiny sailboat *careen* wildly during the electrical storm.
  b.   The drunk *careened* down Broadway, bumping into shoppers and lamp posts.

13.   **chary** (cher'-ē, char'-)—careful; cautious; shy. The Anglo-Saxon word *cearig* meant "sorrowful."
  a.   Having once been burned by a get-rich-quick scheme, Gil was *chary* about investing his money.
  b.   We taught Bertha to be *chary* about accepting auto rides from strangers.

14.   **nabob** (nā'-bäb)—a very rich or influential man. A *nabob* was a native district ruler or a European who became very wealthy in India.
  a.   All of the union *nabobs* gathered in Miami Beach to plan for industry negotiations.
  b.   Mr. Onassis, the Greek shipping *nabob,* owned dozens of private planes.

15.   **onus** (ō'-nəs)—task; burden; responsibility.
  a.   For the rest of his life, Mr. Chillingworth bore the *onus* of his sin.
  b.   The fiery manager of the soccer team accepted the *onus* for their long losing streak.

EXERCISES

I. Which Word Comes to Mind?

In each of the following, read the statement, then circle the word that comes to mind.

1. An arm covered with costume jewelry

(addle,   bauble,   nabob)

2. Walking through the cemetery at night

(amulet,   bilk,   chary)

3. Peering into the camera lens

(onus, blithe, aperture)

4. A beggar on the streets of Calcutta

(alms,   bevy,   askew)

5. An angry crowd gathers to protest

(ado,   careen,   acrid)

II. True or False?

In the space provided, indicate whether each statement is true or false.

____ 1. An expensive *amulet* is a *bauble*.
____ 2. It's easy to be *blithe* when everything is going wrong.
____ 3. *Addle*-pated individuals are clear thinkers.
____ 4. People are likely to seek favors and money from *nabobs*.
____ 5. Saying good-by to poverty is bidding a "farewell to *alms*."

III. Find the Words

Somewhere in this box of letters, reading up, down, across, or diagonally, eleven vocabulary words that were taught in this lesson are hidden. As you locate each one, draw a circle around it.

S	T	E	L	D	D	A	G
N	W	H	O	B	M	C	E
A	G	A	E	U	O	R	H
B	D	V	L	P	N	I	T
O	Y	E	H	M	U	D	I
B	T	W	E	K	S	A	L
F	K	L	I	B	R	O	B

IV. Anagrams

In each of the following, add or subtract the indicated number of letters from the word, then rearrange the letters to form the new word whose meaning is given.

1. aperture – 3 letters = candle_____
2. bilk – 1 letter = sort, kind_____
3. chary – 2 letters = meal for horses_____
4. nabob – 2 letters = restriction_____
5. onus + 1 letter = extra money_____

V. Matching

Match the word in column A with its correct definition in Column B by writing the letter of that definition in the space provided.

A	*B*
___ 1. acrid	a. group
___ 2. addle	b. confuse
___ 3. ado	c. cautious
___ 4. alms	d. cheerful
___ 5. amulet	e. trouble
___ 6. aperture	f. responsibility
___ 7. askew	g. assistance given to the poor
___ 8. bauble	h. to cheat
___ 9. bevy	i. opening; gap
___ 10. bilk	j. rich man
___ 11. blithe	k. trinket
___ 12. careen	l. crooked
___ 13. chary	m. toss from side to side
___ 14. nabob	n. a charm
___ 15. onus	o. sharp; irritating

Answers are on pages 209–210.

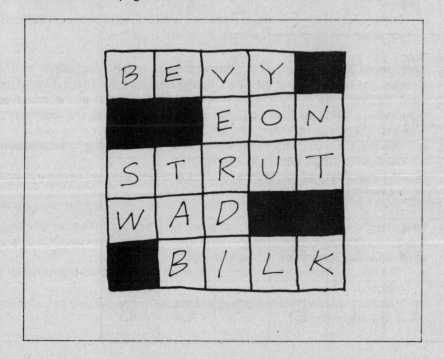

Mythology (II)

Why would you hear hisses from a *gorgon*?

What were the *Argonauts* seeking?

Why would a *Cyclops* tend to turn his head more than a normal being?

Were the *Harpies* vicious creatures or lovers of refined music?

Is a *paean* a peasant, a song, or a serious injury?

---

antaean
argonaut
calliope
cyclopean
gorgon
harpy
homeric
myrmidon
oracular
paean
plutonian
Promethean
stygian
terpsichorean
thespian

1. **antaean** (an-te′-ən)—possessed of superhuman strength with suggestions of earthiness. Antaeus was an African giant, the son of Poseidon and Gaea, who was invincible while touching the ground, but was lifted into the air by Hercules and crushed.
   a. The hapless flood victims harbored the *antaean* hope that they were safe as long as they remained in their homes, but the rushing waters washed them away.
   b. The artist portrayed the peasant leader like an *antaean* figure gaining strength from his contact with the land.

2. **argonaut** (är′-gə-nôt)—adventurer; one who sailed with Jason on the Argo in search of the Golden Fleece. Specifically, the word refers to a participant in the California Gold Rush of 1849.
   a. The *Argonauts* included many famous Greek heroes like Hercules, Theseus, and Orpheus.
   b. Most of the *argonauts* in the California Gold Rush had little to show for their adventure.

3. **calliope** (kə-lī′-ə-pē, kal′-ē-ōp)—a musical instrument fitted with steam whistles, played from a keyboard, and usually heard at carnivals and circuses. It is named after Calliope, the Greek Muse of epic poetry.
   a. The music of the *calliope* has become an integral part of the merry-go-round ride.
   b. The sneezing of the diners, caused by the overdose of pepper in the food, sounded like an off-key *calliope*.

4. **cyclopean** (sī-klə-pē′-ən)—vast, massive and rough; suggestive of the Cyclops, the race of one-eyed giants, descended from the Titans. One of the most exciting tales in the *Odyssey* recounts the blinding of the one-eyed Polyphemus, who had confined Odysseus' crew in his cave and promised to "reward" Odysseus by eating him last.
   a. The mountain climbers found shelter from the avalanche in a *cyclopean* cave, surprisingly vast in its interior.
   b. The eye of the cyclone, like that of some suddenly aroused *cyclopean* bird, moved ominously closer to the terrified city.

5. **gorgon** (gôr′-gən)—a repulsively ugly or terrifying woman. In Greek mythology, the Gorgon sisters included the mortal Medusa, who had snakes for hair, and eyes which, if looked into, turned the beholder into stone.
   a. Ted returned home early, claiming his blind date could have doubled for a *gorgon*.
   b. Perseus managed to slay the *Gorgon* Medusa by viewing only her reflection in his bright shield.

6. **harpy** (här′ pē)—a shrewish woman; a predatory person. The name is derived from the Harpies, one of several loathsome, voracious monsters, having a woman's head and trunk, and a bird's tail, wings and talons.
   a. The mistrustful bachelor looked upon every new female acquaintance as a potential *harpy* who wanted to get her claws into him.
   b. The bars were crowded by day as well as by night with screaming *harpies.*

7. **homeric** (hō-mer′-ik)—suggestive of Homer or his poetry; of heroic dimensions; grand; imposing.
   a. Pulitzer prizes are awarded annually for *homeric* feats of reporting.
   b. Landing on the moon was an achievement of *homeric* proportions.

8. **myrmidon** (mur′-mə-dän, -dən)—a faithful follower who carries out orders without question. The Myrmidons were the legendary Greek warriors of ancient Thessaly who followed their king Achilles on the expedition against Troy.
   a. The Mafia chieftain assigned one of his *myrmidons* the task of removing the threat to his leadership.
   b. A new spirit has swept across the youth of today and they no longer follow like *myrmidons* the wills of their parents or mentors.

9. **oracular** (ô-rak′-yə-lər)—uttered or delivered as if divinely inspired or infallible; ambiguous or obscure; portentous; ominous. Priests or priestesses in the shrines of ancient Greece would give ambiguous answers as the response of a god to an inquiry. One famous shrine was the oracle of Apollo at Delphi.
   a. Some modern poetry is a jumble of *oracular* statements.
   b. Exposing witches by *oracular* means smacks of witchcraft itself.

10. **paean** (pē′-ən)—any song of praise, joy or triumph. In classical mythology, a Paean was a god serving as a physician to the Olympian gods, later identified with Apollo.
    a. The bicentennial celebration was a great *paean* to liberty.
    b. With the appearance of the celebrity, a great cheer rose in a wild *paean* of frenzy.

11. **plutonian** (plōō-tŏ′-nē-ən)—pertaining to the planet Pluto or the underworld; grim and gloomy; harsh and unpleasing. The Greek god of the subterranean world of the dead was Pluto, after whom our solar system's farthest planet was named.
    a. With the disappearance of the last rays of the sun, a *plutonian* darkness descended upon the moonless night.
    b. The artist's strong penchant for *plutonian* landscapes suggests a pessimistic view of the world.

12. **Promethean** (prō-mē′-thē-ən)—creative and boldly original. Prometheus was a Titan who taught mankind various arts and confined all its troubles in the box that Zeus treacherously gave to Epimetheus as the dowry of Pandora. For having stolen fire from Olympus and given it to mankind in defiance of Zeus, Prometheus was chained to a rock where an eagle daily tore at his liver, until he was finally released by Hercules.
    a. There will always be nonconformists, rebels, *Promethean* pioneers.
    b. Do not confuse an ornery or contrary attitude with the true *Promethean* spirit.

13. **stygian** (stij′-ē-ən, stij′-ən)—gloomy and dark; hellish; infernal; inviolable (safe from profanation). The river Styx was one of the rivers of Hades, across which Charon ferried the souls of the dead.
    a. Wordsworth describes the kiss of death as follows: "Upon those roseate lips a *stygian* hue."
    b. Mr. Stone took a *stygian* oath never to reveal his secret pact with the devil.

14. **terpsichorean** (turp-si-kə-rē'-ən)—pertaining to dancing. Terpsichore was the Muse of dancing and choral singing.
   a. Anna's *terpsichorean* talents earned her the leading role in the musical.
   b. Two stars of the *terpsichorean* art, Gene Kelly and Fred Astaire, teamed up to produce a nostalgic movie.

15. **thespian** (thes'-pē-ən)—dramatic (adj.); an actor or actress (noun). Thespis was the Greek poet of the sixth century B.C. who was the reputed originator of tragic drama.
   a. The director got excellent *thespian* cooperation.
   b. John Barrymore was a *thespian* of great renown.

EXERCISES

I. Which Word Comes to Mind?

In each of the following, read the statement, then circle the word that comes to mind.

1. Music like a hundred steam whistles

   (harpy,   calliope,   plutonian)

2. I would do anything you ask.

   (myrmidon,   homeric,   paean)

3. Not recommended to give exact directions

   (gorgon,   argonaut,   oracular)

4. He is an outstanding dramatic actor

   (terpsichorean,   thesplan,   antaean)

5. Beneficial to mankind

   (cyclopean,   stygian,   Promethean)

II. True or False?

In the space provided, indicate whether each statement is true or false.

___ 1. Both *stygian* and *plutonian* have some association with gloom.
___ 2. A *terpsichorean* would be ideal for a comic role.
___ 3. An *antaean* creature would relish being thrown to the earth.
___ 4. *Homeric* laughter refers to the humorous passages in the *Iliad* and the *Odyssey*.
___ 5. A *calliope* is a means of conveyance.

III. Synonyms and Antonyms

Find and circle the two words in each line that are either synonyms or antonyms.

1. harpy	musical	calliope	termagant
2. gorgon	antaean	obdurate	frail
3. myrmidon	paean	anguish	servant
4. loquacious	awkward	oracular	terpsichorean
5. puny	homeric	infallible	graceful

IV. Missing Letters

Each word below has a missing letter. Fill in these missing letters and then rearrange them to form a word meaning "hymn of praise."

1. Ataean
2. tersichorean
3. stygin
4. cyclopan
5. orcular

V. Matching

Match the word in column A with its correct definition in column B by writing the letter of that definition in the space provided.

A	B
____ 1. antaean	a. a scolding, bad-tempered woman
____ 2. argonaut	b. ugly woman
____ 3. calliope	c. grand
____ 4. cyclopean	d. extraordinarily strong
____ 5. gorgon	e. slavish follower
____ 6. harpy	f. grim and unpleasing
____ 7. homeric	g. huge and rough
____ 8. myrmidon	h. original
____ 9. oracular	i. gloomy and dark
____ 10. paean	j. having to do with dancing
____ 11. plutonian	k. adventurer
____ 12. Promethean	l. an actor
____ 13. stygian	m. ambiguous
____ 14. terpsichorean	n. musical instrument
____ 15. thespian	o. exultant outburst

Answers are on page 210.

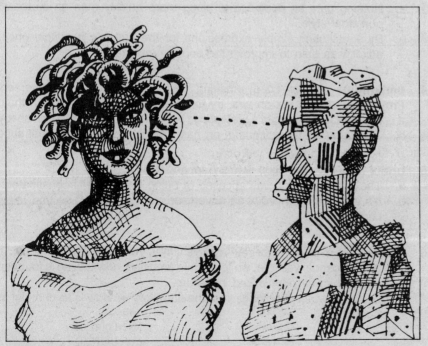

Look on a Gorgon — turn to stone.

Appearances and Attitudes (IV)

Is the Pontiff (Pope) *pontifical* in his prose?

Even if you didn't know the meaning of *sleazy,* why wouldn't you buy a *sleazy* suit?

Supercilious comes from "raised eyebrows." Does that give you a clue to its meaning?

Can you tell a *ribald* story in mixed company without raising someone's eyebrows?

Why is a *pedantic* person likely to be *prolix?*

pedantic
pertinacious
pontifical
pretentious
prolix
puerile
quiescent
recalcitrant
restive
ribald
sardonic
sedulous
sleazy
supercilious
voluptuous

1. **pedantic** (pi-dan'-tik)—stressing trivial points of learning; lacking a sense of proportion in scholarship. A *pedant* is a narrow-minded teacher who insists on rigid adherence to a set of arbitrary rules.
   a. Professor Valentine knows how to communicate with his students; and although he is brilliant, he is never *pedantic.*
   b. Janie's father turned her off with his *pedantic* lectures about diet, drugs, and dating.

2. **pertinacious** (pur-tə-nā'-shəs)—stubborn; unyielding; holding firmly to some belief.
   a. I had a *pertinacious* fever which hung on for weeks despite all the medicines I had been given.
   b. Because both management and labor took *pertinacious* positions, we expected a long strike.

3. **pontifical** (pän-tif'-i-k'l)—ornate; stiff; having the pomp and dignity of a high priest or Pope.
   a. Nothing puts an audience to sleep more quickly than an orator with a *pontifical* style.
   b. By substituting simple expressions for the author's *pontifical* ones, the editor was able to improve the book dramatically.

4. **pretentious** (pri-ten'-shəs)—making claims to some distinctions; showy. *Pretentious* people put on airs, try to appear more important than they are.
   a. Don't encourage Anita's *pretentious* pose of being related to Danish royalty.
   b. That which is *pretentious* in art has little chance of permanent success.

5. **prolix** (prō-liks', prō'-liks)—wordy; long-winded.
   a. The *prolix* senator was accused of being intellectually constipated.
   b. It's amazing how *prolix* an advertiser can get in a 60-second television commercial.

6. **puerile** (pyoo'-ər-əl, pyoor'-əl)—childish; silly; young. In Latin it means "boy."
   a. When Joshua was four, we found him amusing; now that he is fourteen, we regard him as *puerile* and immature.
   b. Dropping water-filled bags from the dormitory window is as criminal as it is *puerile.*

7. **quiescent** (kwī-es'-nt)—inactive; in repose; latent.
   a. The sea monster, *quiescent* for centuries, was awakened by the earthquake.
   b. Although Richard Rodgers has been *quiescent* for some years, he is preparing a new musical for Broadway.

8. **recalcitrant** (ri-kal'-si-trənt)—unruly; refusing to obey authority. In Latin it meant "to kick one's heels *(calx)* in defiance."
   a. Our principal can handle the most *recalcitrant* pupil.
   b. Thurman Munson, the N.Y. Yankees' *recalcitrant* catcher, refused to shave his beard off.

9. **restive** (res'-tiv)—hard to control; restless; contrary.
   a. On the eye of the big fight, Ali remained *restive* and impatient.
   b. Dr. Mitchell prescribed a strong sedative for his *restive* patient.

10. **ribald** (rib'-əld)—coarse; vulgar in language; irreverent.
    a. Eddie's *ribald* humor was better suited to the saloon than it was to our party.
    b. Some people who enjoy a *ribald* story told by a man will object to hearing it from a woman.

11. **sardonic** (sär-dän'-ik)—sarcastic; bitterly sneering. It is believed that this word can be traced back to a Sardinian plant whose bitter taste caused facial distortion.
    a. The movie cameras recorded Bogart's *sardonic* smile as he squeezed the trigger.
    b. Harold's laugh was heard but I was frightened by its *sardonic* quality.

12. **sedulous** (sej'-oo-ləs)—busy; working hard; diligent.
    a. Through *sedulous* study Joan was able to get her degree in three years.
    b. The bee hive was the hub of *sedulous* activity by hundreds of bustling drones.

13. **sleazy** (slē'-zē)—flimsy or thin in texture or substance; of poor quality. This word can be traced back to cloth made in Silesia, Germany.
    a. Once Mr. Mansfield lived in a mansion but today his home is in a *sleazy* slum neighborhood.
    b. The glib storekeeper was trying to get a high price for his *sleazy* merchandise.

14. **supercilious** (soo-pər-sil'-ē-əs)—haughty; arrogant; contemptuous.
    a. The saleslady with the *supercilious* manner made Emma tongue-tied.
    b. Most of the prisoners were friendly but Count Palozzi maintained a *supercilious* attitude.

15. **voluptuous** (və-lup'-choo-əs)—sensuous; full of sensual delights and pleasures.
    a. He fell into a *voluptuous* sleep, buoyed by the clear mountain air.
    b. The oriental delicacies, combined with the subtle flavors of the rare herbs and spices, made the dinner a *voluptuous* experience.

EXERCISES

I. Which Word Comes to Mind?

In each of the following, read the statement, then circle the word that comes to mind.

1. A gangster's cruel smile

(puerile,   sedulous,   sardonic)

2. Second-rate fabric which wears poorly

(quiescent,   pertinacious,   sleazy)

3. Someone who uses a dozen words when one would do

(prolix,   supercilious,   recalcitrant)

4. The natives were nervous before the battle

(pontifical,   restive,   pretentious)

5. A night club comic's suggestive monologue

(pedantic,   ribald,   voluptuous)

II. True or False?

In the space provided, indicate whether each statement is true or false.

____ 1. Mules and oxen are frequently described as being *pertinacious.*
____ 2. *Sleazy* products deserve the high price they command.
____ 3. Gary Cooper, famed for using words sparingly, drew compliments for that *prolix* style.
____ 4. Although we strive to be young, no one wants to be described as *puerile.*
____ 5. *Quiescent* talent can often be brought to the surface through patient teaching techniques.

III. Find the Words

Somewhere in this box of letters, reading up, down, across, or diagonally, three vocabulary words that were taught in this lesson are hidden. As you locate each one, draw a circle around it.

C	E	L	L	I	W	T	A
A	B	X	C	R	S	E	S
S	D	R	I	B	A	L	D
N	O	V	D	L	E	G	K
Q	U	F	G	A	O	W	Y
M	P	E	Z	T	G	R	C
G	R	Y	H	F	Z	V	P

IV. Extra Letters

In each of the vocabulary words below there is an extra letter. Put all the extra letters together and you will be able to spell out a word taught in a previous lesson. Its meaning is "possessed of superhuman strength."

raibald   prolaix   pueraile
sendulous   peedantic   supercilinous
sleatzy

V. Matching

Match the word in column A with its correct definition in column B by writing the letter of that definition in the space provided.

	A		B
____	1. pedantic		a. childish
____	2. pertinacious		b. of poor quality
____	3. pontifical		c. haughty
____	4. pretentious		d. unruly

_____ 5. prolix
_____ 6. puerile
_____ 7. quiescent
_____ 8. recalcitrant
_____ 9. restive
_____ 10. ribald
_____ 11. sardonic
_____ 12. sedulous
_____ 13. sleazy
_____ 14. supercilious
_____ 15. voluptuous

e. sensuous
f. ornate; overdone; high-sounding
g. restless
h. diligent
i. stressing trivial points
j. irreverant
k. in repose
l. sarcastic
m. stubborn
n. wordy
o. showy

Answers are on page 210.

Foreign Terms (II)

Would a good golfer know about *par excellence?*

What is meant by *de facto* segregation?

Have you ever been chosen to serve on an *ad hoc* committee?

Why is *a cappella* a challenge for a singer?

How does the public respond to a *nolo contendere* plea in court?

---

a cappella
ad hoc
bon vivant
de facto
gemütlich
leitmotif
nolo contendere
par excellence
parvenu
pièce de résistance
postprandial
quid pro quo
qui vive
savoir faire
sub rosa
vis-à-vis

1. **a cappella** (ä kə-pel′ə)—without instrumental accompaniment. Usually used to describe choral singing. In Italian, the meaning is "in the chapel style."
   a. When her pianist failed to appear, Helen had to sing *a cappella.*
   b. I have arranged to hire one of the greatest *a cappella* performers alive today.

2. **ad hoc** (ad häk′)—for this case only; temporary. The most frequent use of this Latin term is to describe a committee which is organized to deal with a specific issue and will be disbanded later.
   a. I was pleased to be selected for the *ad hoc* committee for the Senior Prom.
   b. When the *ad hoc* fund raising project proved so successful, it was made into a permanent unit of our club.

3. **bon vivant** (bän vi-vänt′)—one who enjoys good food and other pleasant things.
   a. Although Charles was quite thin, he was known in restaurant circles as a *bon vivant.*
   b. Yesterday a *bon vivant,* today the unemployment line!

4. **de facto** (di-fak′-tō)—in fact; actual. The law may require one thing *(de jure),* but as a matter of fact *(de facto)* the reality is quite different.
   a. Segregated schools are not lawful, but *de facto* segregation is common in this country.
   b. The former army colonel was the head of his *de facto* government until his assassination.

5. **gemütlich** (gə-müt′-liH)—agreeable; cheerful. This German word is often used to describe a sense of well-being.
   a. Jerry lit the fire, and we settled down to a *gemütlich* evening at home.
   b. Adding colorful tablecloths and flowers gave a *gemütlich* touch to the Princess Pat Tea Room.

6. **leitmotif** (līt′-mō-tēf)—a short musical phrase which recurs and is associated with a given character, situation, or emotion in an opera. This technique was first used by the German composer, Richard Wagner.
   a. Everytime the evil sorcerer appeared, the orchestra struck up a chilling *leitmotif.*
   b. We agreed that even though the play would be serious, a *leitmotif* of comic relief was required.

7. **nolo contendere** (nō′-lō-kən-ten′-də-rē)—a defendant's plea declaring that he will not make a defense but not admitting his guilt.
   a. Because Buddy's lawyer did not want to put him on the witness stand, he suggested a *nolo contendere* plea.

129

b. Although a *nolo contendere* defense does not admit to guilt, most people are likely to assume that only a guilty person would follow such a course.

8. **par excellence** (pär ek′-sə-läns)—in the greatest degree of excellence. This French term also means "beyond comparison."
   a. In the 1976 Olympiad, the Rumanian girl proved to be a gymnast *par excellence.*
   b. Julia Childs, the TV chef, is a cook *par excellence.*

9. **parvenu** (pär′-və-noo′,-nyoo′)—one who has suddenly acquired wealth or power; a person who is considered an upstart because he does not conform to the standards of the class into which he has risen. This word has the same "put down" connotation as "nouveau riche."
   a. After winning a million dollars in the lottery, the *parvenu* bought two pink Cadillacs.
   b. At the elegant dinner party, Mr. Fischer was constantly reminded of his status as a *parvenu.*

10. **pièce de résistance** (pyeś-də-rā-zēs′-täns′)—the principal dish of a meal; the main item or event in a series.
    a. At the end of the seven-course dinner, our hostess brought out the *pièce de résistance*—a scrumptious strawberry shortcake.
    b. The *pièce de résistance* in the magician's act came when he sawed his assistant in half.

11. **postprandial** (pōst-pran′-dē-əl)—after dinner. In Latin, *prandium* means "noonday meal."
    a. Ben Green's greatest delight was his *postprandial* cigar.
    b. We gathered on the porch for *postprandial* cordials and a discussion of politics.

12. **quid pro quo** (kwid′-prō-kwō′)—one thing in return for another.
    a. The mayor helped us but we knew he expected a *quid pro quo.*
    b. In politics, the term for a *quid pro quo* is "log-rolling."

13. **qui vive** (kē-vēv′)—to be on the lookout or on the alert is to be on the *qui vive.* The literal French meaning is "who lives?" or "who goes there?" and, as such, was a term used by sentries.
    a. Our firm likes to hire young people who are on the *qui vive.*
    b. Anyone who makes a day-to-day living in the stock market must be on the *qui vive.*

14. **savoir faire** (sav′-wär-fer′)—a ready knowledge of what to do or say; tact.
    a. I have always been impressed with Cousin Gloria's *savoir faire.*
    b. Totally lacking in *savoir faire,* Eloise kept saying the wrong things and embarrassing her family.

15. **sub rosa** (sub-rō′-zə)—secretly; confidentially. In Latin, "under the rose." The rose was a symbol of silence or secrecy in ancient times.
    a. Our agreement was made *sub rosa,* and I hoped that it would never be made public.
    b. Donald whispered, "Let's just keep this between the two of us, *sub rosa,* you might say."

16. **vis-à-vis** (vēz-e-vē′) —a person or thing that is face to face with another; opposite; in reference to; opposed to.
    a. When she stands *vis-à-vis* her competitors, she will not be so confident.
    b. The mayor's point of view, *vis-à-vis* capital punishment, is well known.

EXERCISES

I. Which Word Comes to Mind?

In each of the following, read the statement, then circle the word that comes to mind.

1. A person who enjoys good food and fine wine

(bon vivant,   postprandial,   pièce de résistance)

2. A group of citizens form a committee to beautify their town

(a cappella,   qui vive,   ad hoc)

3. In court, the defendant rises to plead

(nolo contendere,   parvenu,   de facto)

4. Everytime the camera switches to the cavalry, trumpets are heard

(par excellence,   leitmotif,   sub rosa)

5. You are asked to repay a favor

(savoir faire,   quid pro quo,   gemütlich)

II. True or False?

In the space provided, indicate whether each statement is true or false.

____ 1. Publication of a sub rosa agreement can prove embarrassing.
____ 2. An opportunist may be described as one who is on the qui vive.
____ 3. Minority groups are likely to protest about de facto segregation.
____ 4. In her a cappella performance, the star criticized her accompanist.
____ 5. Sophisticated people are expected to possess savoir faire.

III. Find the Words

Somewhere in this box of letters, reading up, down, acoss, or diagonally, four vocabulary words that were taught in this lesson are hidden. As you locate each one, draw a circle around it.

O	S	L	H	Q	U	I	P
T	A	S	O	U	C	A	L
C	M	B	G	I	R	D	U
A	P	E	R	V	S	H	T
F	C	S	E	I	N	O	M
E	S	N	L	V	D	C	W
D	U	F	T	E	S	H	A

IV. Extra Letters

In each of the vocabulary words below there is an extra letter. Put all the extra letters together and you will be able to spell out a word taught in a previous lesson. Its meaning is "childish."

ap cappella

postpraundial

savoire faire

ard hoc

pair excellence

parlvenu

sub erosa

V. Matching

Match the word in column A with its correct definition in column B by writing the letter of that definition in the space provided.

	A		*B*
____	1. a cappella	a.	temporary
____	2. ad hoc	b.	no defense
____	3. bon vivant	c.	actual

_____ 4. de facto
_____ 5. gemütlich
_____ 6. leitmotif
_____ 7. nolo contendere
_____ 8. par excellence
_____ 9. parvenu
_____ 10. pièce de résistance
_____ 11. postprandial
_____ 12. quid pro quo
_____ 13. qui vive
_____ 14. savoir faire
_____ 15. sub rosa
_____ 16. vis-à-vis

d. after dinner
e. recurring musical phrase
f. something in return for another
g. alert
h. without instrumental accompaniment
i. chief dish
j. secretly
k. cheerful
l. tact
m. one who enjoys good food
n. outstanding
o. upstart; newly rich
p. in reference to

Answers are on pages 210–211.

Appearances and Attitudes (V)

Is there a connection between crochet and *crotchety*?

Would a *dilatory* person win a punctuality award?

What is the relationship between spleen and *splenetic*?

Are the police pleased to get a *loquacious* stool pigeon?

What medicine is appropriate for a *bucolic* condition?

---

ambivalent
bucolic
crotchety
dilatory
disconsolate
dudgeon
froward
genteel
jocund
loquacious
splenetic
tendentious
truculent
vacuous
venal

1. **ambivalent** (am-biv′-ə-lənt)—having conflicting feelings toward a person or thing, such as love and hate.
   a. I've read a great deal on the topic of capital punishment but I'm still *ambivalent* about it.
   b. On the surface, Sloan was loyal to the chemical company but she maintained *ambivalent* feelings about its defense policies.

2. **bucolic** (byoo-käl′-ik)—rural; rustic; pastoral. The Greek word *boukolikos* means "herdsman."
   a. The artist was celebrated for his *bucolic* canvases painted at the Ohio farm.
   b. Two hours out of the big city, our eyes were refreshed by *bucolic* countryside scenes.

3. **crotchety** (kräch′-it-ē)—full of peculiar whims; ill-tempered; eccentric. Crochet work was done with a small, twisted hook; from "twisted" it was an easy jump to "eccentric"—thus the connection between crochet and *crotchety*.
   a. No one took Uncle Sid seriously when he asked for watermelon pudding because he had a reputation for being *crotchety*.
   b. The *crotchety* old millionaire left his fortune to his twelve cats.

4. **dilatory** (dil′-ə-tôr-ē)—slow; late in doing things; inclined to delay; meant to gain time.
   a. The crooked sheriff's *dilatory* tactics prevented Columbo from watching the thieves that night.
   b. Phyllis' *dilatory* habits drove her punctual husband up the wall.

5. **disconsolate** (dis-kän′-sə-lit)—sad; dejected; cheerless.
   a. After the bad news arrived in a telegram from the Secretary of Defense, the new widow was understandably *disconsolate*.
   b. When Zelda Fitzgerald was *disconsolate,* she sought relief through alcohol.

6. **dudgeon** (duj′-ən)—resentment; an angry or offended feeling. It comes from the Anglo-French expression *en digeon* which meant "the hand on the dagger hilt."
   a. Captain Ralston was in high *dudgeon* after having been demoted.
   b. Filled with *dudgeon,* Edgar sought revenge against his stepbrother, Edmund.

7. **froward** (frō′-ərd,-wərd)—contrary; not easily controlled; stubbornly willful.
   a. The *froward* colt was led into the ring by three handlers who were careful not to be kicked.
   b. Petruchio displayed one way to deal successfully with a *froward* woman in *The Taming of the Shrew.*

8. **genteel** (jen-tēl')—well-bred; refined; excessively polite.
   a. Mrs. Berman's *genteel* manners were quite out of place in the sailors' bar she operated.
   b. Etiquette and *genteel* behavior are taught by Emily Post and Amy Vanderbilt.

9. **jocund** (jäk'-ənd, jō'-kənd)—pleasant; agreeable; genial. Our word *joke* can be traced back to *jocund*.
   a. One of the things that gets me off to a good start each morning is our elevator operator's *jocund* face.
   b. The company's *jocund* mood was shattered by the blackout.

10. **loquacious** (lō-kwā'-shəs)—talkative. Some synonyms are *garrulous, voluble, prolix, verbose,* and *prating*.
    a. With a few drinks under his belt, my normally quiet cousin can become quite *loquacious*.
    b. The *loquacious* talk-show host never gave his guests a chance to tell about themselves.

11. **splenetic** (spli-net'-ik)—irritable; bad-tempered; spiteful. The word derives from *spleen,* the abdominal organ which the ancients regarded as the seat of emotions.
    a. Frieda's *splenetic* outburst at the dinner table was in poor taste.
    b. One way to drive Albie into a *splenetic* frenzy is to discuss income taxes with him.

12. **tendentious** (ten-den'-shəs)—opinionated; advancing a definite point of view or doctrine.
    a. Although the Post's political columns are often *tendentious,* I find them very informative.
    b. Our school board rejected several history texts, objecting to the *tendentious* writing they contained.

13. **truculent** (truk'-yoo-lənt)—fierce; cruel; savage.
    a. In a *truculent* editorial, the newspaper's owner ripped the Supreme Court decision to shreds.
    b. Lord Hastings was unprepared for Richard's *truculent* outburst.

14. **vacuous** (vak'-yoo-was)—empty; purposeless; stupid; senseless.
    a. Two years on drugs had changed Roger's alert look to a *vacuous* stare.
    b. The judge dropped the assault charges when he realized how *vacuous* they were.

15. **venal** (vē'-n'l)—that which can readily be bribed or corrupted.
    a. Originally there was enough money to cover all expenses but *venal* officials took most of it.
    b. When caught for speeding, George tried to set up a *venal* bargain with the arresting officer.

EXERCISES

I. Which Word Comes to Mind?

In each of the following, read the statement, then circle the word that comes to mind.

1. Cows in the meadow, sheep in the corn

    (venal,   bucolic,   disconsolate)

2. First, I want to go—then I want to stay

> (ambivalent,   truculent,   dudgeon)

3. "What's your rush? So what if we're late?"

> (jocund,   dilatory,   genteel)

4. The millionaire asked to be buried in his Rolls Royce

> (crotchety,   tendentious,   froward)

5. "Were you vaccinated with a phonograph needle?"

> (vacuous,   loquacious,   splenetic)

II.   True or False?

In the space provided, indicate whether each statement is true or false.

___ 1. A *jocund* person has a good chance of being hired as a receptionist.
___ 2. *Splenetic* behavior is always a sign of good breeding.
___ 3. Truly great bullfighters welcome an animal which is *froward*.
___ 4. Watergate has become synonomous with *venal* arrangements.
___ 5. Skyscrapers and subways are integral parts of the *bucolic* life.

III.   Find the Words

Somewhere in this box of letters, reading up, down, across, or diagonally, four vocabulary words that were taught in this lesson are hidden. As you locate each one, draw a circle around it.

B	J	F	G	W	B	A	R
L	O	T	D	P	U	V	X
E	C	F	O	Z	C	E	T
D	U	D	G	E	O	N	S
I	N	P	A	B	L	A	V
A	D	Q	U	P	I	L	M
R	O	H	L	N	C	U	E

IV. Extra Letters

In each of the vocabulary words below there is an extra letter. Put all the extra letters together and you will be able to spell out a word taught in a previous lesson. Its meaning is "cowardly."

buccolic   vevnal
durdgeon   dileatory
disconsoalate   trunculent

V. Matching

Match the word in column A with its correct definition in Column B by writing the letter of that definition in the space provided.

A	*B*
____ 1. ambivalent	a. resentment
____ 2. bucolic	b. not easily controlled
____ 3. crotchety	c. having conflicting feelings
____ 4. dilatory	d. ill-tempered
____ 5. disconsolate	e. talkative
____ 6. dudgeon	f. irritable
____ 7. froward	g. opinionated
____ 8. genteel	h. empty
____ 9. jocund	i. refined
____ 10. loquacious	j. rural
____ 11. splenetic	k. inclined to delay
____ 12. tendentious	l. genial
____ 13. truculent	m. able to be bribed
____ 14. vacuous	n. savage
____ 15. venal	o. dejected

Answers are on page 211.

NOT A WORD ALL EVENING BUT MR. LOQUACIOUS AT NIGHT!

Size and Shape (II)

What is the trouble with a *tenuous* plan?

To which author are we indebted for the word *gargantuan*?

How is an artist likely to feel about his *magnum opus*?

Who would have reason to rely on a *micrometer*?

What traffic sign would you expect to find on a *serpentine* road?

amorphous
gargantuan
iota
lissome
macrocosm
magnitude
magnum opus
microcosm
micrometer
scabrous
scintilla
serpentine
sinuous
smidgen
tenuous

1. **amorphous** (ə-môr'-fəs)—without definite form; shapeless.
    a. The science fiction movie featured an *amorphous* monster who preyed on Chicago.
    b. As a result of numerous mergers, the conglomerate presented an *amorphous* picture.

2. **gargantuan** (gär-gan'-chōō-ən)—huge; gigantic; prodigious. The word comes from Rabelais' 16th-century political satire, *Gargantua and Pantagruel*.
    a. After skipping breakfast and lunch, I had a *gargantuan* appetite for dinner.
    b. When the Russian men came on the basketball court, we saw that they had a *gargantuan* center.

3. **iota** (ī-ōt'-ə)—a very small quantity; a jot. Iota is the ninth letter of the Greek alphabet.
    a. I don't care one *iota* for your relatives' wishes.
    b. If Larry had an *iota* of sense, he would propose to Vivian.

4. **lissome** (lis' əm)—supple; limber; flexible.
    a. Ballet dancers are apt to be *lissome*.
    b. The heavyweight champion slimmed down from a ponderous 250 lbs. to a *lissome* 210.

5. **macrocosm** (mak'-rə-käz'm)—the great world; the universe. The opposite of this is *microcosm* (see definition 8 below).
    a. My philosophy professor is constantly concerned with the vastness of the *macrocosm*.
    b. Space explorers have unlocked some of the mysteries of the *macrocosm*.

6. **magnitude** (mag'-nə-tōōd)—greatness of size or extent; importance or influence.
    a. District Attorney Hogan unveiled the *magnitude* of the corruption.
    b. After his death, the *magnitude* of the "pauper's" wealth first came to light.

7. **magnum opus** (mag'-nəm ōpəs)—a great work, especially of art or literature.
    a. Picasso's *Guernica* is considered by some to be his *magnum opus*.
    b. When the composer's *magnum opus* was panned by the critics, he killed himself.

8. **microcosm** (mi'-krə-käz'm)—a little world; miniature universe. It is the opposite of *macrocosm*.
    a. Spencer spent six years developing his unique *microcosm* made out of matchsticks.
    b. That which is in the *microcosm* I can grasp, but *macrocosmic* concepts are beyond me.

9. **micrometer** (mī-kräm′-ə-ter)—an instrument for measuring very small distances, angles, diameters. In Latin, *micro* means "small" and *meter* means "to measure."
   a. With the aid of a surgical *micrometer,* the doctor was able to undertake the difficult operation.
   b. Since the size of the angle was in dispute, we sent for a *micrometer* to settle the argument.

10. **scabrous** (skab′-rəs, skā′-brəs)—rough with small points or knobs; bumpy; scaly; full of difficulties. In Latin, *scabere* means "to scratch."
    a. Dr. Weldon was greatly concerned as he ran his hand over Edgar's *scabrous* back.
    b. My Toyota had a bad time over the *scabrous* back country roads.

11. **scintilla** (sin-til′-ə)—the least trace; a particle. In Latin, *scintilla* means "a spark."
    a. There is not a *scintilla* of truth in the accusations.
    b. Unless new evidence is produced, Richie does not have a *scintilla* of a chance of getting out of jail.

12. **serpentine** (sur′-pən-tēn, -tīn)—evilly cunning or subtle; treacherous; coiled; twisting.
    a. As our bus snaked its way down the narrow, *serpentine* road, all of the passengers prayed silently.
    b. The extortionist's *serpentine* plot failed because of a careless oversight.

13. **sinuous** (sin′-yoo-wəs)—bending; wavy. The word *sinus* ("a cavity in the bones of the skull") is related to *sinuous.*
    a. With *sinuous* movements, the dancer portrayed a venomous snake.
    b. Driving along the California coast, we took a *sinuous* route.

14. **smidgen** (smij′-ən)—a small amount; a bit. This word is related to "midge" or midget.
    a. My mother added just a *smidgen* of paprika to the recipe.
    b. In the Crimean battle, the British general did not display even a *smidgen* of intelligence.

15. **tenuous** (ten′-yoo-wəs)—unsubstantial; flimsy; physically thin.
    a. Our company's plans to move to New Jersey are *tenuous* at this time.
    b. The rope bridge over the river was so *tenuous* that only one person at a time could use it.

EXERCISES

I. Which Word Comes to Mind?

In each of the following, read the statement, then circle the word that comes to mind.

1. A writer spends ten years preparing his masterpiece

   (macrocosm, magnum opus, micrometer)

2. Cyclops had an enormous appetite

   (scintilla, gargantuan, microcosm)

3. A graceful gymnast

   (lissome, smidgen, iota)

4. An indefinite proposal

(serpentine,   scabrous,   tenuous)

5. The actress adopted a sexy walk

(amorphous,   magnitude,   sinuous)

II. True or False?

In the space provided, indicate whether each statement is true or false.

_____ 1. The *microcosm* of man reflects the *macrocosm* of the universe.
_____ 2. The *magnitude* of the Grand Canyon frequently awes travelers.
_____ 3. A *tenuous* idea is often offered hesitantly.
_____ 4. Two words in this lesson which are closely related are *smidgen* and *iota*.
_____ 5. The *amorphous* scheme was spelled out in such detail that it was grasped by all.

III. Find the Words

Somewhere in this box of letters, reading up, down, across, or diagonally, five vocabulary words that were taught in this lesson are hidden. As you locate each one, draw a circle around it.

R	O	L	T	M	H	A	N
H	D	S	E	Q	U	S	E
A	X	C	N	U	F	H	G
B	T	Q	U	M	P	O	D
W	A	T	O	I	S	V	I
S	I	N	U	O	U	S	M
L	I	S	S	O	M	E	S

IV. Extra Letters

In each of the vocabulary words below there is an extra letter. Put all the extra letters together and you should be able to spell out a vocabulary word taught in a previous lesson. Its meaning is "reversion to a primitive type."

scaintilla   scabrious
sintuous   mascrocosm
serpentaine   ammorphous
magnivtude

V. Matching

Match the word in column A with its definition in column B by drawing a line between the two.

A	B
____ 1. amorphous	a. shapeless
____ 2. gargantuan	b. bending, wavy
____ 3. iota	c. greatness of size
____ 4. lissome	d. a very small quantity
____ 5. macrocosm	e. supple
____ 6. magnitude	f. a great work
____ 7. magnum opus	g. winding
____ 8. microcosm	h. precision measuring instrument
____ 9. micrometer	i. scaly
____ 10. scabrous	j. a tiny jot
____ 11. scintilla	k. the least trace
____ 12. serpentine	l. the universe
____ 13. sinuous	m. flimsy
____ 14. smidgen	n. the little world
____ 15. tenuous	o. huge

Answers are on pages 211–212.

MAGNUM OPUS, EH?

Review

A. The Out-of-Place Word

In each of the following groups, find and circle the one vocabulary word that is out of place. You should be able to explain what the other three words have in common.

1. licentious, pusillanimous, libidinous, ribald
2. lissome, voluptuous, bucolic, sinuous
3. bon mot, mot juste, non sequitur, repartee
4. mercurial, pontifical, argonaut, Promethean
5. quid pro quo, sub rosa, amicus curiae, qui vive
6. minatory, sinuous, bête noire, truculent
7. gauche, savoir faire, sangfroid, nonchalant
8. pertinacious, obdurate, officious, recalcitrant
9. miscreant, oracular, omniscient, tendentious
10. amorphous, mutable, ambivalent, amulet

B. Rearranging Words

Rearrange the following groups of words using the first letter of each word to spell out one of the new words in this unit.

1. barrister, amulet, obdurate, nonchalant, bucolic

_____

2. noxious, avant-garde, restive, sine qua non, onus

_____

3. éclat, élan, malaise, addle, nolo contendere, gemütlich, leitmotif

_____

4. embezzle, vacuous, ad hoc, niggardly, loquacious

_____

5. nabob, gargantuan, iota, truculent, tendentious, entrepreneur, extradition, venal

_____

C. Finding Partners

Which word best describes a person or thing you would need in each of the following situations? Circle the correct answer.

1. You want to pour your heart out

(*parvenu,   tête-à-tête,   magnum opus,   pièce de résistance*)

2. You are in a legal jam

(*cul-de-sac,   perpetrator,   barrister,   entrepreneur*)

3. You have a million questions

(*deus ex machina,   amicus curiae,   omniscient,   bête noire*)

4. You have a yen to trip the light fantastic

(scintilla,   terpsichorean,   junta,   amulet)

5. You're a director looking for an actress to play a young innocent

(ingenue,   vignette,   miscreant,   gorgon)

D. Making Pairs

From the group below, find the pairs of words that have something in common and record them in the spaces provided. You should be able to find ten such pairs. List them numerically, using the same number for each pair.

scabrous _____	pontifical _____	jocund _____	cul-de-sac _____
impasse _____	embezzle _____	bon mot _____	homeric _____
mercurial _____	perpetrator _____	miscreant _____	Promethean _____
bilk _____	libidinous _____	gemütlich _____	mutable _____
iota _____	mot juste _____	oracular _____	scintilla _____

E. Cliché Time

Which of the words from this unit fit into the following familiar expressions? Choose the correct word from the choices given and record it in the space provided.

1. The _____ old miser never knew the joys of companionship.

(sardonic,   chary,   tenuous,   crotchety)

2. The president appointed an _____ committee to select a band for the next affair.

(officious,   prolix,   ad hoc,   onus)

3. The opera star's _____ temper was well known to her audiences.

(mercurial,   jejune,   avant-garde,   indeterminate)

4. There is a little _____ in all of us.

(myrmidon,   leitmotif,   larceny,   bauble)

5. After a beautiful afternoon spent experiencing the _____ delights of a walk through the woods, the couple dined by candlelight.

(sedulous,   voluptuous,   sub rosa,   de facto)

F. Find the Words

Somewhere in this box of letters, reading up, down, across, or diagonally, twenty-eight vocabulary words that were taught in Unit 3 are hidden. As you locate each one, draw a circle around it.

A	D	U	D	G	E	O	N	A	B	O	B
R	G	P	E	D	A	N	T	I	C	N	O
T	J	U	N	T	A	K	A	D	A	H	N
L	A	D	O	M	L	C	D	E	F	T	M
Q	U	I	V	I	V	E	H	F	A	W	O
Y	N	P	B	V	I	T	O	A	Y	P	T
N	E	L	A	N	E	W	C	C	R	Y	A
E	V	Y	F	M	E	N	Y	T	A	V	M
C	R	P	O	K	A	R	A	O	H	E	U
R	A	R	S	O	N	U	S	L	C	B	L
A	P	A	L	M	S	O	A	D	D	L	E
L	E	H	C	U	A	G	E	C	L	A	T

Answers are on page 212.

Language

Is "reading Shakespeare" an example of *metonymy* or *synecdoche*?

Is "granite jaw" an example of a *simile* or *metaphor*?

Is *oxymoron* a paradoxical expression or an act of animal folly?

Is "he saw with his own eyes" an example of *panegyric* or *pleonasm*?

Is "damning with faint praise" a form of *paralipsis* or *bathos*?

---

bathos
malapropism
metaphor
metonymy
onomatopoeia
oxymoron
panegyric
paradigm
paralipsis
pleonasm
polyglot
semantics
simile
synecdoche
threnody

1. **bathos** (bā'-thäs, bā'-thôs)—anticlimax; triteness or triviality in style; sentimentality. *Bathos* is also used to denote an insincere pathos, an evocation of pity or compassion.
   a. In his summation to the jury, the defense attorney stooped to *bathos* to portray his client as a misunderstood and unhappy victim of circumstances.
   b. The drama suffered from *bathos,* the strongest and most telling point having been made in the first act.

2. **malapropism** (mal'-ə-präp-iz'm)—ridiculous misuse of words, especially by confusion of words that are similar in sound. Mrs. Malaprop, a character in Sheridan's famous Restoration play, *The Rivals,* is noted for her misapplication of words.
   a. One or two unfortunate faux pas established Richard as a master of *malapropism.*
   b. In an obvious *malapropism,* Mrs. Farrell said she was bemused by the exciting circus performance.

3. **metaphor** (met'-ə-fôr, -fər)—the application of a word or phrase to an object or concept which it does not literally denote, in order to suggest a comparison with another object or concept. The use of *metaphors* may help to clarify or ennoble an idea, but one must not mix *metaphors.* This practice results in humorous effects, such as "We must put our noses to the grindstone and push."
   a. "A mighty fortress is our God" is a *metaphor* expressing the permanence, power, and protectiveness of the Deity.
   b. William explained to the police that he was only speaking *metaphorically* when he described the strangers as men from Mars.

4. **metonymy** (mə-tän'-ə-mē)—the use of the name of one object or concept for that of another to which it is related, or of which it is a part, as "the bottle" for strong drink.
   a. "Taking to the streets" is a *metonymy* that refers to rioting.
   b. The *metonymy* "Go fight City Hall" has become the frustrated cry of the average citizen overwhelmed by government bureaucracy.

5. **onomatopoeia** (än-ə-mät-ə-pē'-ə)—formation of words in imitation of natural sounds; the use of words whose sound suggests the sense. The "bow-wow theory" of language maintains that language originated in imitation of natural sounds. By contrast, the "pooh-pooh theory" says language originated in interjections which gradually acquired meaning.
   a. *Onomatopoeic* words have a strong appeal to children.
   b. A study of the poet's frequent use of *onomatopoeia* shows he had an unusual ear for natural sounds, as if he were listening to Nature and letting it speak for itself.

6. **oxymoron** (äk-si-môr'-än)—a figure of speech by which a particular phrasing of words produces an effect by seeming self-contradiction, as in "cruel kindness" or "laborious idleness." The Greek meaning is "pointed foolishness."
   a. The *oxymoron* "make haste slowly" has been a piece of folk wisdom for centuries.
   b. To indicate Romeo's shallow feelings for Rosaline as opposed to his deep love for Juliet, Shakespeare has him utter a string of *oxymorons* like "loving hate, heavy lightness, cold fire."

7. **panegyric** (pan-ə-jir'-ik, -jī'-rik)—an oration, discourse, or writing in praise of a person or thing; eulogy.
   a. Forgetting partisanship, representatives of all parties delivered *panegyrics* at the funeral of the late president.
   b. The board chairman felt the revolutionary fuel substitute had merit but had not yet earned the *panegyrics* that had been heaped upon it.

8. **paradigm** (par'-ə-dim, -dīm)—example or pattern; a set of forms in grammar all of which contain a particular element, especially the set of all inflected forms based on a single stem (as in verb declensions).
   a. Watergate shocked the American people because the leaders who were supposed to be *paradigms* of honesty proved themselves unscrupulous and deceptive.
   b. In the past, language was studied by reciting lists of *paradigms;* modern methodology stresses correct usage and conversation.

9. **paralipsis** (par-ə-līp'-sis)—the suggestion, by deliberately concise treatment of a topic, that much significant material is being omitted, as in the use of the phrase "not to mention other faults." Another name for *paralipsis* is *preterition.*
   a. By using such *paralipses* as "I confine my account of the defendant's treacheries to only his first year in office," the prosecuting attorney left the jury with the impression that the misuse of power continued for many years.
   b. *Paralipsis* is one of many techniques used in the courtroom to exaggerate and magnify the crimes of which a defendant is accused.

10. **pleonasm** (plē'-ə-naz'm)—the use of more words than necessary to express an idea; redundancy; superfluity. It is derived from the Greek word for "to be or have more than enough."
    a. Sensational advertising is replete with *pleonasms.*
    b. Some expressions that are *pleonasms* in our language, such as "the man he said," are perfectly correct in other languages.

11. **polyglot** (päl'-i-glät)—knowing many or several languages; containing, composed of, or in several languages; a confusion of languages; a person with a speaking or reading knowledge of a number of languages; a book, especially a Bible, containing the same text in several languages.
    a. The population of our city ranges from the very rich to the masses of *polyglot* poor.
    b. His travels around the world have made our neighbor something of a *polyglot.*

12. **semantics** (sə-man'-tiks)—the study of meaning; the study of linguistic development by classifying and examining changes in meaning and form. *Semantics* is also called *significi,* a branch of *semiotics* (signs and symbols) dealing with the relationship between signs and what they denote. *General semantics* is an educational discipline concerning the relationship between symbols and reality and with improving the adjustment of people to each other and to the environment.
    a. We now find it hard to believe that an entire nation swallowed the racist *semantics* of the fanatical Nazi propaganda.

    b. The word "soon" has undergone *semantic* change from the Old English meaning of "immediately."

13. **simile** (sim'-ə-lē)—a figure of speech in which two unlike things are explicitly compared using the words "like" or "as," as in "she is like a rose."

    a. *Similes* are not confined to poetry, for they appear frequently in our daily use, adding spice and wit to the commonplace.

    b. *Similes* like "as tight as a drum," and "as sweet as sugar," have become clichés and hence lost their effectiveness.

14. **synecdoche** (si-nek'-də-kē)—a figure of speech in which a part is used for a whole or the whole for a part, the special for the general or the general for the special, as in "ten sail" for "ten ships" or "a Croesus" for "a rich man" or the name of the material for the thing made ("willow" for "bat").

    a. Sympathetic voodoo uses *synecdochism* by treating part of an object as representing the whole in an attempt to produce or prevent a particular result.

    b. A humanistic critic has objected to the *synecdoche* "All hands on deck" because it reduces a human being to one function that serves an impersonal cause.

15. **threnody** (thren'-ə-dē)—a poem, speech, or song of lamentation, especially for the dead; dirge; funeral song.

    a. William Cullen Bryant's "Thanatopsis" is one of the most famous *threnodies* in our literature.

    b. A failure is to be deplored but is not cause for a *threnody*.

EXERCISES

I. Which Word Comes to Mind?

In each of the following, read the statement, then circle the word that comes to mind.

1. She was too young to die

(polyglot,   simile,   threnody)

2. The allegories on the banks of the Nile

(malapropism,   metonymy,   synecdoche)

3. Snap! Crackle! Pop!

(paradigm,   oxymoron,   onomatopoeia)

4. A true fact

(bathos, pleonasm,   semantics)

5. The least of his crimes is his complicity with drugs

(metaphor,   panegyric,   paralipsis)

II. True or False?

In the space provided, indicate whether each statement is true or false.

_____ 1. Both *metaphor* and *simile* use forms of comparison.
_____ 2. *Synecdoche* and *metonymy* are similar figures of speech in which an object or idea is described by reference to only a part of it.
_____ 3. A *polyglot* is a person with a taste for exotic foods.
_____ 4. *Semantics* is concerned with the syntax of a language.
_____ 5. A *panegyric* is a test devised to determine the linguistic level of a speaker.

III. Find the Impostor

Find and circle the one word on each line that is not related to the other three.

1. metaphor	simile	literary	comparative
2. threnody	legacy	elegy	dirge
3. encomium	panegyric	panorama	accolade
4. paradox	paradigm	paragon	touchstone
5. insinuation	intuition	innuendo	paralipsis

IV. Find the Words

Somewhere in this box of letters, reading up, down, across, or diagonally, six vocabulary words that were taught in this lesson are hidden. As you locate each one, draw a circle around it.

M	E	T	O	N	O	M	Y
G	B	A	T	H	O	S	D
I	P	P	L	N	I	O	O
D	A	E	O	M	O	X	N
A	N	N	I	A	R	Y	E
R	E	L	S	M	O	M	R
A	E	G	Y	R	I	C	H
P	O	L	Y	G	L	O	T

V. Matching

Match the word in column A with its correct definition in column B by writing the letter of that definition in the space provided.

A

_____ 1. bathos
_____ 2. malapropism
_____ 3. metaphor
_____ 4. metonymy
_____ 5. onomatopoeia
_____ 6. oxymoron
_____ 7. panegyric
_____ 8. paradigm
_____ 9. paralipsis
_____ 10. pleonasm
_____ 11. polyglot
_____ 12. semantics
_____ 13. simile
_____ 14. synecdoche
_____ 15. threnody

B

a. commendation
b. humorous misapplication of a word
c. deliberate withholding of facts for effect
d. specific for the general
e. substituting one name for another
f. study of words as symbols
g. echoic sounds
h. a resemblance made explicit
i. funeral song
j. implied comparison
k. multi-lingual
l. paradox; contradiction
m. anticlimax
n. standard or example
o. redundancy

Answers are on pages 212–213.

"Who's an *oxymoron*?"

Speech

Is *harangue* a salty fish, a lemon pit, or a buttonholing tirade?

Which is harder on the ego, being censored or *censured*?

Does a *guttural* sound come from an alcoholic, the abdomen, or the throat?

Would you expect the *argot* of the underworld to be the same as its *jargon*?

Is *gobbledegook* the same as talking turkey?

---

argot
aspersion
badinage
bombast
braggadocio
censure
countermand
gainsay
gobbledegook
guttural
harangue
jargon
mellifluous
resonant
sententious

1. **argot** (är'-gō, -gət)—the specialized vocabulary and idioms of those in the same work or way of life, especially of the underworld. The French origin, meaning "to beg," associates beggary with thievery.
   a. The sociologists' *argot* describing juvenile delinquency amounts to a condemnation of a permissive society that fosters its development.
   b. It is hard to keep up with the *argot* of teenagers, which changes almost daily.

2. **aspersion** (ə-spur'-zhən, -shən)—act of defaming; a damaging or disparaging remark; a sprinkling of water, as in baptizing. This final definition, now rare, is based on an archaic meaning of the original Latin word for "sprinkle." The modern definition refers to "sprinkling" a few maliciously chosen words to vilify someone.
   a. The last few days of the campaign were marked by vicious attempts by the candidates to cast *aspersions* on each other.
   b. Such vehement *aspersions* that defame our sacred ideals and institutions cannot be ignored.

3. **badinage** (bad-ən-äzh', bad'-in-ij)—playful, teasing talk; banter.
   a. In one brief moment, the speaker rose from the level of *badinage* to grandiloquence.
   b. Raoul was a master of *badinage* but he could not be relied upon to serve in position of leadership.

4. **bombast** (bäm'-bast)—originally a soft material used for padding; talk or writing that sounds grand or important but has little meaning; pompous language. *Bombastic* refers to speech or writing that is heavily padded with words; *grandiloquent* suggests grandiose language and an oratorical tone; *euphuistic* writing is characterized by artificiality and a straining for effect; *turgid* suggests the style has obscured the meaning.
   a. Some enjoy the rant and *bombast* of politics while others are more comfortable simply to exercise their voting rights at the polls.
   b. *Bombast* and extravagance are no longer fashionable in the press; instead we follow the dictum of "telling it like it is."

5. **braggadocio** (brag-ə-dō'-shē-ō, -dō'-shō)—a braggart; pretentiousness; vain, noisy, or bragging swaggering manner. The word was coined by Edmund Spenser for his personification of boasting in the "Faerie Queene."
   a. The *braggadocio* of Uganda's Idi Amin has become a source of embarrassment to other African leaders.
   b. Muhammad Ali's *braggadocio* in claiming to be "the greatest" is a mixture of showmanship, psychology, and conformity to championship style.

6. **censure** (sen'-shər)—strong disapproval; a judgment or resolution condemning a person for misconduct.

    a. To explain the light sentence, the judge said the defendant was more to be pitied than *censured.*

    b. Newspapers were unanimous in their *censure* of the bill raising gasoline taxes as a means of discouraging energy waste.

7. **countermand** (koun'-tər-mand, koun-tər-mand')—to cancel or revoke a command; to call back by a contrary order.

    a. Realizing the futility of continuing the defense of the island, McArthur *countermanded* his original order to fight to the last man.

    b. Business fell sharply when the auto companies *countermanded* the order to reduce prices by six percent.

8. **gainsay** (gān'-sā)—to deny; to speak or act against; contradiction; denial.

    a. Beyond *gainsay,* the picture is a genuine Rembrandt.

    b. Our purpose in supporting the huge military budget is to make certain that no nation can *gainsay* us.

9. **gobbledegook** (gäb'-'l-dē-gook')—wordy and generally unintelligible jargon; specialized language of a group that is usually wordy and complicated and often incomprehensible to an outsider; a meaningless jumble of words.

    a. Laws now require the *gobbledegook* on insurance policies to be changed to understandable language.

    b. College professors claim that the average freshman composition is nothing but *gobbledegook.*

10. **guttural** (gut'-ər-əl)—of the throat; harsh, rasping sound.

    a. Certain *guttural* sounds, like the glottal stop and the *ch* in German *Buch,* do not exist in English.

    b. Part of the evening music of the country is the *guttural* symphony of the frogs.

11. **harangue** (hə-raŋ')—a long, blustering, noisy, or scolding speech; tirade. The original Italian word meant "a site for horse races and public assemblies."

    a. I recall that every poor grade on my report card brought forth a *harangue* on the subject of studying.

    b. The long, tiresome *harangue* by the director was full of bombast and ended with the firing of three actors.

12. **jargon** (jär'-gən)—a language or dialect unknown to one so that it seems incomprehensible; a mixed or hybrid language or dialect, especially pidgin; specialized idioms of those in the same work, profession; speech or writing full of long, unfamiliar, or roundabout words or phrases. The Middle French root means "a chattering of birds." The word is ultimately of echoic origin.

    a. Can you imagine anyone being so ethnocentric as to consider all foreign languages rude *jargons?*

    b. Medical *jargon* conceals from the public facts about diseases and medicines that all are entitled to know.

13. **mellifluous** (me-lif'-loo-wəs)—sounding sweet and smooth; honeyed.

    a. Juanita's mother wondered if her daughter wasn't more attracted by the suitor's *mellifluous* voice than by his character.

    b. Everyone was enraptured by the *mellifluous* tones of the Mozart opera.

14. **resonant** (rez'-ə-nənt)—echoing; reinforced and prolonged by reflection or by sympathetic vibration of other bodies. The word has specialized uses in various fields—chemistry, electricity, medicine, phonetics, physics.

    a. To develop a *resonant* voice, Carlos was willing to practice many hours.

    b. All talking stopped when the *resonant* thundering of cannons reverberated through the dark night.

15. **sententious** (sen-ten'-shəs)—abounding in pithy aphorisms or maxims; terse; self-righteous.
   a. One type of judge is magisterial; another is *sententious*.
   b. Paul's idea of a valedictory address was a compilation of *sententious* platitudes.

EXERCISES

I. Which Word Comes to Mind?

In each of the following, read the statement, then circle the word that comes to mind.

1. Sports lingo

(harangue,   jargon,   resonant)

2. A snide remark

(countermand,   badinage,   aspersion)

3. Coughing sound

(gobbledegook,   guttural,   censure)

4. Sweet-sounding talk

(mellifluous,   sententious,   bombast)

5. A thousand times no!

(braggadocio,   argot,   gainsay)

II. True or False?

In the space provided, indicate whether each statement is true or false.

_____ 1. *Argot* and *jargon* have one meaning in common.
_____ 2. *Bombast* may be a cover for weak content.
_____ 3. *Countermanding* is equivalent to sticking to your guns.
_____ 4. *Sententious* is more concerned with sense than sound.
_____ 5. *Badinage* is a minor vice that indicates immaturity.

III. Missing Letters

Each word below has a missing letter. Fill in these missing letters and then rearrange them to form a word meaning "the speech and idiom of the underworld."

1. bragadocio
2. gutturl
3. countemand
4. sentenious
5. resnant

IV. Synonyms and Antonyms

Find and circle two words on each line that are either synonyms or antonyms.

1. glorification   release   aspersion   dismay
2. mellifluous   ethos   attitudes   soft
3. timidity   paranoid   braggadocio   freedom
4. plebescite   gainsay   votary   deny
5. rhapsodic   peccadillo   falsetto   bombastic

V. Matching

Match the word in column A with its correct definition in column B by writing the letter of that definition in the space provided.

A	B
____ 1. argot	a. damaging remark
____ 2. aspersion	b. tirade
____ 3. badinage	c. pompous language
____ 4. bombast	d. terse
____ 5. braggadocio	e. dialect
____ 6. censure	f. gibberish
____ 7. countermand	g. criticism
____ 8. gainsay	h. harsh; rasping
____ 9. gobbledegook	i. oppose
____ 10. guttural	j. honeyed
____ 11. harangue	k. echoing
____ 12. jargon	l. pretentiousness
____ 13. mellifluous	m. specialized language
____ 14. resonant	n. revoke
____ 15. sententious	o. banter

Answers are on page 213.

History and Government (I)

Would you attack an enemy with a *canon?*

Does *renascent* refer to something new, young, or old?

Is a *subversion* a view of a secondary problem?

Is a *regicide* one who always sides with the king?

Is *peonage* a condition of certain laborers, a period of history, or a species of flowers?

---

canon
hegemony
oligarchy
peonage
pharisaical
plebescite
plenipotentiary
proxy
recession
regicide
renascent
reprisal
subversion
surrogate
votary

1. **canon** (kan' ən)—an ecclesiastical or secular law or code of laws; a basis for judgment; any officially recognized set of books. *Canon* has many specialized meanings in religion and in literature referring to the authoritative list of accepted books.
   a. According to newspaper *canon,* a big story calls for a lot of copy.
   b. There are thirty-seven plays in the Shakespearean *canon.*

2. **hegemony** (hi-jem'-ə-nē; hej'-ə-mō-nē)—leadership; preponderant influence or authority, especially of a government or state.
   a. Until the rise of rival city-states, the *hegemony* of ancient Greece was in the hands of Athens.
   b. In an uninformed electorate, the *hegemony* of the party passes to the one who promises more than any other contender.

3. **oligarchy** (äl'-ə-gär-kē)—form of government in which the ruling power lies in the hands of a select few.
   a. The founders of the new country set up an *oligarchy* in order to maintain tight control.
   b. There is a wide philosophical gap between those who choose democracy and those who favor *oligarchy.*

4. **peonage** (pē'-ə-nij)—a system by which debtors are bound in servitude to their creditors until debts are paid; the condition of being an unskilled day laborer, especially in Latin America and the southwestern U.S. The word *peon* ultimately is traceable to the Latin word for "walker" and therefore also developed a meaning of "foot soldier."
   a. *Peonage* at one time involved convict labor leased to contractors in parts of the southeastern U.S.
   b. The fallacy of the *peonage* system consisted in the inability of a person in prison to earn the money to repay the debt for which he was sent to prison.

5. **pharisaical** (far-ə-sā'-i-kəl)—making an outward show of piety but lacking the inward spirit; hypocritical. Orginally, *Pharisaism* referred to the doctrine and practices of the Pharisees, the Hebrew sect which followed the path of withdrawal, separation, and dedication and became the mainstream of Jewish belief. Later christological history gave the work a negative connotation.
   a. When we continually censure others, we are likely to sound *pharisaical.*
   b. A strong leader is not deterred from his goals by the *pharisaical* comments of his detractors.

6. **plebescite** (pleb'-ə-sīt)—a direct vote of the qualified electors of a state in

regard to some important public question. The word is derived from the Latin words *plebis scitum* ("the people's decree").

   a. A *plebescite* was held to determine whether the people of the disputed territory preferred autonomy or unification with their giant neighbor.

   b. *Plebescites* are the most democratic way of settling political or legislative questions, but they are too cumbersome and costly to be used on every issue.

7. **plenipotentiary** (plen-i-pə-ten′-shē-er-ē)—invested with or conferring full power; a diplomatic agent fully authorized to represent his government.

   a. As a *plenipotentiary* of the American government, Mr. Linowitz concluded the Panama Canal Treaty talks.

   b. *Plenipotentiary* powers were not entrusted to the minister as his mission was only of an exploratory nature.

8. **proxy** (präk′-sē)—an agent or substitute; a document giving one authority to act for another.

   a. Legal status has been given to voting or marriage by *proxy*.

   b. Books are not *proxies* for experience.

9. **recession** (rē-sesh′-ən)—the act of withdrawing or going back; a moderate and temporary decline in economic activity that occurs during a period of otherwise increasing prosperity.

   a. Economists for a time could not agree on whether the business decline was a *recession* or a depression.

   b Climatologists were concerned that a *recession* of the lakes and streams would endanger the water supply.

10. **regicide** (rej′-ə-cīd)—the killing of a king; one who kills or helps to kill a king.

   a. The judges who condemned Charles I to death were guilty of *regicide*.

   b. With the number and power of kings greatly reduced, *regicide* no longer looms as a probability in modern times.

11. **renascent** (ri-nās′-ənt)—coming into being again; showing renewed growth or vigor. The word is related to *Renaissance,* the humanistic revival of classical art, literature and learning that originated in Italy in the fourteenth century and later spread throughout Europe.

   a. In recent years there has been a *renascent* interest in Egyptology.

   b. The new freedom has brought with it a *renascent* individualism that some consider detrimental to society.

12. **reprisal** (rə-prī′-zəl)—the practice of using political or military force without actually resorting to war; retaliation for an injury with the intent of inflicting at least as much injury in return.

   a. *Reprisals* can run the gamut from embargo to military attack.

   b. Hanafi gunmen seized three Washington buildings and over 100 hostages in *reprisal* for murders by Black Muslims that were committed in an internal power struggle.

13. **subversion** (sub-vur′-zhən)—ruination or complete destruction; corruption; complete overthrow. As the meaning implies, the original Latin word meant "to turn upside down."

   a. Economic assistance, it was felt, would cause the *subversion* of the existing tribal order.

   b. We cannot tolerate schemes of *subversion* when the liberties our country has cherished for two centuries are at stake.

14. **surrogate** (sur′-ə-gāt, sur′-,-git)—a substitute; in some states, a judge having

jurisdiction over the probate of wills and the settlement of estates. As a verb, the word means "to substitute or to put into the place of another."
a. Some people regard teachers as parent *surrogates.*
b. Those who de-emphasize correctness in writing regard it as only a *surrogate* of oral communication.

15. **votary** (vō′-tə-rē)—a person bound by vows to live a life of religious worship and service, as a monk or nun; any person fervently devoted to a religion, activity, leader, or ideal.
a. Pagan worshippers tried to cultivate the good will of their gods, and so induce them to bestow their benefits on their *votaries.*
b. In Las Vegas, gaming tables are thronged all night by the *votaries* of chance.

EXERCISES

I. Which Word Comes to Mind?

In each of the following, read the statement, then circle the word that comes to mind.

1. Sharecroppers or migrant workers

    (surrogate,   proxy,   peonage)

2. You can't judge a book by its cover

    (pharisaical,   reprisal,   renascent)

3. Vox populi

    (votary,   plebescite,   subversion)

4. A man to be reckoned with

    (regicide,   canon,   plenipotentiary)

5. Times are bad but they could be worse

    (oligarchy,   recession,   hegemony)

II. True or False?

In the space provided, indicate whether each statement is true or false.

____ 1. *Hegemony* refers to the currency in circulation.
____ 2. A *proxy* and a *surrogate* are similar, both suggesting a substitute.
____ 3. A *votary* is one who keeps his word.
____ 4. A *regicide* favors the restoration of a monarchy.
____ 5. Vengeance is an act of *reprisal.*

III. Missing Letters

Each word below has a missing letter. Fill in these missing letters and then rearrange them to form a word meaning "a secret meeting."

1. plenipoteniary
2. oligachy

3. votar
4. surrogae
5. plebecite

IV. Find the Words

Somewhere in this box of letters there are five vocabulary words that were taught in this lesson. By making one turn for each word, you can find four of these words. The letters of the fifth word, meaning "rule by a select group," are scattered throughout the box.

H	I	V	O	O
E	E	E	T	T
G	Y	N	A	C
E	X	O	R	P
M	O	N	Y	L

V. Matching

Match the word in column A with its correct definition in column B by writing the letter of that definition in the space provided.

A	B
____ 1. canon	a. legal authorization to act for another
____ 2. hegemony	b. being reborn
____ 3. oligarchy	c. undermining
____ 4. peonage	d. hypocritical
____ 5. pharisaical	e. probate judge
____ 6. plebescite	f. basis for judgment
____ 7. plenipotentiary	g. believer
____ 8. proxy	h. economic setback
____ 9. recession	i. referendum
____ 10. regicide	j. slayer of kings
____ 11. renascent	k. control; influence
____ 12. reprisal	l. repayment
____ 13. subversion	m. ambassador
____ 14. surrogate	n. a kind of slavery
____ 15. votary	o. rule by a few

Answers are on page 213.

Travel

Why is *wanderlust* a travel agent's dream?

What do *transmigrate* and *traverse* have in common?

From the name of Aristotle's followers, *Peripatetics,* what can we deduce about Aristotle's method of teaching?

Is a *safari* a kind of gem or a caravan?

Would people be helped or hindered by working in *tandem*?

---

antipodal
cartography
concierge
hegira
hustings
landmark
peripatetic
portmanteau
safari
tandem
transmigrate
traverse
trek
wanderlust
wayfarer

1. **antipodal** (an-tip'-ə-d'l)—on the opposite side of the globe; diametrically opposite.
   a. It was amazing to see the twin brothers with *antipodal* personalities.
   b. While we are awake, night engulfs those who inhabit the *antipodal* part of our world.

2. **cartography** (kär-täg'-rə-fē)—art or business of drawing or making charts or maps. The original meaning of *chart* was a map for the use of navigators indicating the outline of coasts, position of rocks, sandbanks, and channels.
   a. The exploration of the New World was advanced by the science of *cartography.*
   b. Modern astronauts are guided by the *cartography* of incredibly complex maps drawn with the aid of giant computers.

3. **concierge** (kän-sē-urzh')—doorkeeper; caretaker; custodian; janitor. The *concierge* in French and other European hotels has a more important position than is implied by the title of janitor or custodian.
   a. Travelers quickly learn the importance of getting on the good side of their *concierge.*
   b. A *concierge,* looking as stern as Madame de Farge, guarded the lobby night and day.

4. **hegira** (hi-jī'-rə, hej'-ər-ə)—any flight or journey to a more desirable or congenial place than where one is. *Hegira* was the flight of Muhammad from Mecca to Medina to escape persecution in 622 A.D., a date regarded as the beginning of the Muslim era.
   a. Fashion experts are making their annual *hegira* to Paris.
   b. With the onset of the hot weather, the *hegira* to the beach resorts began in earnest.

5. **hustings** (hus'-tiŋz)—the route followed by a campaigner for political office; an election platform; the proceedings at an election. The original Old English word referred to a lord's household assembly as distinct from a general assembly.
   a. Televised debates have replaced the rough give-and-take of the *hustings.*
   b. Taking to the *hustings* required boundless energy, extraordinary endurance, and an unflagging voice.

6. **landmark** (land'-märk)—any fixed object used to mark the boundary of a piece of land; any prominent feature of the landscape, serving to identify a particular locality; an event or discovery considered as a high point or a turning point in the history or development of something.
   a. The huge oak tree was so prominent in the curve of the road it became a *landmark* to travelers.

     b. Our age has seen a *landmark* shift in morals and values.

7. **peripatetic** (per-i-pə-tet′ik)—moving from place to place; itinerant; of the followers of Aristotle, who walked about the Lyceum while he was teaching.
     a. Donald's *peripatetic* habits during his youth came back to haunt him when he later tried to find a steady job.
     b. As a professional photographer, Mr. Randall managed to stay in one place with his camera, avoiding a *peripatetic* life.

8. **portmanteau** (pôrt-man′-tō, -tō′)—a case or bag to carry clothing in while traveling, especially a leather trunk or suitcase which opens into two halves. The literal French meaning is "cloak carrier." A more recent use of the word in linguistics is to define a blend, a word made by putting together parts of other words, as *dandle,* made from *dance* and *handle.*
     a. Lewis Carroll, author of *Alice in Wonderland,* made frequent use of *portmanteau* words, as in his combination of *snort* and *chuckle* to form *chortle.*
     b. Sir Oliver was late for the meeting because his *portmanteau* had been placed on the wrong plane.

9. **safari** (sə-fär′-ē)—a journey or hunting expedition, especially in East Africa; the caravan of such an expedition; a long, carefully planned trip, usually with a large entourage.
     a. Roald Amundsen's *safari* to the Arctic in 1926 won him the title of "Discoverer of the North Pole."
     b. Hemingway wrote of the introspection or confrontation that was a by-product of the *safari.*

10. **tandem** (tan′-dəm)—a two-wheeled carriage drawn by horses harnessed one behind the other; a team of horses harnessed one behind the other; a bicycle with two seats and sets of pedals placed one behind the other; a relationship between two persons or things involving cooperative action and mutual dependence. *Tandem* may be a noun, an adjective, or an adverb.
     a. President Carter expressed the hope that all parties will function in *tandem* to solve the nation's major problems.
     b. A more persuasive *tandem* could not be found, nor were there two women with more desire to bring peace to the struggling factions in Northern Ireland.

11. **transmigrate** (trans-mī′-grāt)—to move from one habitation or country to another; in religion, to pass into some other body at death (of the soul). Believers in *reincarnation* and *metempsychosis* also feel that the souls of the dead successively return to earth in new forms and bodies.
     a. Some people believe that the soul may *transmigrate* into an animal as well as a person.
     b. Early in the Colonial period, the pioneers *transmigrated* from the Rocky Mountain slopes to the fertile plains.

12. **traverse** (tra′-vurs, trə-vurs′)—to pass, move, or extend over or across; oppose; to survey or inspect carefully; to swivel or pivot; to move across a mountain slope in an oblique direction (as in skiing); a zigzagging course.
     a. I accept no precepts that *traverse* my moral freedom.
     b. The new discovery opens a wide area of investigation that must now be *traversed* by historians.

13. **trek** (trek)—to travel by ox wagon; to travel slowly or laboriously. Colloquially, the word means "to go, especially on foot." *Trek* is also used as a noun.
     a. The shortage of new housing led to a consequent *trek* into older apartments.

b. George Washington Carver's *trek* up from slavery was a harbinger of the civil rights advances made in the latter half of the twentieth century.

14. **wanderlust** (wän'-dər-lust, wôn'-)—an impulse, longing, or urge to travel or wander.
   a. Modern traveling comforts and conveniences have simplified the problems of those who are afflicted with *wanderlust*.
   b. No one could figure out why a *wanderlust* seized the successful business man and drew him to a life of vagabondage.

15. **wayfarer** (wā'-fer-ər)—a person who travels, especially from place to place on foot.
   a. We are all *wayfarers* on the road to eternity.
   b. Some of the old virtues, like showing kindness to the weary *wayfarer*, have been lost in the hubbub of city life.

EXERCISES

I. Which Word Comes to Mind?

In each of the following, read the statement, then circle the word that comes to mind.

1. A train makes whistle-stops across the Midwest

   (trek, hustings, hegira)

2. Infanticipate, slithy, swalm

   (peripatetic, concierge, portmanteau)

3. The Supreme Court decision on school integration

   (cartography, landmark, antipodal)

4. Tracking lions in their native habitat

   (safari, wayfarer, wanderlust)

5. A bicycle built for two

   (transmigrate, tandem, traverse)

II. True or False?

In the space provided, indicate whether each statement is true or false.

_____ 1. A *safari* can properly be described as a *trek* through the jungle.
_____ 2. The art of *cartography* can be used to chart the skies.
_____ 3. The early *Peripatetics* were philosophers.
_____ 4. *Transmigration* is a form of ESP.
_____ 5. *Wanderlust* describes the sensuality of the homeless criminal.

III. Find the Impostor

Find and circle the one word on each line that is not related to the other three.

1. peripatetic	hegira	globe-trotting	parabolic
2. vagabondage	wayfarer	valediction	nomadism
3. tirade	trek	harangue	diatribe
4. astronaut	travail	navigator	pilgrim
5. anticipate	antipodal	different	antithetic

IV. Find the Words

Somewhere in this box of letters, reading up, down, across, or diagonally, four vocabulary words that were taught in this lesson are hidden. As you locate each one, draw a circle around it. Then find two words whose letters are scattered throughout the box.

H	K	F	A	R	M
W	E	E	R	E	D
A	R	G	D	P	A
Y	T	N	I	O	L
S	A	F	A	R	I
T	A	N	T	I	A

V. Matching

Match the word in column A with its correct definition in Column B by writing the letter of that definition in the space provided.

	A		B
____	1. antipodal	a.	map-making
____	2. cartography	b.	two-seated carriage
____	3. concierge	c.	traveler
____	4. hegira	d.	itinerant
____	5. hustings	e.	journey from one place to another
____	6. landmark	f.	luggage
____	7. peripatetic	g.	hunting expedition
____	8. portmanteau	h.	addiction to traveling
____	9. safari	i.	opposite
____	10. tandem	j.	travel with difficulty
____	11. transmigrate	k.	event marking the turning point
____	12. traverse	l.	flight
____	13. trek	m.	oppose
____	14. wanderlust	n.	election platform
____	15. wayfarer	o.	caretaker

Answers are on pages 213–214.

Foods and Taste

Is *cuisine* a traditional family recipe?

Which would be served at a *refection, viands* or *manna*?

Can *piquant condiments assuage* one's hunger?

Would you find *comestibles* at a *repast*?

Which usually offers more food, a *refection* or a *repast*?

---

a la carte
assuage
comestible
condiment
cuisine
culinary
gastronomic
gourmand
manna
palatable
piquant
refection
repast
subsistence
viands

1. **a la carte** (ä-lə-kärt')—by the card or by the bill of fare. It is used to describe a meal that is ordered dish by dish, with each dish having a separate price. The opposite is *table d'hôte*, a complete meal of several courses offered at a fixed price.
    a. An *a la carte* dinner is usually more expensive than a complete dinner offered at a set price.
    b. The advantage of an *a la carte* meal is that you order and pay for only what you choose to eat.

2. **assuage** (ə-swäj')—to satisfy and slake; to lessen (pain or distress); allay; calm (passion); relieve. The Latin root *suavis* ("sweet") suggests that sweets play an important role in our eating habits.
    a. Upon our return from the arduous climb, we were treated to more than enough food to *assuage* our hunger.
    b. There was little anyone could say to the widow to *assuage* her grief.

3. **comestible** (kə-mes'-tə-b'l)—suitable to be eaten. The plural, *comestibles*, is used as a noun and means "food."
    a. When the city inhabitants realized the imminent danger of a siege, they began to store up *comestibles*.
    b. Not every green plant is *comestible*.

4. **condiment** (kän'-də-mənt)—seasoning or relish for food, such as pepper, mustard, or sauce. The Latin root means "to pickle."
    a. Gourmets are very careful with the kinds and amounts of *condiments* used in the preparation of their food.
    b. It is no exaggeration to say that the search for *condiments* for the royal tables of Europe led to the discovery of the New World.

5. **cuisine** (kwə-zēn')—style of cooking or preparing food; the food prepared, as at a restaurant. In French it means "kitchen."
    a. Nowhere can you find as many restaurants offering international *cuisine* as in New York.
    b. The advertisement caught our eye because it claimed quite frankly that the restaurant had no atmosphere but offered an excellent *cuisine*.

6. **culinary** (kyōō'-lə-ner-ē, kul'-ə-ner-ē)—of the kitchen or cooking; suitable for use in cooking. *Culinary* comes from the Latin word for "kitchen" or "kiln," *culina*.
    a. It is paradoxical that while a woman's place was once thought to be in the kitchen, the greatest *culinary* experts were men.
    b. These dishes are prepared with the finest *culinary* herbs.

7. **gastronomic** (gas-trə-näm'-ik)—pertaining to the art and science of good

eating; epicurian; pertaining to the enjoyment of food with a discriminating taste. *Gaster* is the Greek word for "stomach." *Gastronome* is the Russian name for a delicatessen.

   a. *Gastronomic* experts, like Craig Clayborne, have influenced our choice of foods.

   b. Television chefs have introduced the *gastronomic* delights of Oriental dishes to the Western household.

8. **gourmand** (goor'-mənd, goor'-mänd)—a glutton; a person with a hearty liking for good food and drink and a tendency to indulge in them to excess; a luxurious eater or epicure. *Gourmet* has only the second meaning, that is, a connoisseur in eating and drinking.

   a. Randolph was too much of a *gourmand* to appreciate rare and fragile flavors.

   b. It took a team of chefs to satisfy the *gourmand* appetite of Diamond Jim Brady.

9. **manna** (man'-ə)—food miraculously provided for the Israelites in the wilderness; divine and spiritual sustenance; anything badly needed that comes unexpectedly.

   a. The hard-pressed family regarded the unexpected bonus as *manna.*

   b. Dr. Mount's optimistic mood after learning the results of the tests surrounded the worried patient like *manna* from heaven.

10. **palatable** (pal'-it-ə-b'l)—pleasing or acceptable to the taste; acceptable to the mind.

   a. The root, when properly cooked, was converted into a *palatable* and nutritious food.

   b. It took Darryl hours and several modifications to make his plan *palatable* to the rest of the committee.

11. **piquant** (pē'-kənt, -känt)—agreeably pungent or stimulating to the taste; pleasantly sharp or bitter; exciting agreeable interest or curiosity; stimulating.

   a. Joan had a delightful, *piquant* smile.

   b. Murray Kempton's columns are always *piquant* and sometimes blistering.

12. **refection** (ri-fek'-shən)—refreshment, especially with food or drink. *Refection* comes from a Latin word meaning "to restore" and refers to a light meal taken after a point of hunger or fatigue.

   a. After the lengthy speeches, the audience was anxious to partake of the *refection*.

   b. In our weight-conscious society, the grand *refections* at social gatherings challenge our will power and tempt us to gluttony.

13. **repast** (ri-past')—a meal; mealtime. Like other words in this list, *repast* has nonmaterialistic associations as well. *Pastor,* for example, is derived from the same Latin word *pascere* meaning "to feed."

   a. The Berensons preferred to be alone at the evening *repast*.

   b. How I envy people who are satisfied with a light *repast* of simple and nourishing food.

14. **subsistence** (sub-sis'-təns)—existence; means of support or livelihood, often the barest.

   a. Early pioneers to the Dakotas found a barren land providing no more than the barest *subsistence*.

   b. Without a skill or trade, Mr. Jenkins could not hope to reach a standard of living beyond a mere *subsistence* level.

15. **viands** (vī'-əndz)—foods of various kinds, especially choice dishes. The ultimate root is the Latin *vivere*, "to live."
    a. The grocery shelves were stocked with *viands* of the most exotic kind.
    b. To our surprise, the grizzled traveler pulled *viands* from his tattered knapsack that were unobtainable locally in the finest stores.

EXERCISES

I. Which Word Comes to Mind?

In each of the following, read the statement, then circle the word that comes to mind.

1. Catsup, curry, vinegar

    (a la carte,   refectory,   condiment)

2. Pennies from heaven

    (cuisine,   manna,   gourmand)

3. Living on the edge of poverty

    (subsistence,   assuage,   gastronomic)

4. Wake-up flavor

    (repast,   comestibles,   piquant)

5. "Something's cooking."

    (culinary,   palatable,   viands)

II. True or False?

In the space provided, indicate whether each statement is true or false.

_____ 1. *A la carte* refers to food brought to the table in a wagon.
_____ 2. *Assuage* refers to both hunger and thirst.
_____ 3. *Gourmand* can be used with a complimentary or derogatory connotation.
_____ 4. *Palatable* applies to foods that can be served on a plate.
_____ 5. *Gastronomic* describes a condition caused by excessive indulgence in foods that are rich in fats and carbohydrates.

III. Find the Impostor

Find and circle the one word on each line that is not related to the other three.

1. comestible	edifying	esculent	eatable
2. slake	assuage	determine	sate
3. sustenance	subsistence	essential	aliment
4. palatable	pungent	toothsome	agreeable
5. banquet	refection	repast	relish

IV. Anagrams

In each of the following, add the letter indicated, then rearrange the letters to form the two new words whose definitions are given.

1. gourmand + e = a *scoundrel* and *condemn*_____
2. piquant + s = *to look obliquely* and *broadcast system*_____
3. viands = *forefront* and *divisions of the psyche*_____
4. refection + s = *shoal* and *warning system*_____
5. assuage + h = *estimate* and *expression of triumph or pleasure*_____

V. Matching

Match the word in column A with its correct definition in column B by writing the letter of that definition in the space provided.

A

_____ 1. a la carte
_____ 2. assuage
_____ 3. comestible
_____ 4. condiment
_____ 5. cuisine
_____ 6. culinary
_____ 7. gastronomic
_____ 8. gourmand
_____ 9. manna
_____ 10. palatable
_____ 11. piquant
_____ 12. refection
_____ 13. repast
_____ 14. subsistence
_____ 15. viands

B

a. lover of food and drink
b. divine food
c. provocative
d. pacify
e. meal
f. edible
g. choice dishes
h. style of cooking
i. existence
j. suitable for cooking
k. dish by dish
l. tasteful
m. flavor enhancer
n. refreshment
o. pertaining to the science of good eating

Answers are on page 214.

Fun and Frolic

Why is a king well equipped to *regale* his subjects?

Would adding yeast to dough make it more *risible*?

Which is not likely to be *waggish*—a cat, a clown, or a tiger?

Which character trait makes a better friend, *bonhomie* or *insouciance*?

Is a *japery* an Oriental joke?

---

antic
beguile
bonhomie
dalliance
divertissement
euphoria
guffaw
insouciance
japery
regale
risible
roguish
roister
squib
waggish

1. **antic** (an'-tik)—odd and funny; ludicrous; a playful or silly act, trick, prank, or caper. Shakespeare has Hamlet hide his real intent by assuming an *antic* disposition.
   a. How can we seriously consider Frank for the promotion when he is continually involved with such juvenile *antics*?
   b. Fletcher's *antics* may be fun to watch but I wouldn't want to be on the receiving end.

2. **beguile** (bi-gīl')—to charm; to divert attention in some pleasant way; to while away; to deceive.
   a. We often allow ourselves to be *beguiled* by false hopes and vain promises.
   b. To *beguile* the time, Carrie spent hours on the telephone.

3. **bonhomie** (bän-ə-mē', bän'-ə-mē)—frank and simple good-heartedness; a good-natured manner. The word is a combination of two French words meaning "good" and "man." *Bonhomie* was the name given to an order of begging friars and finally to French peasants in general.
   a. An affectionate *bonhomie* radiated from Mrs. Goren, endearing her to all she came in contact with.
   b. The alumni gathering was marked by the cheerfulness and *bonhomie* of a fraternity reunion.

4. **dalliance** (dal'-ē-əns, dal'-yəns)—a trifling away of time; amorous toying; flirtation. In *Hamlet,* Ophelia reminds her brother Laertes not to give her moral advice while he follows "the primrose path of *dalliance.*"
   a. Marco's short *dalliance* with the drug cult ended when he realized the terrible havoc it had wrought among its followers.
   b. Mrs. Farren warned her daughter that Steve's interest might be a mere amatory *dalliance*.

5. **divertissement** (di-vurt'-is-mənt, dī-ver-tēs-man')—a diversion or amusement; a short ballet or other entertainment performed between the acts of a play.
   a. The detective story has an honorable history as an intellectual *divertissement*.
   b. With the legalization of certain forms of gambling, lotteries have become a popular *divertissement*.

6. **euphoria** (yoo-fôr'-ē-ə)—a feeling of well-being or high spirits, especially one that is groundless, disproportionate to its cause, or inappropriate to one's life situation.
   a. Michael's *euphoria* was of a suspicious nature.
   b. Making the team in his sophomore year put Arnold into a state of *euphoria* that made it hard for him to settle down to his schoolwork.

7. **guffaw** (gə-fô′)—a loud, coarse burst of laughter. This is an echoic onomatopoeic word. Laughs range from chuckles, giggles, and titters to snickers and *guffaws.*
   a. Mr. Bumble's loud *guffaw* could be heard above the din of the train station.
   b. As the clown continued his antics, the chuckles soon changed to howls and roars and *guffaws.*

8. **insouciance** (in-sōō′-sē-əns)—calmness; freedom from anxiety; indifference.
   a. Disregarding the snickers around her, Alice walked to the stage with an elegant *insouciance* and delivered her speech.
   b. The diva's *insouciance* concealed a growing concern about her fading youth.

9. **japery** (jā′-pə-rē)—jesting talk; mockery; a trick or practical joke.
   a. Milton Berle was the sort of comic who indulged in flippant *japeries.*
   b. You cannot fault a man for his *japeries* if he is honest and productive in his work.

10. **regale** (ri-gāl′)—to entertain by providing a splendid feast; to delight with something pleasing or amusing. The first meaning is related etymologically to the word *regal,* as it was customary for a king to treat his courtiers to sumptuous feasts.
    a. Washington hostesses must *regale* their guests with the best foods and good companionship if they wish to maintain their reputation in that competitive society.
    b. The purple mountains unfolding in grandeur to meet the rising sun were a sight to *regale* the eyes.

11. **risible** (riz′-ə-b′l)—able or inclined to laugh; laughable; funny. Most people are familiar with Leoncavallo's opera *Pagliacci,* in which the major character sings "Ride, Pagliacci." Our word *ridiculous* shows the close relationship to *risible.*
    a. "Heaven," said Christopher Morley, "is not for pallid saints but for raging and *risible* men."
    b. The manager was ordered off the field for his *risible* antics.

12. **roguish** (rō′-gish)—dishonest; unprincipled; pleasantly mischievous.
    a. With a *roguish* wink, the magician stepped into the box with the money he had "borrowed" and disappeared in a cloud of orange smoke.
    b. Blanche decided to return to her husband despite his *roguish* past.

13. **roister** (rois′-tər)—to boast or swagger; to have a noisy, disorderly good time, especially under the influence of alcohol. This word can be traced to *rustic* and *rural,* indicating the low esteem in which the country ruffian and boor was held by the sophisticated city dweller.
    a. Poor Charlie had gambled and *roistered* and drunk until he dropped in his tracks.
    b. The critics felt the play had been rushed to a *roistering* conclusion.

14. **squib** (skwib)—a firecracker that burns with a hissing, spurting noise before exploding; a short, humorous satiric writing or speech; a short news item or filler.
    a. Teachers have become accustomed to being the subjects of versified *squibs* in yearbooks.
    b. Once famous and lionized, the old movie idol could not even rate a *squib* among the used-car ads.

15. **waggish** (wag′-ish)—roguishly merry; playful.

a. A *waggish* disposition is not the best qualification for the position of class president.

b. Albert's distorted idea of a *waggish* trick was to call in false fire alarms.

EXERCISES

I. Which Word Comes to Mind?

In each of the following, read the statement, then circle the word that comes to mind.

1. A pleasant intermission

(insouciance,   divertissement,   roister)

2. The laughter of the jolly green giant

(guffaw,   euphoria,   dalliance)

3. A ten-course banquet

(japery,   regale,   risible)

4. Racy humor

(bonhomie,   waggish,   beguile)

5. A satire

(antic,   roguish,   squib)

II. True or False?

In the space provided, indicate whether each statement is true or false.

—— 1. You cannot trust a man with *bonhomie*.
—— 2. A *waggish* person would be likely to indulge in *japery*.
—— 3. A *dalliance* is a brightly colored flower.
—— 4. A *roisterer* would be found at a bacchanal.
—— 5. A *squib* is a variety of an octopus that has ten tentacles.

III. Missing Letters

Each word below has a missing letter. Fill in these missing letters and then rearrange them to form a word meaning "pixyish."

1. daliance
2. gufaw
3. divertissment
4. isouciance
5. rosterer

IV. Find the Words

Somewhere in this box of letters, reading up, down, across, or diagonally, five vocabulary words that were taught in this lesson are hidden. As you locate each one, draw a circle around it.

G	U	F	F	A	W
E	C	I	T	N	A
L	N	C	E	B	G
A	E	J	P	I	G
G	L	I	A	U	I
E	A	Y	R	Q	S
R	L	A	D	S	H

V. Matching

Match the word in column A with its correct definition in column B by writing the letter of that definition in the space provided.

A
- ____ 1. antic
- ____ 2. beguile
- ____ 3. bonhomie
- ____ 4. dalliance
- ____ 5. divertissement
- ____ 6. euphoria
- ____ 7. guffaw
- ____ 8. insouciance
- ____ 9. japery
- ____ 10. regale
- ____ 11. risible
- ____ 12. roguish
- ____ 13. roister
- ____ 14. squib
- ____ 15. waggish

B
- a. a short ballet
- b. indifference
- c. high spirits
- d. ludicrous
- e. revel
- f. mockery
- g. frolicsome
- h. lampoon
- i. boisterous laughter
- j. disreputable
- k. dawdling
- l. refresh with sumptuous food
- m. deceive
- n. laughable
- o. geniality

Answers are on page 214.

History and Government (II)

Is *suffrage* a matter of high tolerance to pain?

Who is opposed to progressive changes, the *reactionary* or the liberal?

Why does a vote count more in a democracy than in a *totalitarian* state?

What are the drawbacks to government *bureaucracy*?

Why would a *muckraker* be feared by people in high office?

---

anarchy
bourgeois
bureaucracy
demagogue
ethos
gerrymander
imperialism
Machiavellian
martial
muckraker
partisan
reactionary
schism
suffrage
totalitarian

1. **anarchy** (an'-ər-kē)—the complete absence of government; political disorder and violence; disorder in any sphere of activity. The anarchist opposes all direct or coercive government and proposes the voluntary association of people as the mode of organized society.
   a. The death of the king was followed by a period of *anarchy*.
   b. For some people liberty often means only license and *anarchy*.

2. **bourgeois** (boor-zhwä', boor'-zhwä)—typical of the social middle class; characterized by selfish concern for material comfort and for property values. *Bourgeois* virtues are thriftiness and a serious attitude toward life; its faults are a preoccupation with moneymaking and anxiety about respectability. It all depends on one's point of view.
   a. Communists say that all capitalists are *bourgeois*.
   b. The Martins were social climbers who followed a *bourgeois* mediocrity in their opinions and tastes.

3. **bureaucracy** (byoo-rä'-krə-sē)—a system that rigidly adheres to rules, forms, and routines. In American usage, the term is almost invariably derogatory unless the context establishes otherwise.
   a. Government has become a huge *bureaucracy* with agencies and departments that often duplicate each other.
   b. In his election campaign, the President promised to streamline the Washington *bureaucracy* and eliminate inefficiency.

4. **demagogue** (dem'-ə-gäg)—a leader who obtains power by means of impassioned appeals to the emotions and prejudices of the populace. In ancient Greece, the *demagogue* was the leader who championed the cause of the common people.
   a. Oversimplification and single-minded pursuit of an inflammatory issue are characteristics of the modern *demagogue*.
   b. The mayoral candidate seized upon the blackout to make a *demagogic* attack upon the ability of the incumbent.

5. **ethos** (ē'-thäs)—the disposition, character, or attitude that distinguishes a particular group, epoch, or region.
   a. From her youth, Althea Gibson had a distinctly athletic *ethos* about her, as if she might have majored in physical education.
   b. America has expressed its *ethos* in its basic allegiance to the principles of the Constitution.

6. **gerrymander** (jer'-i-man-dər, ger'-)—to divide an area into voting districts to give unfair advantage to one party in an election. The word comes from a

reference to Elbridge Gerry, governor of Massachusetts, whose party redistricted the state in 1812, combined with *salamander,* because the map of Essex County, Massachusetts, seemed to resemble this animal after the redistricting.

a. Federal law prohibits *gerrymandering* of school districts so that de facto segregation can be maintained.

b. Only through a complex *gerrymander* was the entrenched union chief able to avoid a disastrous defeat.

7. **imperialism** (im-pir′-ē-al-iz′m)—the policy of extending the rule or authority of an empire or nation over countries, or of acquiring and holding colonies and dependencies.

a. Communist Russia, like Nazi Germany before it, aims at autocratic control and *imperialistic* expansion.

b. It is conceivable that small nations can follow the path of *imperialism* through nuclear blackmail.

8. **Machiavellian** (mak-ē-ə-vel′-ē-ən, -vel′-yən)—acting in accordance with the principles of government in which political expediency is placed above morality; subtly or unscrupulously cunning or deceptive. Nicolo Machiavelli in *The Prince* expounded the doctrine of political expediency.

a. Few people openly support the *Machiavellian* position that the end justifies the means.

b. With *Machiavellian* cunning, the political newcomer gradually built a power base from which he hoped to seize power.

9. **martial** (mär′-shəl)—inclined or disposed to war; brave; warlike. The blood-red planet Mars was named after the Roman god of war.

a. John Philip Sousa is the best known composer of *martial* music.

b. When it became obvious that police were unable to contain the riot, *martial* law was declared to restore peace and order.

10. **muckraker** (muk′-rā-kər)—one who searches for and exposes real or alleged corruption and scandal. *Muckrake,* a rake for use on muck or dung, was first used in the work of Lincoln Steffens and his contemporaries.

a. Who can feel safe if the *muckraking* journalists turn over every stone in a person's life?

b. Unwilling to stoop to *muckraking* to discredit his opponent, Mr. Barios felt he could win on his own merit.

11. **partisan** (pärt′-ə-z′n, -s′n)—an adherent or supporter of a person, party, or cause; a member of an irregular troop engaged in harassing an enemy.

a. *Partisans* in World War II, fighting against the Nazi occupation of their countries, carved a niche of honor and glory for their courage and determination.

b. When the fabric of American society is disintegrating, it is useless and dangerous to play *partisan* politics.

12. **reactionary** (rē-ak′ shə-ner-ē)—a person who favors political conservatism or extreme rightism.

a. *Reactionary* movements sometimes develop in response to unsuccessful or unhappy liberal politics.

b. Aided by disunity and splintering among the progressives, the *reactionary* forces were able to achieve victory with their appeal for a return to "the good old days."

13. **schism** (siz′-əm, skiz′-əm)—a separation or division into factions. The term "The Great Schism" was used in connection with the Christian church to describe the split between the Western and Eastern sects.

a. Despite their denials, a *schism* seemed to be developing between the President and the secretary of state.

b. "Let there be no *schism* in our ranks," the prime minister admonished, "or we will fritter away our energies and strength in useless contention."

14. **suffrage** (suf'-rij)—the right to vote; a vote given in favor of a proposed measure or candidate.

a. The U.S. Constitution guarantees that "no state shall be deprived of its equal *suffrage* in the Senate."

b. The struggle for universal *suffrage* is behind us; ahead looms the battle to assure a decent standard of living for everyone.

15. **totalitarian** (tō-tal-ə-ter'-ē-ən)—of or pertaining to a centralized government in which those in control grant neither recognition nor toleration to parties of differing opinions.

a. The children suffered under the *totalitarian* rule of the father in their patriarchal household.

b. Almost all countries adopt *totalitarian* measures in war time.

EXERCISES

I. Which Word Comes to Mind?

In each of the following, read the statement, then circle the word that comes to mind.

1. The Confederacy votes to secede from the Union

(martial,   gerrymander,   schism)

2. Vote the party line all the way

(partisan,   Machiavellian,   reactionary)

3. Russia tries to expand its influence in the Middle East

(anarchy,   imperialism,   bureaucracy)

4. The Amish object to TV and other modern inventions and conveniences

(ethos,   totalitarian,   suffrage)

5. A spellbinding speaker

(demagogue,   muckraker,   bourgeois)

II. True or False?

In the space provided, indicate whether each statement is true or false.

_____ 1. *Bourgeois* manners tend to be different from the manners of those who have been born with "a silver spoon in their mouth."

_____ 2. To *gerrymander* is to vote on the basis of issue rather than party.

_____ 3. *Martial* refers to a rank in the army.

_____ 4. A *Machiavellian* attitude could lead to power but also to unpopularity.

_____ 5. Anarchy is a form of government that is built upon *bureaucracy*.

III. Find the Impostor

Find and circle the one word on each line that is not related to the other three.

1. anarchy   narcissism   terrorism   nihilism
2. demagogue   instigator   pedant   agitator
3. partisan   coherent   zealot   adherent
4. schism   disjunction   fissure   quarry
5. Machiavellian deceptive   artistic   sinister

IV. Mistaken Letters

In each of the words below, one letter is mistakenly used. Correct all the mistakes and use the discarded letters to form a word meaning "a basis for judgment."

1. ethas
2. boorgeois
3. marcial
4. gerrynander
5. mucknaker

V. Matching

Match the word in column A with its correct definition in column B by writing the letter of that definition in the space provided.

	A		B
____	1. anarchy	a.	one who appeals to the emotions
____	2. bourgeois	b.	warlike
____	3. bureaucracy	c.	right to vote
____	4. demagogue	d.	disorder
____	5. ethos	e.	one who exposes public misdeeds
____	6. gerrymander	f.	system of beliefs
____	7. imperialism	g.	supporter
____	8. Machiavellian	h.	expansionism
____	9. martial	i.	ultra-conservative
____	10. muckraker	j.	conventional
____	11. partisan	k.	breach
____	12. reactionary	l.	deceitful
____	13. schism	m.	belief in established routines
____	14. suffrage	n.	total power of the state
____	15. totalitarian	o.	divide into districts unfairly

Answers are on pages 214–215.

Legal Language (III)

Should you be pleased to receive a *bequest*?

Is *altercation* related to alter (to change)?

Who would be likely to have an interest in *contraband*?

Would a labor leader necessarily welcome an *injunction*?

Why do consumer advocates use the phrase *caveat emptor*?

---

abnegation
abscond
affidavit
altercation
battery
bequest
cause célèbre
caveat emptor
codicil
contiguous
contraband
contumacious
disenfranchise
injunction
jurisprudence

1. **abnegation** (ab-nə-gā′-shən)—giving up of rights; self-denial.
   a. After years of *abnegation,* the timid relative decided to demand what was rightfully his.
   b. The *abnegation* of his citizenship was the painter's final move before going off to live in Tahiti.

2. **abscond** (əb-skänd′, ab-)—to run away and hide in order to escape the law.
   a. When our trusted bookkeeper *absconded* with the money, I lost all faith in the human race.
   b. Because of adequate government insurance, we were not too concerned when the banker *absconded.*

3. **affidavit** (af′-ə-dā-vit)—a written statement made on oath, usually before a notary public. In Medieval Latin, the verb *affidare* meant "he has made an oath."
   a. In order to get the job, Maria needed an *affidavit* testifying to her character.
   b. When we checked into the salesman's *affidavits,* we found that they had all been forged.

4. **altercation** (ôl-tər-kā′-shən, al-)—a quarrel; an angry or heated dispute. Other synonyms are *spat* and *squabble. Wrangle* suggests a noisy dispute.
   a. When the *altercation* led to violence, the police were called.
   b. I hesitate to get involved in any *altercation* between a husband and his wife.

5. **battery** (bat′-ər-ē, bat′-rē)—a pounding; illegal beating. A person who commits *assault and battery* inflicts physical harm upon his victim.
   a. Mrs. Grimes dropped the *battery* complaint when her assailant agreed to pay all the medical bills.
   b. It was hard to see how such a puny youngster could be accused of assault and *battery.*

6. **bequest** (bi-kwest′)—that which is given by inheritance; a gift specified in a will. In Middle English, *bicewste* meant "a saying."
   a. John Barrymore always said that his acting talent was a *bequest* from his father.
   b. The *bequest* of $10 million allowed the university to go ahead with its plans for a new library.

7. **cause célèbre** (kōz′ sā-leb′r′)—a celebrated law case, trial, or controversy.
   a. Let's settle this matter quietly before it becomes a *cause célèbre.*
   b. The famous Dreyfus Case was a genuine *cause célèbre* of the late nineteenth century.

8. **caveat emptor** (kā′-vē-at emp′-tôr)—let the buyer beware; one buys at his own risk. The implication is that the vendor is trying to sell inferior merchandise.

a. The unscrupulous retailer followed the cynical policy of *caveat emptor.*

b. None of the large department stores can afford to practice the doctrine of *caveat emptor.*

9. **codicil** (kod'-i-s'l)—an addition to a will; an appendix or supplement. The Latin word *codex* means "tree trunk" or a "wooden tablet covered with wax for writing."

   a. In an interesting *codicil*, Uncle Herbert set aside $10,000 for the care of his six cats.

   b. The outraged relatives went to court to try to get the offending *codicil* revoked.

10. **contiguous** (kən-tig'-yoo-wəs)—adjacent; touching.

   a. I wanted a wall built where Tom's property was *contiguous* to mine.

   b. Before the redesigning of the building, our offices were *contiguous.*

11. **contraband** (kän'-trə-band)—goods forbidden by law to be exported. This word was first used in the 16th century to refer to illicit trade with Spanish colonies.

   a. At Kennedy Airport, the customs officials make a thorough search for *contraband.*

   b. The *contraband* was discovered in the car trunk when the smugglers tried to cross the border.

12. **contumacious** (kän-too-mā'-shəs)—insubordinate; disobedient. Its original Latin meaning was "to swell up."

   a. The principal's *contumacious* behavior brought him headlines and disciplinary action.

   b. Our terrier used to be easy to manage but lately he has developed a *contumacious* personality.

13. **disenfranchise** (dis'-in-fran'-chīz)—to deprive of the rights of citizenship; to deprive of a privilege. This word is sometimes written as *disfranchise.*

   a. The punishment that the criminal fears the least is that he will be *disenfranchised.*

   b. Betty Friedan paid tribute to those feminists who had fought against the *disenfranchisement* of women.

14. **injunction** (in-junk'-shən)—a command or order; a court order stopping a person or group from carrying out a given action.

   a. Our attorney went into court to seek an *injunction* against the strikers.

   b. When I was a boy, no morning would be complete without my mother's *injunction:* "Brush your teeth!"

15. **jurisprudence** (joor'-is-proo-d'ns)—the science or philosophy of law; a system of laws.

   a. The law professor's religion was to worship at the shrine of *jurisprudence.*

   b. The proudest day of my father's life was when I became a Doctor of *Jurisprudence.*

EXERCISES

I. Which Word Comes to Mind?

In each of the following, read the statement, then circle the word that comes to mind.

1. When the financier could not be found, the scandal came to light

(injunction,   codicil,   abscond)

2. A soldier is absent without leave

    (contumacious,   jurisprudence,   disenfranchise)

3. The plight of the whales attracts world-wide attention

    (cause célèbre,   caveat emptor,   abnegation)

4. Hidden weapons are discovered by the airport's X-ray machine

    (contraband,   contiguous,   altercation)

5. Relatives gather to hear the reading of the will

    (battery,   affidavit,   bequest)

II. True or False?

In the space provided, indicate whether each statement is true or false.

_____ 1. When a dog displays his *contumacious* spirit, obedience training is often prescribed.
_____ 2. Merchants follow the policy of *caveat emptor* when competition is fierce.
_____ 3. Our houses are *contiguous,* and I wish we were closer together.
_____ 4. An important *codicil* is like the tail that wagged the dog.
_____ 5. Following the *altercation* on the field, both players were ejected.

III. Find the Words

Somewhere in this box of letters, reading up, down, across, or diagonally, four vocabulary words that were taught in this lesson are hidden. As you locate each one, draw a circle around it.

Y	A	B	X	L	R	B	H
R	C	E	N	I	Z	P	M
E	K	Q	O	C	A	S	T
T	W	U	D	I	E	H	G
T	L	E	S	D	F	S	Y
A	B	S	C	O	N	D	C
B	F	T	G	C	P	I	J

IV. Extra Letters

In each of the vocabulary words below there is an extra letter. Put all of the extra letters together and you will be able to spell out a word taught in a previous lesson. Its meaning is "a surgical procedure to determine malignancy."

abbnegation	abscoond	caveat empstor
alitercation	contumpacious	beyquest

V. Matching

Match the word in column A with its correct definition in Column B by writing the letter of that definition in the space provided.

A
____ 1. abnegation
____ 2. abscond
____ 3. affidavit
____ 4. altercation
____ 5. battery
____ 6. bequest
____ 7. cause célèbre
____ 8. caveat emptor
____ 9. codicil
____ 10. contiguous
____ 11. contraband
____ 12. contumacious
____ 13. disenfranchise
____ 14. injunction
____ 15. jurisprudence

B
a. statement written under oath
b. a quarrel
c. illegal beating
d. touching
e. deprive of a privilege
f. famous law case
g. self-denial
h. system of laws
I. supplement
j. an order
k. let the buyer beware
l. gift specified in a will or testament
m. disobedient
n. forbidden merchandise
o. run away and hide

Answers are on page 215.

Philosophy and Logic

Does the *dogma* of a church have any relationship to its canons?

Why would a *utilitarian* reject "art for art's sake"?

Is a *syllogism* a foolish belief or a form of reasoning?

What is the ultimate goal of the *theosophists*?

What fallacy do the underprivileged see in *hedonism*?

---

aphorism
dogma
empirical
epistemology
eschatology
fallacy
hedonism
pragmatism
predestination
ratiocination
syllogism
teleology
tenet
theosophy
utilitarian

1. **aphorism** (af'-ə-riz'm)—a brief statement of a principle; a tersely phrased statement of a truth or opinion.
   a. *Aphorisms*, like proverbs, may sometimes seem contradictory, but the wise person knows what counsel a particular situation calls for.
   b. Speeches that string together a list of *aphorisms* betray a lack of creativity.

2. **dogma** (dôg'-mə, däg'-)—a system of principles or tenets as of a church; prescribed doctrine; an established opinion or belief. *Dogmas*, derived from the Greek *dokein*, "to seem good," are sometimes put forth without adequate grounds and arrogantly or vehemently proclaimed.
   a. Despite efforts at detente, communist *dogma* assumes the ultimate eradication of capitalism.
   b. Modern pedagogy is based on the *dogma* that every child is educable.

3. **empirical** (em-pir'-i-k'l)—guided by practical experience and not theoretical.
   a. Much medical lore has had an *empirical* origin—centuries of trial-and-error groping after remedies.
   b. It is safer to be *empirical* and practical in dealing with reality.

4. **epistemology** (i-pis-tə-möl'-ə-jē)—the division of philosophy that investigates the nature, origin, methods, and limits of human knowledge.
   a. According to *epistemology*, it is impossible to transcend the confines of one's own civilization.
   b. *Epistemology* differs from ontology in that the former is concerned with knowledge, the latter with being.

5. **eschatology** (es-kə-täl'-ə-jē)—the branch of theology that is concerned with the ultimate or last things—such as death, judgment, heaven, and hell.
   a. Medieval philosophers and theologians were hypnotized by a horrible *eschatology*.
   b. Our civilization has become increasingly indifferent to *eschatology*, and guilty of mistaking means for ends.

6. **fallacy** (fal'-ə-sē)—an idea or opinion founded on mistaken logic or perception. There are several types of logical *fallacies:* the fallacy of accident, of composition, of division, of the antecedent, and of the consequence.
   a. Among some ardent admirers of Shakespeare, the *fallacy* exists that the bard was superhuman.
   b. Magellan and other explorers disproved the popular *fallacy* that the world is flat.

7. **hedonism** (hēd'-'n-iz'm)—pursuit of or devotion to pleasure; the ethical doctrine that that which is pleasant or has pleasant consequences is intrinsically good. In psychology, *hedonism* refers to the doctrine that behavior is motivated by the desire for pleasure or the avoidance of pain.

    a.   The later Roman emperors were notorious for their *hedonism*.

    b.   In the way she chose and cast off friends, Margaret was a perfect example of selfish *hedonism*.

8.   **pragmatism** (prag'-mə-tiz'm)—the theory, developed by Charles S. Peirce and William James, that the meaning of a proposition or course of action lies in its observable consequences, and that the sum of these consequences constitutes its meaning; a method or tendency in the conduct of political affairs characterized by the rejection of theory and precedent, and by the use of practical means and expedients. A *pragmatic* person is practical and active rather than contemplative. He may also tend to be meddlesome and officious.

    a.   *Pragmatism* takes the position that whatever works is right.

    b.   Think tanks are a strange combination of *pragmatism* and idealism, not trying on the one hand to extract sunbeams from cucumbers, nor on the other hand to avoid pure speculation.

9.   **predestination** (prē-des-tə-nā'-shən)—the doctrine that God has foreordained whatever comes to pass, especially the salvation or damnation of individual souls.

    a.   Theologians have long struggled with the apparent contradiction between *predestination* and man's freedom of will.

    b.   It is easy to attribute one's lack of ambition or success to some act of *predestination*, but there are many examples to prove to us that we are the "masters of our fate."

10.   **ratiocination** (rash-ē-os-ə-nā'-shən)—the act of reasoning methodically or logically.

    a.   *Ratiocination* works in the cold light of reason, leaving no room for emotions and feelings.

    b.   Edgar Allan Poe's detective stories are masterpieces of *ratiocination*.

11.   **syllogism** (sil'-ə-jiz'm)—in logic, a form of deductive reasoning consisting of a major premise (all men are foolish), a minor premise (Smith is a man), and a conclusion (therefore, Smith is foolish); a subtle or specious piece of reasoning. Opposed to *syllogistic* reasoning is inductive reasoning, known as the scientific method, which reasons from a part to the whole, from the particular to the general, or from the individual to the universal.

    a.   A *syllogism* based on a false premise will of course lead to a mistaken conclusion.

    b.   Francis Bacon, known as the father of the scientific method, rejected *syllogisms* in favor of the procedure of gathering sufficient facts through experiment before formulating a general principle by which to test further data.

12.   **teleology** (tel-ē-äl'-ə-jē)—the doctrine that final causes exist; design, purpose, or utility as an explanation of any natural phenomenon. In philosophy, *teleology* looks upon natural processes as determined by the design of a divine Providence rather than as purely mechanical determinism.

    a.   Darwinism and *teleology* both take into account design and utility in natural development but differ on whether this design is a temporal accident or an act of God.

    b.   In ethics, *teleology* evaluates human conduct in relation to the end it serves; hence, behavior which has a beneficial purpose would be considered good.

13.   **tenet** (ten'-it)—an opinion or doctrine held to be true.

    a.   Observation and deduction are the two great *tenets* of the physical sciences.

    b. Political *tenets* are easily abandoned when the mood of the people changes.

14. **theosophy** (thē-äs'-ə-fē)—a system of philosophy or religion that proposes to establish direct, mystical contact with divine principles through contemplation or revelation. The doctrines of the modern Theosophical Societies incorporate elements of Buddhism and Brahmanism.
    a. As a believer in *theosophy,* the mahatma claimed superior wisdom and insight into the mastery of nature.
    b. Despite the U.N. and similar world-unifying attempts, we are far from attaining universal brotherhood, which is the goal of *theosophy.*

15. **utilitarian** (yoo-til-ə-ter'-ē-ən)—stressing the value of practical over aesthetic values. The theory of *utilitarianism,* proposed by Jeremy Bentham and John Stewart Mill, held that all moral, social, or political action should be directed toward achieving the greatest good for the greatest number of people.
    a. The original *utilitarians* believed that each individual was the best judge of his own welfare.
    b. Love of truth for its own sake is becoming rare in this hasty, *utilitarian* age.

EXERCISES

I. Which Word Comes to Mind?

In each of the following, read the statement, then circle the word that comes to mind.

1. How do we know what we know?

      (eschatology, epistemology, pragmatism)

2. If *A* is *B* and *B* is *C,* then *A* is *C*

      (fallacy, dogma, syllogism)

3. Sherlock Holmes is a prime example

      (tenet, ratiocination, teleology)

4. Don't do it; it might hurt

      (hedonism, aphorism, theosophy)

5. Daniel and Pearl forever

      (empirical, utilitarian, predestination)

II. True or False?

In the space provided, indicate whether each statement is true or false.

_____ 1. A *pragmatist* and an *empiricist* are both more concerned with results than theories.
_____ 2. *Eschatology* is deeply involved with daily rituals.
_____ 3. The explanation for the lion's mane, the elephant's trunk, the leopard's spots falls in the province of *teleology.*
_____ 4. A *tenet* is one of the ten basic principles of faith.
_____ 5. *Aphorism* is the belief that natural phenomena can be understood only by a study of original causes.

III. Find the Impostor

Find and circle the one word in each line that is not related to the other three.

1. eschatology	teleology	utilitarian	predestination
2. document	dogma	tenet	doctrine
3. pragmatic	experiential	romantic	empirical
4. laconic	aphoristic	pointed	conjectural
5. hedonism	affliction	malaise	paroxysm

IV. Cryptogram

The first letters of each of the "words" below, when arranged in the proper order, spell out a vocabulary word from this lesson. The same is true for the second, third, and fourth letters. Find the four words. Hint: The initial letters of the words are in ETTS.

MHEY	LYYM	IOEL
RSOO	AHGS	IOLG
CPOI	ETTS	PELL

_____

_____

_____

_____

V. Matching

Match the Word in column A with its correct definition in column B by writing the letter of that definition in the space provided.

	A		B
____	1. aphorism	a.	seek pleasure, avoid pain
____	2. dogma	b.	fate
____	3. empirical	c.	giving greatest happiness for most people
____	4. epistemology	d.	brief statement of principle
____	5. eschatology	e.	deductive reasoning
____	6. fallacy	f.	false notion
____	7. hedonism	g.	study associated with mysticism
____	8. pragmatism	h.	based on observation
____	9. predestination	i.	belief in final causes
____	10. ratiocination	j.	study of last things
____	11. syllogism	k.	logical reasoning
____	12. teleology	l.	prescribed doctrine
____	13. tenet	m.	theory that results, not procedure, give meaning
____	14. theosophy	n.	belief
____	15. utilitarian	o.	study of the nature of knowledge

Answers are on page 215.

Beliefs and Religion

Is a *mantra* a hymn, a sacred object, or a clothing worm?

What do an *apostate,* an *infidel,* and a *blasphemer* have in common?

Is *apotheosis* a theory, a religious chant, or a glorification?

How does an *agnostic* differ from an atheist?

Does *theodicy* deal with a pilgrimage, the existence of evil, or the revelations in the Bible?

---

agnostic
apocalyptic
apocryphal
apostate
apotheosis
benediction
blasphemy
deist
infidel
mantra
ontology
pantheism
sacrilegious
syncretism
theodicy

1. **agnostic** (ag-näs′-tik)—a thinker who disclaims any knowledge of God. The agnostic does not deny God but denies the possibility of knowing Him.
   a. The *agnostic* position is midway between the atheist and the believer.
   b. The impassioned speaker claimed that faith, reason, and experience had shattered his *agnostic* beliefs.

2. **apocalyptic** (ə-päk-ə-lip′-tik)—pertaining to a revelation; foretelling imminent disaster and total destruction. *Apocalypse* refers to the last books of the New Testament.
   a. A SALT agreement with Russia is vital in order to avoid the *apocalyptic* horrors of nuclear war.
   b. Books with an *apocalyptic* view of life find many readers in an age of violence.

3. **apocryphal** (ə-päk′-rə-f′l)—of questionable authority or authenticity; false or counterfeit. The *Apocrypha* includes the 14 books of the Septuagint found in the Vulgate but considered uncanonical by the Protestants because they are not part of the Hebrew Scriptures.
   a. The bookseller was careful to point out which works were regarded as authentic and which were *apocryphal.*
   b. *The Wisdom of Ben Sira,* although considered *apocryphal,* should be studied for its wisdom and good counsel.

4. **apostate** (ə-päs′-tāt)—one who forsakes his faith or principles.
   a. The Church excommunicated all *apostates* who professed the radically new doctrine.
   b. O'Connor's statement of support for the Republican nominee was taken to mean that he had become an *apostate* from his own party.

5. **apotheosis** (ə-päth-ē-ō′-sis)—deification; an exalted or glorified ideal.
   a. Elvis Presley was considered the *apotheosis* of the age of Rock and Roll.
   b. In their bestial and brutal policies, the Nazis reached the *apotheosis* of barbarism.

6. **benediction** (ben-ə-dik′-shən)—a blessing; an invocation of divine blessing, usually at the end of a religious service. A newly married man is called a *benedict,* suggesting that marriage brings to a bachelor many blessings.
   a. The gentle rain brought its *benediction* to the parched fields.
   b. His parents' *benediction* ringing in his ears, the young student departed for his first year in college.

7. **blasphemy** (blas′-fə-mē)—any irreverent or impious act or utterance.
   a. The outraged judge branded the witness's language an act of *blasphemy.*
   b. It is not *blasphemy* to question the motives of high officials.

8. **deist** (dē'-ist)—believer in the existence of God as the creator of the universe who after setting it in motion abandoned it, assumed no control over life, exerted no influence on natural phenomena, and gave no supernatural revelation. *Deism* is a natural religion based on human reason and morality.
   a. The *deist* views the world much like a giant clock that God wound up and now allows to run by itself.
   b. *Deistic* principles impose a sense of morality on the human race, but stop short of prescribing rituals and ceremonies.

9. **infidel** (in'-fə-d'l)—a person who does not believe in any religion; among Christians or Muslims, one who does not accept their particular beliefs. The word *infidelity* denotes unfaithfulness to moral or marital obligations.
   a. Those deemed *infidels* by the Inquisition were persecuted and often burned at the stake.
   b. In an atmosphere of tolerance and freedom from bigotry, the so-called *infidel* can still retain a position of dignity.

10. **mantra** (man'-trə)—a mystical formula of invocation or incantation in Hinduism and Buddhism. The word comes from *mens,* the Latin word meaning "mind," and the ancient Sanskrit word for "sacred counsel" or "formula."
    a. Upon entering the temple grounds, we heard the strange rhythms of the *mantra* coming from the inner chambers.
    b. His face suffused with serenity, the priest intoned the *mantra* as the worshippers listened respectfully.

11. **ontology** (än-täl'-ə-jē)—the branch of philosophy dealing with the nature of being.
    a. The *ontological* argument for a Supreme Being asserts that as existence is a perfection and as God is described as the most perfect Being, it follows that God must exist.
    b. *Ontology* is concerned not with material or spiritual existence but with the investigation of what constitutes reality or ultimate substance.

12. **pantheism** (pan'-thē-iz'm)—the doctrine that the universe, conceived of as a whole, is God.
    a. According to *pantheism,* there is no God but the combined forces and laws that are manifested in the existing universe.
    b. Since *pantheism* tends to depersonalize God, identifying the Deity instead with nature, it could accommodate itself to and tolerate the worship of all gods at certain periods in the Roman Empire.

13. **sacrilegious** (sak-rə-li'-jəs)—disrespectful or irreverent toward anything regarded as sacred. The term is derived from the Latin *sacrilegium,* "one who steals sacred things," which of course is one form of *sacrilege.*
    a. The *sacrilegious* thieves stole the $500 that had been collected for charity.
    b. The change from Latin to the vernacular in church services as well as the relaxation of certain rules for the clergy has been regarded as *sacrilegious* by some traditionalists.

14. **syncretism** (sin'-krə-tiz'm)—the attempt or tendency to combine or reconcile differing beliefs, as in philosophy or religion. It comes from the Greek *syr* ("together") and *kret* ("Cretan"), and refers to the uniting of Cretan cities against a common enemy.
    a. While *syncretism* is usually a healthy development, it can lead to an eclecticism that is illogical and inconsistent.
    b. In the field of linguistics, the use of *was* for both singular and plural in nonstandard English is an example of *syncretism.*

15. **theodicy** (thē-ǎd′-ə-sē)—a vindication of divine justice in the face of the existence of evil. *Theodicee* was the title of a work by Leibnitz in 1710. The word combines the Greek roots for "god" and "judgment."
   a. One of the arguments advanced for *theodicy* is that humans have only a limited view of life, whereas God sees everything.
   b. Theologians and philosophers, grappling with the *theodician* problem of the existence of evil in a world created by a Perfect Being, have asserted that good would not be recognizable without evil.

EXERCISES

I. Which Word Comes to Mind?

In each of the following, read the statement, then circle the word that comes to mind.

1. In the Middle Ages this would have brought the harshest punishment

   (ontology,   blasphemy,   apocryphal)

2. God and nature are synonymous

   (benediction,   pantheism,   apocalyptic)

3. This person could be a Christian, Muslim, or Jew, depending on what you are

   (infidel,   mantra,   apotheosis)

4. An attempt to explain why God permitted the rise of Hitlerism

   (theodicy,   apostate,   sacrilegious)

5. If you can't beat them, join them

   (agnostic,   syncretism,   deist)

II. True or False?

In the space provided, indicate whether each statement is true or false.

_____ 1. The *apocryphal* writings have been universally accepted as part of the Bible.
_____ 2. An *apostate* is one who has changed his religious beliefs.
_____ 3. *Pantheists* emphasize the importance of religious services.
_____ 4. The *sacrilegious* person holds a place of honor in the community of believers.
_____ 5. The *apocalyptic* view is definitely pessimistic.

III. Synonyms or Antonyms

Find and circle the two words on each line that are either synonyms or antonyms.

1. apostate	apocryphal	heretic	biblical
2. blasphemous	apotheosis	degradation	occult
3. infidel	mantra	religion	invocation
4. canonical	apocryphal	apocalyptic	orthodox
5. laity	benediction	denominational	anathema

IV. Anagrams

In each of the following, use the letters of the vocabulary words to form the new words whose meanings are given. In one case, you will have to add a letter.

1. syncretism = *sir* and *clipped form of regulate* _____
2. sacrilegious + n = *instruction in boating* _____
3. theodicy = *scold* and *plaything* _____
4. apotheosis = *circular band* and *afternoon nap* _____
5. agnostic = *money* and *markers* _____

V. Matching

Match the word in column A with its correct definition in column B by writing the letter of that definition in the space provided.

A	B
____ 1. agnostic	a. profanity
____ 2. apocalyptic	b. prophetic
____ 3. apocryphal	c. one who doesn't know God
____ 4. apostate	d. atheist
____ 5. apotheosis	e. one who forsakes his faith
____ 6. benediction	f. mystical incantation
____ 7. blasphemy	g. belief that God is the universe
____ 8. deist	h. questionable or fictitious
____ 9. infidel	i. blessing
____ 10. mantra	j. vindication of God
____ 11. ontology	k. deification
____ 12. pantheism	l. fusion
____ 13. sacrilegious	m. one who believes God has a hands-off policy toward life
____ 14. syncretism	n. impious
____ 15. theodicy	o. the study of the nature of reality

Answers are on pages 215–216.

Review

A. The Out-of-Place Word

In each of the following groups, find and circle the one vocabulary word that is out of place. You should be able to explain what the other three words have in common.

1. mellifluous, beguile, roister, assuage
2. palatable, renascent, comestible, regale
3. apotheosis, infidel, blasphemy, sacrilegious
4. injunction, countermand, mantra, gainsay
5. deist, pantheism, theosophy, paralipsis
6. benediction, apostate, anarchist, pharisaical
7. safari, wanderlust, trek, hegira
8. fallacy, malapropism, syncretism, pleonasm
9. guffaw, paradigm, onomatopoeia, guttural
10. censure, muckraker, harangue, aspersion

B. Rearranging Words

Rearrange the following groups of words using the first letter of each word to spell out one of the words in this unit.

1. fallacy, recession, abnegation, abscond, imperialism, semantics

_____

2. oligarchy, deist, gastronomic, anarchist, metonymy

_____

3. squib, insouciance, cause célèbre, metaphor, subsistence, hedonism

_____

4. eschatology, risible, theosophy, suffrage, anarchist, predestination

_____

5. epistemology, landmark, subversion, mellifluous, infidel, injunction

_____

C. Making the Right Connection

In each of the following, which word best describes the person or thing named? Circle the correct answer.

1. A language expert

(mantra, polyglot, oxymoron, demagogue)

2. Light entertainment

(euphoria, peonage, divertissement, portmanteau)

3. A government representative

(plenipotentiary, votary, schism, partisan)

4. Hotel accommodations

(apostate,   concierge,   tenet,   bureaucracy)

5. A food expert

(codicil,   teleology,   gourmand,   safari)

6. Property boundaries

(caveat emptor,   dalliance,   landmark,   condiment)

7. A way to slake your thirst

(squib,   panegyric,   tandem,   viands)

8. Someone who would appreciate your hospitality

(argot,   wayfarer,   cuisine,   surrogate)

9. Someone to discredit your opponent

(muckraker,   gobbledegook,   refection,   bourgeois)

10. A substitute

(japery,   antipodal,   proxy,   threnody)

D. Making Pairs

From the group below, find the pairs of words that have something in common and record them in the spaces provided. You should be able to find ten such pairs. List them numerically, using the same number for each pair.

simile _____	metonymy _____	waggish _____	codicil _____
repast _____	tenet _____	utilitarian _____	canon _____
pragmatism _____	refection _____	surrogate _____	badinage _____
jargon _____	oligarchy _____	bequest _____	synechdoche _____
metaphor _____	argot _____	proxy _____	totalitarian _____

C. Cliché Time

Which of the words from this unit fit into the following familiar expressions? Choose the correct word from the choices given and record it in the space provided.

1. Don't cast any _____ .

(semantics,   aspersions,   viands,   braggadocio)

2. In the _____ of the underworld

(censure,   bathos,   jargon,   cuisine)

3. To order ——————

(harangue,   squib,   japery,   à la carte)

4. A —————— delight

(pharisaical,   culinary,   martial,   contiguous)

5. The basic —————— of his argument

(subsistence,   fallacy,   affidavit,   hustings)

6. The —————— seized by the customs inspector

(contraband,   paradigm,   bathos,   mantra)

7. Fed up with government ——————

(peonage,   subversion,   bureaucracy,   votary)

8. Vote by ——————

(tandem,   ethos,   proxy,   bequest)

9. With —————— guile

(apocryphal,   piquant,   apocalyptic,   Machiavellian)

10. To —————— her grief

(assuage,   beguile,   censure,   countermand)

F. Find the Words

Somewhere in this box of letters, reading up, down, across, or diagonally, twenty-two vocabulary words that were taught in this lesson are hidden. As you locate each one, draw a circle around it.

C	T	H	E	O	D	I	C	Y	C	I	S
E	O	R	E	G	A	L	E	I	A	A	S
N	V	N	T	E	N	E	T	N	C	Q	N
S	O	H	T	A	B	N	N	R	U	K	O
U	J	L	R	U	A	A	I	I	E	A	G
R	A	S	S	D	M	L	B	R	T	I	R
E	P	K	M	O	E	A	T	O	G	R	A
L	E	P	S	G	H	I	C	G	W	O	J
I	R	R	I	M	B	T	S	I	C	H	L
M	Y	O	H	A	J	P	E	T	O	P	F
I	U	X	C	M	A	N	T	R	A	U	H
S	G	Y	S	C	I	T	N	A	M	E	S

Answers are on page 216.

Final Review Test — SAT Style

For each of the fifty questions below, choose the best answer and blacken the corresponding space. Each question consists of a capitalized word, followed by five choices. Pick the word or phrase that is most nearly OPPOSITE in meaning to the word in capital letters. Since some of the answers are fairly close in meaning, consider all the choices before deciding which is best.

Example

TALL: (A) huge (B) high (C) short (D) sad (E) rich   Ⓐ Ⓑ ● Ⓓ Ⓔ

1. CONTUMACIOUS: (A) obedient (B) sinful (C) considerate (D) tearful (E) stiff
   1. Ⓐ Ⓑ Ⓒ Ⓓ Ⓔ

2. QUIXOTIC: (A) lively (B) urbane (C) adventurous (D) warlike (E) practical
   2. Ⓐ Ⓑ Ⓒ Ⓓ Ⓔ

3. SATURNINE: (A) obvious (B) youthful (C) talented (D) vengeful (E) cheerful
   3. Ⓐ Ⓑ Ⓒ Ⓓ Ⓔ

4. TAWDRY: (A) sweet (B) sour (C) tasteful (D) trustworthy (E) sleepy
   4. Ⓐ Ⓑ Ⓒ Ⓓ Ⓔ

5. BELLICOSE: (A) ancient (B) peaceful (C) slow (D) inquisitive (E) trembling
   5. Ⓐ Ⓑ Ⓒ Ⓓ Ⓔ

6. COMPLAISANT: (A) impolite (B) slick (C) rugged (D) hesitating (E) rare
   6. Ⓐ Ⓑ Ⓒ Ⓓ Ⓔ

7. CONVIVIAL: (A) ruthless (B) hostile (C) studious (D) nervy (E) tardy
   7. Ⓐ Ⓑ Ⓒ Ⓓ Ⓔ

8. CRAVEN: (A) brave (B) dull (C) infallible (D) original (E) succinct
   8. Ⓐ Ⓑ Ⓒ Ⓓ Ⓔ

9. LACHRYMOSE: (A) tortured (B) unwise (C) ingenious (D) intolerant (E) jolly
   9. Ⓐ Ⓑ Ⓒ Ⓓ Ⓔ

10. CORNUCOPIA: (A) foot ailment (B) sadness (C) ship's mast (D) shortage (E) doldrums
    10. Ⓐ Ⓑ Ⓒ Ⓓ Ⓔ

11. HERCULEAN: (A) unintelligible (B) puny (C) mythical (D) furtive (E) intolerable
    11. Ⓐ Ⓑ Ⓒ Ⓓ Ⓔ

12. EXTROVERT: (A) imitator (B) pious person (C) braggart (D) lout (E) withdrawn person
    12. Ⓐ Ⓑ Ⓒ Ⓓ Ⓔ

13. RENEGADE: (A) partisan (B) recluse (C) fugitive (D) loyalist (E) veteran
    13. Ⓐ Ⓑ Ⓒ Ⓓ Ⓔ

14. ANTEBELLUM: (A) serene   (B) post war   (C) incorruptible
(D) previous   (E) subsequent   14. Ⓐ Ⓑ Ⓒ Ⓓ Ⓔ

15. DIURNAL: (A) investigative   (B) somber   (C) nightly
(D) unconditional   (E) chaotic   15. Ⓐ Ⓑ Ⓒ Ⓓ Ⓔ

16. EON: (A) fleeting moment   (B) mortal thing   (C) light year
(D) land mass   (E) oration   16. Ⓐ Ⓑ Ⓒ Ⓓ Ⓔ

17. EPHEMERAL: (A) eroded   (B) permanent   (C) blasé   (D) robust
(E) repetitious   17. Ⓐ Ⓑ Ⓒ Ⓓ Ⓔ

18. SVELTE: (A) resistant   (B) obese   (C) humid   (D) curved
(E) inane   18. Ⓐ Ⓑ Ⓒ Ⓓ Ⓔ

19. COMATOSE: (A) lively   (B) stubborn   (C) rugged   (D) tenacious
(E) dour   19. Ⓐ Ⓑ Ⓒ Ⓓ Ⓔ

20. DICHOTOMY: (A) degree   (B) advice   (C) inversion
(D) harmony   (E) opening   20. Ⓐ Ⓑ Ⓒ Ⓓ Ⓔ

21. EXHUME: (A) invent   (B) nurture   (C) cover up   (D) reject
(E) tranquilize   21. Ⓐ Ⓑ Ⓒ Ⓓ Ⓔ

22. CIRCUMSPECT: (A) sightless   (B) monstrous   (C) troublesome
(D) obtuse   (E) careless   22. Ⓐ Ⓑ Ⓒ Ⓓ Ⓔ

23. DEMURE: (A) imaginative   (B) fruitful   (C) brash   (D) sinister
(E) vocal   23. Ⓐ Ⓑ Ⓒ Ⓓ Ⓔ

24. FLACCID: (A) strong   (B) stern   (C) severe   (D) sacrificial
(E) sacred   24. Ⓐ Ⓑ Ⓒ Ⓓ Ⓔ

25. FLIPPANT: (A) solemn   (B) stable   (C) deceitful   (D) corrosive
(E) two-faced   25. Ⓐ Ⓑ Ⓒ Ⓓ Ⓔ

26. FLORID: (A) ambiguous   (B) pale   (C) businesslike   (D) doubtful
(E) cool   26. Ⓐ Ⓑ Ⓒ Ⓓ Ⓔ

27. GLABROUS: (A) objectionable   (B) weighty   (C) imperceptible
(D) hairy   (E) devious   27. Ⓐ Ⓑ Ⓒ Ⓓ Ⓔ

28. INTRANSIGENT: (A) beneficial   (B) rotund   (C) malicious
(D) flexible   (E) morose   28. Ⓐ Ⓑ Ⓒ Ⓓ Ⓔ

29. INSCRUTABLE: (A) understandable   (B) vicious   (C) salient
(D) concerned   (E) ambitious   29. Ⓐ Ⓑ Ⓒ Ⓓ Ⓔ

30. MEGALOPOLIS: (A) unknown locale   (B) plateau   (C) slope
(D) deserted area   (E) small nation   30. Ⓐ Ⓑ Ⓒ Ⓓ Ⓔ

31. DRACONIAN: (A) tyrannical   (B) mild   (C) topical   (D) out of tune
(E) fabulously wealthy   31. Ⓐ Ⓑ Ⓒ Ⓓ Ⓔ

32. LICENTIOUS: (A) surreptitious   (B) prudish   (C) illegal
    (D) savage   (E) grasping

32. Ⓐ Ⓑ Ⓒ Ⓓ Ⓔ

33. MERETRICIOUS: (A) unworthy   (B) thoughtful   (C) forgiving
    (D) logical   (E) plain

33. Ⓐ Ⓑ Ⓒ Ⓓ Ⓔ

34. MUTABLE: (A) dull   (B) constant   (C) rosy   (D) proud
    (E) horrid

34. Ⓐ Ⓑ Ⓒ Ⓓ Ⓔ

35. NOXIOUS: (A) wholesome   (B) rusty   (C) gentle   (D) abrasive
    (E) meddlesome

35. Ⓐ Ⓑ Ⓒ Ⓓ Ⓔ

36. PUSILLANIMOUS: (A) approving   (B) carping   (C) brave
    (D) receptive   (E) glowing

36. Ⓐ Ⓑ Ⓒ Ⓓ Ⓔ

37. IMMATERIAL: (A) relevant   (B) thin   (C) suspicious   (D) moot
    (E) temporary

37. Ⓐ Ⓑ Ⓒ Ⓓ Ⓔ

38. GAUCHE: (A) critical   (B) tactful   (C) vehement
    (D) commonplace   (E) onerous

38. Ⓐ Ⓑ Ⓒ Ⓓ Ⓔ

39. ASKEW: (A) circuitous   (B) rigid   (C) contemplative   (D) straight
    (E) timorous

39. Ⓐ Ⓑ Ⓒ Ⓓ Ⓔ

40. CHARY: (A) unscrupulous   (B) cheap   (C) careless   (D) willful
    (E) bombastic

40. Ⓐ Ⓑ Ⓒ Ⓓ Ⓔ

41. PUERILE: (A) mature   (B) antiquarian   (C) ghastly   (D) significant
    (E) enraged

41. Ⓐ Ⓑ Ⓒ Ⓓ Ⓔ

42. SEDULOUS: (A) terminal   (B) lavish   (C) corpulent   (D) lazy
    (E) distraught

42. Ⓐ Ⓑ Ⓒ Ⓓ Ⓔ

43. AD HOC: (A) litigious   (B) sub rosa   (C) truncated   (D) of
    moderate means   (E) permanently established

43. Ⓐ Ⓑ Ⓒ Ⓓ Ⓔ

44. DILATORY: (A) prompt   (B) constructive   (C) hopeful
    (D) contracted   (E) skeptical

44. Ⓐ Ⓑ Ⓒ Ⓓ Ⓔ

45. GENTEEL: (A) profitable   (B) irreligious   (C) charitable
    (D) coarse   (E) synthetic

45. Ⓐ Ⓑ Ⓒ Ⓓ Ⓔ

46. JOCUND: (A) classical   (B) informed   (C) disagreeable
    (D) solitary   (E) vengeful

46. Ⓐ Ⓑ Ⓒ Ⓓ Ⓔ

47. LOQUACIOUS: (A) careless with words   (B) benevolent   (C) willing
    to negotiate   (D) moody   (E) silent

47. Ⓐ Ⓑ Ⓒ Ⓓ Ⓔ

48. TENUOUS: (A) substantial   (B) beyond doubt   (C) modest
    (D) threatening   (E) deaf to all pleas

48. Ⓐ Ⓑ Ⓒ Ⓓ Ⓔ

49. CENSURE: (A) trial   (B) approval   (C) lack of concern
    (D) critique   (E) evaluation

49. Ⓐ Ⓑ Ⓒ Ⓓ Ⓔ

50. ANTEDILUVIAN: (A) decrepit   (B) restored   (C) modern
    (D) lacking in culture   (E) ambulatory

50. Ⓐ Ⓑ Ⓒ Ⓓ Ⓔ

Answers are on page 216.

ANSWERS TO EXERCISES

Lesson 1: Words from Proper Names

I. 1. philippic   2. jingoism   3. maverick   4. quixotic   5. procrustean

II. 1.T 2.T 3.F 4.T 5.F

III.

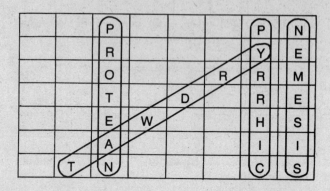

IV. *Canterbury Tales*

V. 1. c   6. n   11. o
    2. j   7. m   12. f
    3. d   8. b   13. a
    4. g   9. l   14. h
    5. i   10. e   15. k

Lesson 2: Appearances and Attitudes (I)

I. 1. contrite 2. churlish 3. neurasthenic 4. dyspeptic 5. bilious

II. 1. F 2. T 3. T 4. T 5. F

III.

IV. tawdry

V. 1. d   6. n   11. b
    2. h   7. c   12. k
    3. o   8. l   13. g
    4. m   9. j   14. i
    5. a   10. f   15. e

Lesson 3: Words About Groups

I. 1. rapprochement 2. caste 3. camaraderie 4. hobnob 5. ecumenical

II. 1. F 2. T 3. T 4. T 5. T

III.

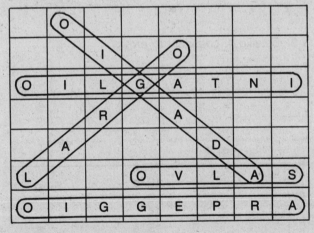

IV. bilious

V.
1. d	6. j	11. e
2. o	7. f	12. b
3. l	8. g	13. c
4. h	9. n	14. i
5. m	10. k	15. a

Lesson 4: Sounds Italian

I. 1. largo 2. salvo 3. imbroglio 4. bravura 5. staccato

II. 1. F 2. T 3. F 4. T 5. T

III.

IV. captious

V.
1. f	6. c	11. g
2. 1	7. k	12. j
3. o	8. n	13. i
4. a	9. b	14. d
5. h	10. e	15. m

Lesson 5: Job and Professions

I.   1. osteopath   2. graphologist   3. entomologist   4. dermatologist   5. ornithologist

II.   1. T   2. F   3. T   4. T   5. F

III.

Y	R	A	D	I	P	A	L
			B				
			E				
			A				
			D				
			L				
A	L	I	E	N	I	S	T

IV.   adagio

V.
1. d	6. j	11. g
2. o	7. b	12. i
3. h	8. c	13. k
4. a	9. l	14. n
5. f	10. e	15. m

Lesson 6: Mythology (I)

I.   1. erotic   2. cornucopia   3. iridescent   4. herculean   5. bacchanal

II.   1. T   2. T   3. F   4. T   5. F

III.   1. dramatic 2. baccalaureate 3. metallic 4. corpulent 5. erotic

IV.   1. Bacchus or Dionysus
2. Hermes or Mercury
3. Hercules
4. Eros or Cupid
5. Iris

V.
1. m	6. o	11. k
2. a	7. h	12. c
3. j	8. f	13. d
4. g	9. b	14. l
5. n	10. i	15. e

Lesson 7: Social Sciences

I.   1. euthanasia   2. epidemiology   3. aberrant   4. demography   5. trauma

II.   1. F   2. F   3. T   4. F   5. T

III.

IV.   odyssey

V.   1. h   6. k   11. j
     2. c   7. a   12. e
     3. g   8. m   13. f
     4. o   9. b   14. l
     5. n   10. d   15. i

Lesson 8: From Sunny Spain

I.   1. torero   2. mañana   3. machismo   4. bonanza   5. desperado

II.   1. T   2. T   3. T   4. T   5. F

III.

IV.   trauma

V.   1. j   6. m   11. 1
     2. a   7. c   12. g
     3. f   8. d   13. i
     4. b   9. n   14. e
     5. o   10. k   15. h

Lesson 9: Time on Our Hands

I.   1. antediluvian   2. anachronism   3. atavism   4. biennial   5. augury

II.   1. T   2. T   3. F   4. T   5. T

III.

L	M	S	I	V	A	T	A
A			N		N		Y
N		E	R	O	C	S	R
R		P	E		N		U
U		O			A		G
I		C					U
D		H					A

IV.   barrio

V. 1. f   6. o   11. a
    2. h   7. l   12. m
    3. n   8. e   13. j
    4. b   9. k   14. c
    5. d   10. i   15. g

Lesson 10: Short but Challenging Words

I. 1. eke   2. mete   3. quail   4. tryst   5. bane

II. 1. F   2. F   3. T   4. T   5. F

III. 1. O   2. S   3. U   4. S   5. O

IV. 1. meek   2. meter   3. motor   4. stele   5. Eban

V. 1. d   6. o   11. l
    2. h   7. i   12. n
    3. j   8. m   13. g
    4. c   9. k   14. e
    5. f   10. a   15. b

Unit I Review (Lessons 1–10)

A. 1. nemesis   2. thrall   3. philippic   4. odyssey   5. anachronism
    6. farrier   7. echelon   8. siesta   9. palladium   10. lapidary

B. 1. jingoist   2. adagio   3. cortege   4. lariat   5. solecism

C. 1. osteopath   2. graphologist   3. tryst   4. cabal   5. dermatologist

D. lothario-philanderer   acidulous-dyspeptic
    augury-Cassandra   esprit de corps-camaraderie
    renegade-desperado   herculean-protean
    ornithologist-phoenix   elite-Olympian
    libretto-contralto   bacchanal-sybarite

E. 1. bane   2. crescendo   3. Pyrrhic   4. staccato   5. elite

F.

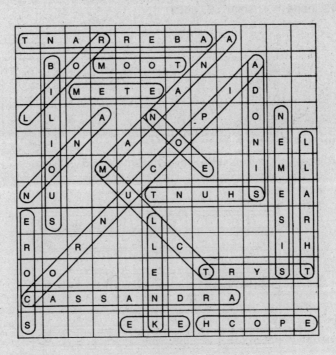

Lesson 11: Medical Science

I. 1. simian   2. carcinogen   3. mastectomy   4. comatose   5. arteriosclerosis

II. 1. T   2. T   3. F   4. T   5. T

III.

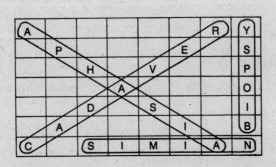

IV. bane, eke

V. 1. n   6. j   11. a
    2. k   7. o   12. m
    3. f   8. h   13. d
    4. e   9. b   14. g
    5. l   10. i   15. c

Lesson 12: Animal World

I. 1. taurine   2. vulpine   3. ovine   4. lupine   5. hircine

II. 1. T   2. F   3. T   4. F   5. T

III. 1. equity   2. feline   3. vexing   4. terrain   5. angular

IV. 1. risen   2. nix   3. bone   4. chin   5. saran

V. 1. m   6. j   11. i
    2. h   7. c   12. k
    3. e   8. n   13. d
    4. o   9. g   14. f
    5. a   10. b   15. l

Lesson 13: Countdown—Words with Numbers

I. 1. dichotomy   2. protocol   3. millennium   4. penultimate   5. nihilism

II. 1. F   2. T   3. F   4. T   5. T

III.

L	O	C	O	T	O	R	P
N	I	H	I	L	I	S	M
D	E	C	I	M	A	T	E
P	R	I	M	E	V	A	L
N	I	A	R	T	A	U	Q

IV. feline

V. 1. k   6. f   11. c
    2. j   7. i   12. n
    3. a   8. h   13. e
    4. b   9. d   14. g
    5. l   10. m   15. o

Lesson 14: Legal Language (I)

I. 1. intestate   2. deposition   3. appellate   4. perjury   5. incommunicado

II. protean

III. 1. F   2. F   3. T   4. T   5. T

IV. 1. d   6. h   11. o
     2. k   7. l   12. m
     3. i   8. n   13. e
     4. a   9. g   14. c
     5. j   10. b   15. f

V. COLLUSION (Intervening letters alternate, first one, then two)
    LIEN (The intervening letters of the first word)
    TRIBUNAL (The remaining intervening letters)

Lesson 15: Appearances and Attitudes (II)

I. 1. circumspect   2. imperious   3. intractable   4. flippant   5. demure

II. 1. T   2. F   3. F   4. T   5. T

III.

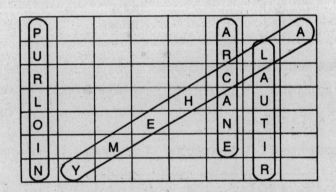

IV.   grandee

V.   1. f
     2. a
     3. o
     4. d
     5. k

6. c
7. e
8. n
9. h
10. j

11. m
12. b
13. g
14. i
15. l

Lesson 16: Mystery and the Occult

I.   1. shamus   2. soothsayer   3. pallor   4. purloin   5. polygraph

II.   1. F   2. F   3. T   4. T   5. T

III.

IV.   beadle

V.   1. g
     2. a
     3. d
     4. f
     5. h

6. k
7. i
8. m
9. o
10. e

11. b
12. j
13. l
14. n
15. c

Lesson 17: Size and Shape (I)

I.   1. infinitesimal   2. megalopolis   3. minimize   4. peccadillo   5. titanic

II.   1. F   2. F   3. F   4. F   5. F

III.   1. infinitesimal—titanic (A)
       2. swarming—teeming (S)
       3. amplitude—range (S)

4. picayune—unbiased (A)
5. exaggerate—minimize (A)

IV. palatial (first letter of each line)
minimize (second letter of each line)
picayune (third letter)
minutiae (fourth letter)
titanic (fifth letter)
teeming (sixth letter)
soupçon (seventh letter)

V. 1. c   6. b   11. a
2. i   7. d   12. e
3. o   8. k   13. g
4. f   9. m   14. h
5. j   10. l   15. n

Lesson 18: Words with Tales Attached

I. 1. proletariat   2. ostracism   3. draconian   4. epicurean   5. accolade

II. 1. F   2. T   3. F   4. F   5. F

III. 1. O   2. S   3. U   4. U   5. S

IV. knell

V. 1. n   6. k   11. a
2. c   7. o   12. f
3. b   8. g   13. d
4. e   9. h   14. l
5. i   10. j   15. m

Lesson 19: Of Loves and Fears and Hates

I. 1. hydrophobia   2. acrophobia   3. misogynist   4. triskaidekaphobia   5. xenophobe

II. 1. F   2. F   3. T   4. T   5. F

III. 1. xenophilia   2. philanthropy   3. bibliophobia   4. acrophilia   5. Francotriskaidekaphilia

IV.

O	I	L	B	I	B
O	R	D	Y	H	
N	C				
E	A				
X					

V. 1. j   6. g   11. b
2. e   7. h   12. i
3. o   8. n   13. m
4. a   9. l   14. f
5. c   10. d   15. k

Lesson 20: Science—"Ology" Words

I. 1. ecology   2. gerontology   3. necrology   4. paleontology   5. speleology

II. 1. T   2. T   3. F   4. F   5. F

III. 1. No   2. Yes   3. No   4. Yes   5. No   6. Yes   7. Yes   8. Yes   9. No   10. No

IV.

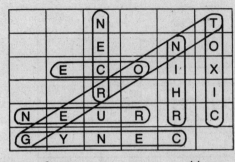

V. 1. c   6. m   11. e
    2. f   7. o   12. k
    3. a   8. b   13. g
    4. j   9. d   14. i
    5. h   10. l   15. n

Unit II Review (Lessons 11–20)

A. 1. quatrain   2. equity   3. alchemy   4. hircine   5. etiology
    6. phenomenology   7. vulpine   8. purloin   9. amplitude   10. elfin

B. 1. conclave   2. lupine   3. comatose   4. titanic   5. decimate

C. 1. cadaver   2. equity   3. soothsayer   4. bibliophile   3. prosthesis

D.   circumspect-demure   Francophile-philogyny
      peccadillo-picayune   Russophobe-misogyny
      intractable-intransigent   abscess-tumescence
      tort-litigation   Decalogue-decimate
      titanic-amplitude   tribunal-adjudicate

E. 1. pallor   2. inscrutable   3. incommunicado   4. teeming   5. junket

F.

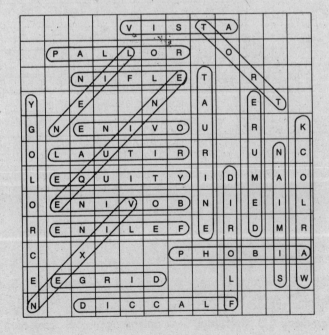

Lesson 21: Appearances and Attitudes (III)

I. 1. omniscient   2. noxious   3. minatory   4. obdurate   5. pusillanimous

II. 1. F   2. F   3. T   4. F   5. T

III.

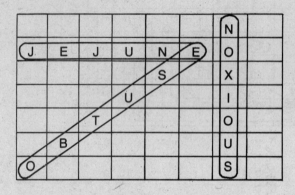

IV. effete

V.
1. g	6. b	11. j
2. o	7. n	12. i
3. a	8. h	13. l
4. c	9. e	14. m
5. k	10. d	15. f

Lesson 22: Legal Language (II)

I. 1. amicus curiae   2. arson   3. extradition   4. plagiarism   5. embezzle

II. 1. F   2. T   3. T   4. T   5. F

III.

IV. junket

V.
1. e	6. a	11. g
2. n	7. c	12. d
3. h	8. m	13. f
4. b	9. j	14. i
5. l	10. o	15. k

Lesson 23: Foreign Terms (I)

I. 1. non compos mentis   2. coup de grace   3. junta   4. non sequitur   5. avant-garde

II. 1. T   2. F   3. T   4. T   5. T

III.

IV. larceny

V. 1. l   6. a   11. f
    2. e   7. n   12. m
    3. h   8. b   13. g
    4. o   9. c   14. i
    5. k   10. d   15. j

Lesson 24: C'est Français

I. 1. sangfroid   2. tour de force   3. tête-à-tête   4. repartee   5. ingenue

II. 1. T   2. T   3. F   4. T   5. T

III.

IV. gauche

V. 1. n   6. a   11. o
    2. h   7. d   12. e
    3. b   8. f   13. g
    4. j   9. c   14. i
    5. k   10. m   15. l

Lesson 25: Crossword Puzzle Words

I. 1. bauble   2. chary   3. aperture   4. alms   5. ado

II. 1. F   2. F   3. F   4. T   5. T

III.

IV.   taper, ilk, hay, ban, bonus

V.			
1. o	6. i	11. d
2. b	7. l	12. m
3. e	8. k	13. c
4. g	9. a	14. j
5. n	10. h	15. f

Lesson 26: Mythology (II)

I.   1. calliope   2. myrmidon   3. oracular   4. thespian   5. Promethean

II.   1. T   2. F   3. T   4. F   5. F

III.   1. harpy—termagant (S)   2. antaean—frail (A)   3. myrmidon—servant (S)   4. awkward—terpsichorean (A)   5. puny—homeric (A)

IV.   paean

V.			
1. d	6. a	11. f
2. k	7. c	12. h
3. n	8. e	13. i
4. g	9. m	14. j
5. b	10. o	15. l

Lesson 27: Appearances and Attitudes (IV)

I.   1. sardonic   2. sleazy   3. prolix   4. restive   5. ribald

II.   1. T   2. F   3. F   4. T   5. T

III.

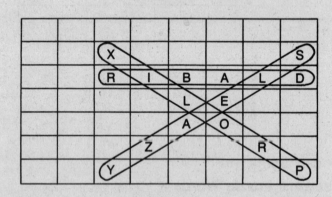

IV.   antaean

V.			
1. i	6. a	11. l
2. m	7. k	12. h
3. f	8. d	13. b
4. o	9. g	14. c
5. n	10. j	15. e

Lesson 28: Foreign Terms (II)

I.   1. bon vivant   2. ad hoc   3. nolo contendere   4. leitmotif   5. quid pro quo

II.   1. T   2. T   3. T   4. F   5. T

III.

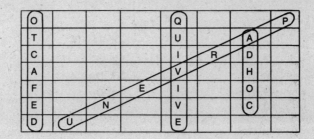

IV.   puerile

V.   1. h   6. e   i1. d   16. p
     2. a   7. b   12. f
     3. m   8. n   13. g
     4. c   9. o   14. l
     5. k   10. i   15. j

Lesson 29: Appearances and Attitudes (V)

I.   1. bucolic   2. ambivalent   3. dilatory   4. crotchety   5. loquacious

II.   1. T   2. F   3. T   4. T   5. F

III.

```
    J           B
    O           U   V
    C           C   E
D   U   D   G   E   O   N
    N           L   A
    D           I   L
                C
```

IV.   craven

V.   1. c   6. a   11. f
     2. j   7. b   12. g
     3. d   8. i   13. n
     4. k   9. l   14. h
     5. o   10. e   15. m

Lesson 30: Size and Shape (II)

I.   1. magnum opus   2. gargantuan   3. lissome   4. tenuous   5. sinuous

II.   1. T   2. T   3. T   4. T   5. F

III.

```
            T               N
            E               E
            N               G
            U               D
    A   T   O   I           I
S   I   N   U   O   U   S   M
L   I   S   S   O   M   E   S
```

IV. atavism

V. 1. a   6. c   11. k
    2. o   7. f   12. g
    3. j   8. n   13. b
    4. e   9. h   14. d
    5. l   10. i   15. m

Unit III Review (Lessons 21–30)

A. 1. pusillanimous   2. bucolic   3. non sequitur   4. pontifical   5. qui vive   6. sinuous   7. gauche
    8. officious   9. miscreant   10. amulet
B. 1. nabob   2. arson   3. melange   4. venal   5. vignette
C. 1. tête-à-tête   2. barrister   3. omniscient   4. terpsichorean   5. ingenue
D. scabrous—libidinous   pontifical—oracular
    impasse—cul-de-sac   miscreant—perpetrator
    iota—scintilla   jocund—gemütlich
    mercurial—mutable   bon mot—mot juste
    bilk—embezzle   homeric—Promethean
E. 1. crotchety   2. ad hoc   3. mercurial   4. larceny   5. voluptuous

F.

Lesson 31: Language

I. 1. threnody   2. malapropism   3. onomatopoeia   4. pleonasm   5. paralipsis

II. 1. T   2. T   3. F   4. F   5. F

III. 1. literary   2. legacy   3. panorama   4. paradox   5. intuition

IV.

V. 1. m   6. l   11. k
    2. b   7. a   12. f
    3. j   8. n   13. h
    4. e   9. c   14. d
    5. g   10. o   15. i

Lesson 32: Speech

I. 1. jargon   2. aspersion   3. guttural   4. mellifluous   5. gainsay

II. 1. T   2. T   3. F   4. T   5. T

III. argot

IV. 1. glorification—aspersion (A)   2. mellifluous—soft (S)   3. timidity—braggadocio (A)   4. gainsay—deny (S)
     5. rhapsodic—bombastic (S)

V. 1. m   6. g   11. b
    2. a   7. n   12. e
    3. o   8. i   13. j
    4. c   9. f   14. k
    5. l   10. h   15. d

Lesson 33: History and Government (I)

I. 1. peonage   2. pharisaical   3. plebiscite   4. plenipotentiary   5. recession

II. 1. F   2. T   3. T   4. F   5. T

III. tryst

IV.

"scattered"
word:
oligarchy

V. 1. f   6. i   11. b
    2. k   7. m   12. l
    3. o   8. a   13. c
    4. n   9. h   14. e
    5. d   10. j   15. g

Lesson 34: Travel

I. 1. hustings   2. portmanteau   3. landmark   4. safari   5. tandem

II. 1. T   2. T   3. T   4. F   5. F

III. 1. parabolic   2. valediction   3. trek   4. travail   5. anticipate

IV.

"scattered"
words:
wayfarer
antipodal

V. 1. i   6. k   11. e
     2. a   7. d   12. m
     3. o   8. f   13. j
     4. l   9. g   14. h
     5. n   10. b   15. c

Lesson 35: Foods and Taste

I. 1. condiment   2. manna   3. subsistence   4. piquant   5. culinary

II. 1. F   2. T   3. T   4. F   5. F

III. 1. edifying   2. determine   3. essential   4. pungent   5. relish

IV. 1. rogue, damn   2. squint, p.a.   3. van, ids   4. reef, tocsin   5. guess, aha

V. 1. k   6. j   11. c
     2. d   7. o   12. n
     3. f   8. a   13. e
     4. m   9. b   14. i
     5. h   10. l   15. g

Lesson 36: Fun and Frolic

I. 1. divertissement   2. guffaw   3. regale   4. waggish   5. squib

II. 1. F   2. T   3. F   4. T   5. F

III. elfin

IV.

G	U	F	F	A	W
E	C	I	T	N	A
L				B	G
A				I	G
G				U	I
E				Q	S
R				S	H

V. 1. d   6. c   11. n
     2. m   7. i   12. j
     3. o   8. b   13. e
     4. k   9. f   14. h
     5. a   10. l   15. g

Lesson 37: History and Government (II)

I. 1. schism   2. partisan   3. imperialism   4. ethos   5. demagogue

II. 1. T   2. F   3. F   4. T   5. F

III. 1. narcissism   2. pedant   3. coherent   4. quarry   5. artistic

IV. canon

V. 1. d   6. o   11. g
    2. j   7. h   12. i
    3. m   8. l   13. k
    4. a   9. b   14. c
    5. f   10. e   15. n

Lesson 38: Legal Language (III)

I. 1. abscond   2. contumacious   3. cause célèbre   4. contraband   5. bequest

II. 1. T   2. F   3. F   4. T   5. T

III.

Y		B		L			
R		E		I			
E		Q		C			
T		U		I			
T		E		D			
A	B	S	C	O	N	D	
B		T		C			

IV. biopsy

V. 1. g   6. l   11. n
    2. o   7. f   12. m
    3. a   8. k   13. e
    4. b   9. i   14. j
    5. c   10. d   15. h

Lesson 39: Philosophy and Logic

I. 1. epistemology   2. syllogism   3. ratiocination   4. hedonism   5. predestination

II. 1. T   2. F   3. T   4. F   5. F

III. 1. utilitarian   2. document   3. romantic   4. conjecture   5. hedonism

IV. empirical, theosophy, teleology, syllogism

V. 1. d   6. f   11. e
    2. l   7. a   12. i
    3. h   8. m   13. n
    4. o   9. b   14. g
    5. j   10. k   15. c

Lesson 40: Beliefs and Religion

I. 1. blasphemy   2. pantheism   3. infidel   4. theodicy   5. syncretism

II. 1. F   2. T   3. F   4. F   5. T

III. 1. apostate—heretic (S)   2. apotheosis—degradation (A)   3. mantra—invocation (S)   4. canonical—orthodox (S)   5. benediction—anathema (A)

IV.   mister, sync   2. sailing, course   3. chide, toy   4. hoop, siesta   5. coin, tags

V.   1. c   6. i   11. o
     2. b   7. a   12. g
     3. h   8. m   13. n
     4. e   9. d   14. l
     5. k   10. f   15. j

Unit IV Review (Lessons 31–40)

A.   1. roister   2. renascent   3. apotheosis   4. mantra   5. paralipsis   6. benediction   7. wanderlust
     8. syncretism   9. paradigm   10. harangue
B.   1. safari   2. dogma   3. schism   4. repast   5. simile
C.   1. polygot   2. divertissement   3. plenipotentiary   4. concierge   5. gourmand   6. landmark   7. viands
     8. wayfarer   9. muckraker   10. proxy

D.   simile-metaphor   tenet-canon
     repast-refection   oligarchy-totalitarian
     pragmatism-utilitarian   waggish-badinage
     jargon-argot   surrogate-proxy
     metonymy-synecdoche   bequest-codicil

E.   1. aspersions   2. jargon   3. à la carte   4. culinary   5. fallacy   6. contraband   7. bureaucracy   8. proxy
     9. Machiavellian   10. assuage

F.

Final Review Test — SAT Style

1. A	11. B	21. C	31. B	41. A
2. E	12. E	22. E	32. B	42. D
3. E	13. D	23. C	33. E	43. E
4. C	14. B	24. A	34. B	44. A
5. B	15. C	25. A	35. A	45. D
6. A	16. A	26. B	36. C	46. C
7. B	17. B	27. D	37. A	47. E
8. A	18. B	28. D	38. B	48. A
9. E	19. A	29. A	39. D	49. B
10. D	20. D	30. D	40. C	50. C